Ka'm-t'em

A Journey Toward Healing

Ka'm-t'em

A Journey Toward Healing

Kishan Lara-Cooper
Walter J. Lara Sr.

Great Oak Press – Pechanga, California

ISBN: 978-1-942279-27-3 (pbk.)
ISBN: 978-1-942279-26-6 (E-Book)
Front Cover: Basket floating down the Klamath River. Courtesy of Gary Colegrove Jr. and Walter Lara Sr.
Back Cover: Kishan Lara-Cooper and Walter Lara Sr. Courtesy of Lau-Lei Lawrence.
For more information regarding *Ka'm-t'em: A Journey toward Healing* visit kamtem-indigenousknowledge.com.

Printed in the United States of America.

Great Oak Press
P.O. Box 2183
Temecula, CA 92593
www.greatoakpress.com

Dedication

To our young people,
May you pick up the basket,
Rejoice in the lessons,
And contribute to its journey.

Contents

Part 5: Pick Up the Basket: Testimonials from our Youth

Bibliography

Figures

Foreword

COLONIZATION IS THE PRACTICE OF DOMINATION. It involves the subjugation of one group by another. Colonization concerns itself with the conquest and exploitation of the lands, waters, resources, labor, and lives of the Indigenous population. Colonizers subjugate Indigenous Peoples using slavery, murder, displacement, theft, abduction, rape, genocide, and religion. Colonization is not something that just happened in the past. Its effects continue to resonant for generations; and through a system of settler colonial processes and structures, it becomes embedded in the laws, regulations, beliefs, and values of a white settler society that compels the allegiance of Indigenous Peoples to a colonial present. But colonization does not end there. Recollections of conquest can remain outwardly in the thinking, feelings, and behavior of the Indigenous survivors as well as inwardly via the molecular, cellular, and genetic memories of the people. Few Indigenous Peoples are exempt from the social, political, and economic injustices that result from colonization.

Increasingly, Indigenous scholars and public intellectuals have turned to various decolonization strategies as the antidote to colonization: Language and culture restoration; renewed assertion of land, cultural, and human rights; a return to traditional governance; food sovereignty and security; revival of ceremony and spiritual practices; truth-telling and the revision of settler history; and return to traditional healing practices. Decolonization is both an idea and concept. As an idea, it is the thinking part of the journey—the mental formations that are imagined and planned to make liberation from colonial oppression possible.

As a concept, it is the doing part of the journey—taking the necessary steps to overcome the shackles of past, present, and future colonization.

The book you hold in your hands shares a number of excellent essays that describe the ideas and concepts of decolonization. The writers share first-hand experiences that range from survival, perseverance, awakening, activism, searching, recovery, renewal, responsibility, revolution, spirituality, remembering, respect, and balance. It also shares the pain and tragedy of the past and present, along with the awakening and the return to, and conservation of, practices and ceremonies to restore and promote healing. Throughout the book there is a beautiful poetry of resistance and renewal that rings in each essay, echoing a renaissance of hope and transformation. Each chapter identifies and critically and fiercely interrogates colonization—imagining, planning, and conceptualizing the approaches necessary to overcome the colonial barriers and oppressions that are fixed in the past and present histories of the people.

The editors of this book, Dr. Kishan Lara-Cooper and Walter J. Lara Sr. are well-known, well-loved, and well-respected leaders in the Indigenous world, in their own community, and in their areas of expertise. We should all be so fortunate to have such learned and powerful allies among us. From 2009 to 2014, my family and I lived in Wiyot and Yurok territory when I was a professor of social work at Humboldt State University, Arcata, California. I had the distinct honor and pleasure of meeting both Kishan and Walt and was able to visit with them at length about their work, their culture, ceremonies, language, and the challenges faced by all of our people in our recovery from colonization. As a visitor to their territory, I was always treated with friendliness, respect, and openness and was inspired and encouraged by their wisdom, energy, and truth-telling.

Dr. Lara-Cooper is an associate professor and the chairperson of the Child Development Department at Humboldt State University in Arcata, California. She is a descendant of Yurok, Hupa, and Karuk peoples and is deeply committed and active in the restoration and preservation of her peoples' culture, ceremonies, and healing. I have listened to her speak and read her work and regard her as a rising star among the next generation of young, brilliant, activist Indigenous academics who are engaged in serious, visionary decolonization practices within and outside of the academy.

I met Kishan when she joined the faculty at Humboldt State University in 2010. However, I had already heard a number of positive comments about her through colleagues such as Arizona State University professors Waziyatawin and James Riding In, who were familiar with, and supportive of, her academic, cultural, and research interests when she was a doctoral student at Arizona State University. I was a professor at this institution prior to her arrival. Dr. Lara-Cooper continues to draw attention through her commitment to recreating educational and institutional paradigms that privilege the knowledge and traditional practices of Indigenous Peoples. As a testament to the influence of her work and presence, in 2016, was recognized "as one of forty emerging leaders under the age of 40 in Indian country by the National Center for American Indian Enterprise Development (NCAIED) for demonstrated leadership, initiative, and dedication and making significant contributions in business and/or in their community."

Walter J. Lara Sr. is a deeply respected spiritual leader and wisdom keeper of the Yurok tribal people. His resume is deep with experience and his knowledge of people, mother earth, ceremony, and history is remarkable. While I was living in northern California, I had heard a great deal about Walter and the amazing work that he has accomplished over his many years of activism, advocacy, and spiritual leadership. However, due to our schedules, we were only able to exchange formal pleasantries the few times we met. It wasn't until his family and I were at Standing Rock amidst the gathering of hundreds of tribal peoples and allies from around the world, who were there to protect the water, that we were able to sit down and visit about his work and contributions. Walt is an eternal optimist and has a good sense of humor. He is an author, a veteran of the Korean War era, a protector of his peoples' graves, and deeply involved in the repatriation of his ancestors skeletal remains and their associated sacred belongings. He is often surrounded by his family, relatives, friends, and those seeking his counsel on matters related to ceremony, spirituality, and culture. I follow Walt and his wife Callie on Facebook.

I think it's fitting to end with what Kishan and Walt hope you will get out of their book. In the preface of Ka'm-t'em: A Journey Toward Healing, Professor Kishan-Lara-Cooper and Walter J. Lara, Sr., write "one purpose of this book is to expose you, the reader, to Indigenous knowledge, the journey to protect it, and the healing that occurs through transmitting it to younger generations." They further share their hopes of a greater transformation of humankind through the words of their contributors: the book, "is intended to share multiple narratives as a form of justice" and "In the sharing and in the listening of Indigenous testimonials, we are reminded of the beauty and strength within us. The precious knowledge shared in this book inspires reclamation of identity and encourages readers to seek, search, embrace, and value their own truth."

—*Michael Yellow Bird (Fargo, North Dakota, April 2019)*

Michael Yellow Bird is the Director of Tribal and Indigenous Peoples Studies and a Professor in the Department of Sociology and Anthropology at North Dakota State University. He is the co-editor of four books that focus on decolonization, including *For Indigenous Eyes Only*, *For Indigenous Minds Only*, and *Decolonizing Social Work*.

Preface

Kishan Lara-Cooper

Many generations ago, along the Klamath River, there lived a wise woman who wove the most beautiful baskets known to humankind. Her baskets were woven so tightly that water could not penetrate them. She was aging and had many experiences to share. Through prayer, she began to weave a basket for the people. The wise woman worked day after day, weaving, praying, and singing. As her strong hands moved gracefully over her materials, she shared a story to be retold, a song to be sung again, and a lesson to be learned. When she finished, she had created a large beautiful basket bowl. She called this basket *Ka'm-t'em* because it held the treasures of the people.

In a Yurok village at Bluff Creek, the woman placed the basket in the water where two rivers join together, and stood silent as the basket began its journey. The basket seemed to tip-toe across the gentle breakers; it moved along more quickly as it hit the swift currents and swirled ever so purposeful into the eddies. Round and round, the basket turned through the trials and tribulations of the water and then burst free into the swift, shallow flow of the river. All life that swam below watched with great interest.

Although the villagers lived within their own unique environment, each village anticipated the basket's presence, for they knew the old woman understood the human need for knowledge and contribution. As such, the people picked up the basket, rejoiced in the lessons, and then they too added prayers and allowed the basket to continue its journey. After many stops, the basket reached Requa, the mouth of the Klamath River. It made three final spins, reflecting a ceremonial journey, and drifted its way over the rough water of the river's mouth and into the belly of the Pacific Ocean. All that the basket had to offer made its final journey into the sunset, where it exists eternally.[1]

KA'M-T'EM: A JOURNEY TOWARD HEALING WAS INSPIRED BY THIS PIECE OF HISTORY. Just as the woven basket was made to share knowledge, one purpose of this book is to expose you, the reader, to Indigenous knowledge, the journey to protect it, and the healing that occurs through transmitting it to younger generations. The roots of this book began when I interviewed my 84-year-old father as part of my dissertation, and he suggested I make a book. I thought he meant simply a transcription of our interview, but what he intended was far greater. He meant a *book*, one that could be used in classrooms, in trainings, or as a mirror of goodness and knowledge in which Indigenous people could see themselves reflected in true, healing, and positive ways. That idea planted the seeds for this book, a project involving almost two dozen authors and written from an Indigenous perspective.

So often, Indigenous children and communities are plagued with a dominant narrative that depicts Indigenous people as deficient, unhealthy, or inadequate. Professionals who work with Indigenous children and families are often inundated with discussions of the alarming social indicators of Indigenous communities, including increased rates of suicide, alcoholism, and violence. Inhaling the social indicators of Indigenous communities and spitting out these statistics as characteristics of Indigenous identity minimizes the worth of Indigenous children and families and often negatively influences their own self-identity.

This book presents Indigenous testimonials of resistance, renewal, advocacy, resilience, beauty, and awakening. For example, a lead plaintiff in Lyng v. NICPA, a case that went to the Supreme Court, shares in-depth Indigenous knowledge and "behind the scenes" influences of the case; a fluent Tolowa speaker describes the impact of colonial education on language loss and his personal journey as a first-language English speaker learning to speak his heritage language; and a regalia maker describes the impact of genocide on communal relationships, the natural environment, and Indigenous spirituality, while relating the journey of reclaiming Indigenous identity through the process of regalia-making. In the sharing and in the listening of Indigenous testimonials, we are reminded of the beauty and the strength within us. The precious knowledge shared in this book inspires reclamation of identity and encourages readers to seek, search, embrace, and value their own truth. All of the royalties from this book will be forwarded to the Ka'm-t'em scholarship for Indigenous California youth.

Tips to Reading this Book

This book is intended to share multiple narratives as a form of testimonial justice. As such, chapter authors may use variated spellings of the same Indigenous words and testimonies may support and/or contradict other testimonies. These variations preserve the integrity of voice; illustrate the rich breadth of humanity; and reflect diversity in generational perspective, worldview, and epistemology.

Interchangeable use of the words Indigenous, Indian, Native American, First Nations, tribal affiliation and/or villages may be used. For example, Nererner (coastal Yurok people) and Puhliklah (river Yurok people) may refer to themselves in this way rather than "Yurok." Also, many Indigenous communities acknowledge the deceased by using terms such as Awok, Ne'en, or Daysri before naming the deceased.

This book highlights Indigenous knowledge and philosophy. Testimonials reflect ways of knowing from a communal perspective. Therefore, multiple authors may be listed on a single testimonial. In these circumstances, the first author listed is the narrator and the second author listed is the primary writer.

Endnotes
1.   Kishan Lara. "Pick up the Basket." *Wicazo Sa Review* 23, no. 2 (2008): 103.

Acknowledgements

A special thank you to Dr. Teresa McCarty, Dr. Michael Yellow Bird, Dr. Bonnie Duran, Dr. Meenal Rana, Dr. Myla Vicenti Carpio, Susie Long, Gary Colegrove Jr., Lori Snyder, Sammy Cooper, and Ellen Colegrove. We also wish to thank the poetry contributors: Brian Tripp, Tene Kremling, and Callie Lara.

In a ceremony, there may only be one singer. It is the responsibility of the singer to pull in the good thoughts and prayers of the people and send them out to the energies of the world through song. The singer is a representative and an orchestrator of knowledge. Through the process of making this book, our contributors have shared some of the treasures within Indigenous knowledge. Each chapter is a song and each author its singer. Thank you to all who have contributed. Our respect and acknowledgment is also extended to those that didn't have an opportunity to share their song this time. We hope that we have represented you in a good way. *Wok-thow* (with sincere gratitude).

Contributing Authors

Dr. George "Pordie" Blake (Hupa/Yurok) is a world-renowned artist known for his sculptures, jewelry, regalia, and contemporary works. He is skilled in feather work, regalia, and elk horn carving. Dr. Blake is one of the few remaining carvers of the Yurok Dugout Canoe. He is a recipient of the National Heritage Fellowship, the highest honor of traditional artists. Dr. Blake is a graduate of the University of California at Davis. He has utilized his artistic skill to preserve traditional ways of the Hupa and Yurok and has taken the opportunity to share this skill with young people. He received a Doctor of Humane Letters from Humboldt State University in 2016.

Loren Me'-lash-ne Bommelyn (Tolowa) is a tradition bearer for the Tolowa Tribe. He has dedicated himself to preserving the traditional songs, language, and basketry. He is the foremost ceremonial leader of the tribe, and its most prolific basketweaver. He holds a Master of Arts degree in linguistics from the University of Oregon and is the Smith River tribal chair, a high school teacher and speaker and teacher of the Tolowa language.

Dr. Kayla Begay (Hupa) earned a Ph.D in Linguistics from University of California at Berkeley. She is an Assistant Professor in Native American Studies at Humboldt State University where she teaches courses in California Indian History and Linguistics. She specializes in languages of northwest California. She is an advocate for language revitalization/restoration and northern California water rights. She is a traditional basketweaver, traditionalist, and singer from the Xontah Nikya:aw (the principle ceremonial big house) on the Hoopa Valley Indian Reservation.

Adrienne Colegrove-Raymond (Hupa) comes from the villages of Medildin on her grandfather's side and Takamildin from her grandmother's side. She was raised on the Hupa Reservation by a traditional family, where she developed her training and guidance. She has devoted a good deal of her energy incorporating cultural relevancy into educational systems serving Indigenous students. She has a Master of Business Administration (MBA) degree where her research has focused on the systemic overhaul of educational policies and practices to create environments conducive to serving Native and underrepresented students, specifically those in the foster care system. As the Coordinator of the Indian Tribal and Educational Personnel Program (ITEPP), established in 1969, she relies on the visionaries of the Native community to guide the university in meeting the needs of local tribes.

Princess Jintcon Colegrove (Hupa/Yurok/Karuk) is a Hoopa Tribal Member from the villages of Me'dildin, Ta'k'imiŁding, and Diyshta:ng'a'de:n . She is also a Ner-er-ner (Coastal Yurok) from the villages of Chapekw and Espew. She is a junior at Hoopa Valley High School, maintaining a 3.6 GPA. She is a cheerleader and a CSF member who excels in the sciences, interning at Hoopa Tribal Fisheries. She is also an advanced Hoopa Language student and is a teaching assistant at the IŁtuq' language center. Princess completed her xoq'it ch'iswa:l when she was thirteen years old. Since then, she has been selected to carry the medicine in healing ceremonies as well as to represent her people in the Jump Dance. Her favorite family activity is paddling traditional redwood canoes on the lagoons. Princess enjoys rodeos and running cattle on the Trinity Summit on her horse Rain, with her three siblings and numerous Colegrove/Jarnaghan cousins.

Kisdyante Joseph (Hupa/Paiute/Shoshone) is seventeen years old and a senior at Hoopa Valley High School. She is an advocate for water and environmental rights. She has participated in numerous conferences, hearings, protests, and documentaries, voicing her concerns and offering solutions. Kisdyante is also an avid athlete, playing basketball and softball, and record-setting in track. She is a singer, dancer, and active participant in the ceremonies of her people.

Julian Lang (Karuk/Wiyot) is a storyteller, poet, artist, graphic designer, and writer. He is a first-language speaker of Karuk and a tribal scholar. Julian is a member of the Board of Directors of the Ink People: Center for the Arts and the author of *Ararapikva: Karuk Indian Literature from Northwest California.*

Callie Lara (Hupa/Karuk) has dedicated her life to preserving the philosophy and teachings of her people. At a young age, her grandmother exposed her to the beauty of ceremony through storytelling, song, and hands-on experience. Callie is a writer, a regalia-maker, and a teacher. She has shared her skill of gathering and regalia-making with numerous young women throughout the community. She has brought life to countless men's and women's regalia items. Often, a ceremony is filled entirely of items that she has created, although she would never want it to be noticed. Callie is an instructor and life-long student of the Hupa language and often resorts to language for a deeper meaning of life.

Shaunna Oteka McCovey (Yurok/Karuk) grew up on the Yurok and Hoopa Valley Indian Reservations, and in Karuk Country in Northern California. Her poetry, articles, and essays have been published in anthologies, magazines, and new journals. She is the author of *The Smokehouse Boys*, a collection of poems about her tribal peoples' experience. She earned undergraduate and graduate degrees in Social Work from Humboldt State University and Arizona State University, respectively, and she holds a Master of Studies in Environment Law and a Juris Doctorate from Vermont Law School. She currently lives in the Pacific Northwest.

Jim McQuillen (Yurok/Tolowa) is the current Education Department Director for the Yurok Tribe. He is a Yurok Tribal member, a father, grandfather, and a dance leader. Jim received a master's degree in Psychology, his PPS credential, and is also a licensed Marriage, Family Counselor with the State of California. Jim is passionate about his work with tribes to educate Yurok people in both traditional and academic learning, addressing the needs of families and children from birth through college. He consistently addresses these needs to the local school districts with the goal of equitable education for native youth. He continues to demand unique needs regarding Yurok language in the schools, trauma-informed practices, restorative justice, and accurate cultural curriculum in the classroom.

Donald Moore (Yurok/Hupa) Donald Moore is eighteen years old and is entering his second year at Fort Lewis College in Durango, Colorado. He is pursuing a degree in Biology, as is working towards becoming a high school teacher so he can motivate our youth and encourage more to get an education. He comes from the villages of Cho-kik, Turip, Morek and Medildin. All throughout his life, he has been dedicated to his culture, ceremonies, and community. He is actively involved in his ceremonies, such as the Jump Dance, Deerskin Dance, Brush Dance, and Flower Dance, and loves the game of Indian Cards. He holds his family and other youth very closely, as he checks in on them often and tries to be a part of their lives as much as he can. Donald also has a lot of knowledge of the Yurok language, as both sides of his family were taught and speak the language. Donald wants to make a positive impact on his native communities and leave a legacy that people will remember for a long time.

Dr. Virgil Moorehead Jr. (Yurok/Tolowa), a member of the Big Lagoon Rancheria, is currently a Lecturer at Humboldt State University and director of Behavioral Health Services at Two Feather Family Services in Mckinleyville, CA. A graduate of University of California at Davis (BA) and California State University, Sacramento (MA), Dr. Moorehead received his Doctorate of Psychology in Clinical Psychology from the Wright Institute in Berkeley, CA in 2015. During his graduate work, he completed his doctoral internship at the University of Michigan, with a post-doctoral fellowship at Stanford University. Dr. Moorehead's research focuses on developing and testing community-based strategies for health promotion with Native American communities. Dr. Moorehead received the Richard Alan Smith Scholar's Award in 2015 for his work on Digital Storytelling with Urban Native Americans in Oakland, CA, and the 19th Annual Anne Medicine Mentorship Award in 2017 for his work with Stanford Native American undergraduate and graduate students.

Jack Norton (Hupa/Cherokee) is Emeritus Professor of Native American Studies at Humboldt State University. He is Hupa/Cherokee descent and an enrolled member of the Yurok Nation. He was the first California Indian appointed to the Rupert Costo Chair in American Indian History at the University of California, Riverside, and is the author of *Genocide of Northwestern California* and *Centering in Two Worlds*.

Michael Orcutt (Hupa) is a descendent of the Karuk and Yurok Tribes and an enrolled member of the Hoopa Valley Tribe (HVT). He graduated from Humboldt State University in 1984 with a Bachelor of Science degree in Fishery Biology. He is married to Vivienna Orcutt and is the father of three daughters: Oni-Rose, Presley, and Peggy. Mr. Orcutt assisted with development of the Tribal Fisheries Program for the HVT. He serves on numerous regional committees that have helped to shape and influence how Tribes co-manage their fishery and water resources. Presently, he serves as the HVT's representative on the Trinity Management Council, California Anadromous Hatchery Review Policy Group, and as Tribal representative on the California Salmon and Steelhead Advisory Committee.

Chisa Oros (Yoeme/Zuni) grew up in Northwestern California and graduated from Humboldt State University with a bachelor's degree in Ethnic Studies and a master's degree in Social Science. Chisa's master's degree research was an interdisciplinary critical analysis of the role of militarism within the Humboldt Bay region during the California Gold Rush, and the implications of settler colonialism on Indigenous female bodies, the balance of the natural world, and spiritual consciousness.

Chris Peters (Pohlik-lah/Karuk) is the President and CEO of the Seventh Generation Fund, dedicated to Indigenous people's self-determination and the sovereignty of Native Nations, and founder and President of Red Deer Consulting. Chris was a lead plaintiff in the *Lyng v. NICPA* case and has more than thirty years of experience in grassroots organizing. He is a spiritual leader among the Pohlik-lah and is a graduate of both the University of California, Davis and Stanford University.

Willie Pink (Luiseño) has been actively involved in the formation of grassroots organizations throughout the State of California. As the Executive Director of the California Indian Heritage Commission, Mr. Pink has worked with many tribes to establish legislation and policy to preserve tribal autonomy, protect sacred and burial sites, and bring awareness to the needs of California tribes.

Dr. Seafha Ramos (Yurok/Karuk) earned a Bachelor of Science degree in Biology from Missouri Southern State University, a Master of Science degree in Wildlife and Conservation Management from the University of Arizona, and a Ph.D. in Natural Resources from the University of Arizona. Dr. Ramos received University of Arizona's School of Natural Resources and Environment Studies Outstanding Dissertation Award for her work on Traditional Ecological Knowledge.

Lyn Risling (Hupa/Yurok/Karuk) came from a family—starting with her grandfather, David Risling Sr.—that has been deeply involved with renewal of culture and ceremony. At a young age, she was taught songs and learned about the dances of her tribal cultures and participated in dance demonstrations. When she was older, she finally had the opportunity to dance in a real ceremony when her grandfather became involved in bringing back the Brush Dance and the World Renewal ceremonies at *Katimiin*, the Karuk Center of the World. Since then, Lyn has continued to be involved in ceremony and other aspects of her cultures. She and her husband, Julian Lang, were instrumental in bringing back the Karuk *Ihuk* ceremony and work to keep it going into the future. Lyn is also an artist whose art focuses primarily on her cultures and can be seen throughout local communities and beyond.

Dr. Cutcha Risling-Baldy (Hupa/Yurok/Karuk) is currently an Assistant Professor of Native American Studies at Humboldt State University. Her research is focused on Indigenous feminisms, California Indians, and decolonization. She received her Ph.D. in Native American Studies with a Designated Emphasis in Feminist Theory and Research from the University of California, Davis and her M.F.A. in Creative Writing and Literary Research from San Diego State University. She also has her B.A. in Psychology from Stanford University. She is a 2011 Ford Foundation Predoctoral Fellow and an American Indian Graduate Center Fellow. In 2007, Dr. Risling-Baldy co-founded the

Native Women's Collective, a nonprofit organization that supports the continued revitalization of Native American arts and culture.

Dr. Rose Soza War Soldier (Mountain Maidu/Cahuilla/Luiseño) is an enrolled member of Soboba Band of Luiseño Indians. She completed a Bachelor of Arts degree in History with a double minor in Political Science and Social/Ethnic Relations at University of California, Davis and earned a doctoral degree in History with an emphasis in American Indian History from Arizona State University. She is a lecturer in Ethnic Studies at Northern Arizona University. Her research and teaching focus on twentieth century American Indian activism, social and cultural history, politics, education, and social justice.

Co-Editors

Dr. Kishan Lara-Cooper (Yurok/Hupa/Karuk) is an Associate Professor and Chair of the Department of Child Development at Humboldt State University, where she teaches courses in child development, language development, history, social and cultural considerations, and instructional practices in American Indian education. She earned her Doctor of Education degree from Arizona State University in Curriculum and Instruction with an emphasis in Indian Education and a specialization in language revitalization, community-based education, and culturally-based pedagogy; her Master of Arts degree in Linguistics from the University of Arizona; and her Bachelor of Arts degree in Native American Studies from Humboldt State University. She has a vested interest and dedication to the preservation of language, culture, and ceremony. She is actively involved in the revitalization of the flower dance (a women's rite of passage ceremony) and the jump dance (a ceremony for the continuance of humankind) on the *Nererner* coast. She cherishes her relationships with elders, the community, the natural environment, and the spiritual elements of the world. As a professional, she understands the impact of language, culture, and ceremony on healing, identity, self-esteem, and self-efficacy. She is an advocate of shifting the paradigm of education and institutional frameworks.

Walt Lara Sr. (Yurok) is a respected spiritual leader and wisdom keeper of the Yurok tribal people. He is recognized as a Native cultural and political luminary among Tribal Nations throughout the State of California. Walter has dedicated his life to the renaissance of Earth Healing and Earth Renewal Ceremonies and the revitalization of spiritual practices and lifeways of the Yurok People. He has been guided in advocacy by his late uncle, Milton Marks. Mr. Lara is the co-founder of the Northwest Indian Cemetery Protective Association (NICPA), a community-based organization established for the protection of tribal burial sites (cemeteries) and sacred places. NICPA was instrumental in the first repatriation of Yurok human remains and artifacts and the passage of the American Indian Religious Freedom Act in 1978. He was appointed as a commissioner of the Native American Heritage Commission of California. The Commission, through the Office of the State's Attorney, was a key litigant in the infamous landmark case *Lyng v. The Northwest Indian Cemetery Protective Association* (NICPA), an American Indian religious freedom case with national precedence. The Heritage Commission, working with California Tribal Nations, was instrumental in the repatriation of human remains and funerary item that were warehoused within the State Parks Department. The Commission also established statutory protection to prevent continued looting and desecration of graves and ceremonial sites. In addition, Mr. Lara served as the chairperson and Area 1 Director of the Inter-Tribal Council; the chair of Tricounties; a member of the Indian Action Council; a member of the California Rural Indian Health Board's (CRIHB) traditional health board; a member of the California State Native American Graves, Protection, and Repatriation Act (NAGPRA) Commission; and the Smithsonian NAGPRA Advisory Board. Mr. Lara is an honored recipient of numerous awards, including the Society for California's Archeology's California Indian Heritage Preservation Award. He is the author of "Blacksnake's Corner" in the *Smoke Signals Journal*, where he shares historical information that is unique to California. Mr Lara has worked alongside his wife, Callie and his seven children: Walt Jr., Lorraine, Willie, Liz, Roberta, Keduescha, and Kishan to preserve and protect Indigenous knowledge. He looks forward to the contributions of his 15 grandchildren: Walt III, Kipoon, Jasper, Lucinda, Lau-lei, Ernie, Chucheesh, Charlene, Mussie Lou, Princess Jintcon, Nijonda, Bronc, Teh-sa'a:nxwe, Tasahce Se:wenah, and Kisdyante as well as his 5 great-grandchildren: Ke-yoh, Moreck, Keech-pooh, Ellie Su, and Nickwich.

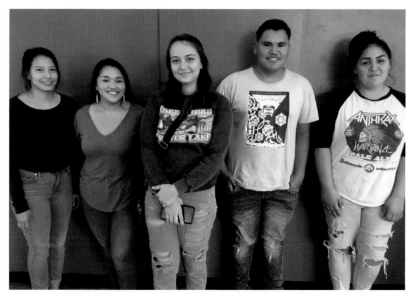

Figure 1: Ka'm-t'em Photography Project students pose for a photograph to commemorate their work. Courtesy of Ka'm-t'em Photography Project.

Ka'm-t'em Photography Project

This project was supported by the Native Cultures Fund and involved cultural mentorship between generations by creating an opportunity for youth to work with an elder, a photographer, a book chapter author, and the book editors. The mentor photographer and authors guided youth in the process of capturing Indigenous knowledge through photography.

A special thank you to our mentor photographer, Gary Colegrove Jr. and youth photographers: Maiya Rainer, Princess Jintcon Colegrove, Ellen Colegrove, Vincent Tracy, and Lozen Nez.

PART 1

The Weaving of the Basket: Foundations of Worldview, Epistemology, History, and Healing

This section gives a glimpse of an ancient people. The testimonials discern an Indigenous worldview and ways of knowing and understanding the world, bring awareness to historical experiences that influence on-going Indigenous experiences, and embrace Indigenous concepts to healing. The content is a journey and a rediscovery of ourselves.

CHAPTER 1

Voices from the Sacred: An Indigenous Worldview and Epistemology of Northwestern California

Chris Peters & Chisa Oros

THIS IS *A LOOK BACK AT A TIME OF TRANSCENDENCE.* We were young Indians in a time of change, intent on making that change in the wake of the devastation and resulting struggles our peoples were facing on Indian reservations and in relocation hubs around the country. In 1976, I was 26 years old, motivated by a deep desire to uncover my own personal identity as a Puhlik/Karuk man and to more fully participate in the spiritual renewal that was already in progress amongst our peoples and within our homelands of what is now called Northern California. We came together, young men and women who had experienced the call for Native cultural renaissance that was sweeping the Indigenous world, all of us driven to bring change and renewal here at home. Everyone brought their own life experiences, desires, and perspectives to our research, learning, labors, and prayer. Today we have at least two generations of Puhlik young people who know no different than a life with ceremonies and cultural protocol. It wasn't always this way. I write these memories with no intention of stirring up challenges of the past, but to remind us all of the obstacles we faced and what we learned in order to return to the ceremonial life we have today as Puhlik-lah. This is a small collection of my own memories and how we came to return here.

This was an exciting time of symbiotic social change. Many young Indigenous men and women were returning to their communities after being the first of their families to attend colleges and universities. Many were returning home from wars and trade schools. And all of us were growing up in the Civil Rights Era, with the American Indian Movement active in our communities and across the nation, linking and working with other movements for equality, rights, and recognition for oppressed peoples. All of this was occurring in the wake of the Indian Wars, the Termination Era, and the loss of our languages and teaching with the passing of elders who had knowledge and memories of lifeways closer to pre-contact times.

In the summer of 1976, shortly after returning to the community, I found myself at the ancient village of Pecwan, along with a gathering of Native youth, unearthing what had been described to us as the oldest house on the Klamath River, the "Men's House," known today as the sweathouse, for the Pecwan Earth Healing Ceremony Wala-we ley ga—or, as referred to in contemporary times, "the Jump Dance Ceremony." We sought to recover this ceremony after the decades of dormancy that followed the California Gold Rush and the subsequent colonial settlement of our homelands by non-Native people. Wala-we ley ga, (translated as "The Raising It Up Ceremony"), was historically performed at this village of Pecwan, within this very same family house that the young camp participants were uncovering. In earlier days, the long redwood roof planks of the family house were removed and all the family's personal belongings were stored elsewhere during the ten-day duration of the ceremony. The last time that Wala-we ley ga was performed here at the Pecwan village was 1937, when it had taken place in the larger family house only a short distance from where we worked that day.

As manager of the Tri-County Indian Development Council, Inc., myself and other community members had organized three summer youth camps that promoted cultural recovery among the Karuk, Tolowa, and Yurok peoples. In each camp, recognized cultural leaders mentored participating native youth on ceremonial protocols, lifeways, and cultural belief systems of our respective Tribal Nations. The primary focus of the teaching and work in the Pecwan camp was the revitalization of the Wala-we ley ga Ceremony. Our primary cultural mentors were Josephine and Jimmy James, and the ceremonial leader and elder Dewey George, advised us all. Dewey and Josephine were siblings and their father had been the last Soo-nay, or Medicine person, for the Pecwan Wala-we ley ga.

From watching and participating in the Hupa's Earth Healing Ceremony, most of the young people at the camp were basically familiar with how the Jump Dance was to be practiced and performed. The Hupa ceremony had been fully recovered after years of pernicious federal laws and policing that criminalized all Native spiritual practices. But still, the mentor of the Pecwan camp offered special presentations and ongoing discussion that described the process and esoteric knowledge of the Pecwan Wala-we ley ga.

From oral history and the mentors' personal recollections of the last ceremonies performed at Pecwan, we learned of a dynamic and beautiful gathering of families and community members who established individual kitchens and camps, which were called Feather Camps, that represented their historic villages. We learned where specific dance leaders would camp. Dewey George would tell us, "This is where my father Sra-gon George would put his dance camp for the village of Sra-gon, and down the river just a short distance Joe Jerry, the dance leader for Kot-tep, would set-up his feather camp, and a short distance up Pecwan Creek, Wak-kel Harry (also known as Pecwan Harry) located the Pecwan dance camp." We also learned about the roles and responsibilities of caretaking the sacred items and regalia used in the ceremony. Condor and eagle feathers and brilliant crimson head rolls (Play-gok, comprised of many pileated woodpecker feathers) would be assembled.

Within each feather camp, the sacred fires and the responsibilities of dance leaders were passed from generation to generation. To fully recover this ceremony, families would have to reassume the responsibility for a balanced world and the continued well-being of the Earth. This means that revitalizing the Pecwan Wala-we ley ga would require that descendants of these families step forward and reassume the inherent spiritual responsibility of their birthright. The spiritual energy associated with the Wala-we ley ga is very strong and must always be respected and held in the utmost highest regard. It must be a lifeway. Diverging from this responsibility could bring about ill health for the Earth and to all living things, including the families that were needed to recover this important ceremony. However, we were also sensitive to the understanding that re-engaging families in the revitalization of the Jump Dance Ceremony would not only require considerable personal and financial investment and sacrifice, but a very serious spiritual learning and engagement process as well.

All this was on our minds as we watched the Native youth camp participants, with picks and shovels, slowly begin to uncover the location of the sacred sweathouse and the ceremonial dance house, and in doing so revealed many memories of our cultural mentors. In the dance house, we found soapstone bowls and other household items that provoked conversations among our advisors of individuals who were birthed in this house and families that lived and grew at this village. In the sweathouse, we uncovered a large black rock that stood about two-and-a-half feet tall and was slightly concave at the top. The entire stone was amazingly polished by the many years of use and handling. Near the foundation of the sweathouse, we unearthed large, rectangular stones of such a size that it must have taken several strong men to move and situate them so tightly in the floor of this sacred house. All of this early effort served to reveal more of what we did not know and/or understand about this ceremony and our ancestors. Our desire as young people grew greater each day, and our drive to learn and reinvigorate ceremonial practice and presentation of this ceremony evolved as the memories uncovered within our cultural leaders and elders of the community suggested the need for more research into the metaphysics of this Earth Healing Ceremony and the spiritual connection with place.

As we had come to better understand the complexity of the ceremony and the work ahead, we now understood that this place and these houses were central to the efficacy of the Earth Healing Ceremony. The sweathouse (Er–geerk) was understood to be a place of contemplative thought and meditation, a place where humans (Auth) can "talk with the fire" and establish a spiritual connection with the energy that links life together, which can be found all around us.

During this process, many community members voiced concern about the ceremony and our effort to further uncover the sacred sweathouse. Perhaps they were already too entrenched in the Christian and settler colonial theologies that for many generations had sought to suppress the unique worldview and spiritual lifeways of the Puhlik people. Many feared the consequences that might befall the families and community should this ceremony and belief system be renewed.

Much of our tribal community had been living as dependents of the settler government since the California Gold Rush. The settlers, their Christian churches, and the United States government, criminalized our ceremonies and oppressed our connection to the Earth. The concern and memories of stigmatization, criminalization, and struggles for survival were fresh and ongoing within our communities.

Even our closest advisors may have been influenced by these oppressive theologies that ravaged our ancestors and continued to hurt us as Native peoples, and we were advised by our cultural leaders and local community members to set aside the renewal of the Wala-we ley ga. Our people were struggling, and their fear was legitimate, although confusing for those of us engaged in revitalization strategies and cultural renewal. Later, when we came to know more of the esoteric knowledge associated with this ceremony, this knowledge would strengthen us to challenge these settler ideologies and the forces of oppositional energy that we met along the way as we worked to uplift the resilience of our ceremonies.

In the years following, the recovery of the Wala-we ley ga was placed as a high priority in the lives of several similarly minded people as myself, despite challenges. We were raising families and wanted to be sure our children and future generations lived with a cultural understanding that our elders were holding but that would soon be gone. The cultural leader Dewey George would spend weeks and months recovering and teaching us songs of the Pecwan sweathouse or Er–geerk. We also learned more about the role of the Taahl, those men who would sacrifice their basic human needs and pleasures for this ceremony. As tradition mandates, the preparation for the Wala-we ley ga requires that the Taahl fast and complete journeys to sacred places in the mountains, seeking to reconnect to the spirit of the Earth and to request the power or medicine to carry out the Earth Healing Ceremony. The Taahl would also reside in the sacred sweathouse for the ten-day duration of the ceremony, coming out only to gather wood for the sweathouse fire. During the night, they burned medicine root (angelica root), "talked to the fire," and sang the songs that our mentor Dewey was still recovering from within his blood memory, songs that were critical to the efficiency of the ceremony.

I recall many evening hours were dedicated to learning the basic rhythm of songs and dance movements associated with this and other ceremonies. As these songs were recovered and given life, the important esoteric knowledge transferred to a younger generation and the

Wala-we ley ga ceremony begin to reveal itself in all of the brilliance and dynamic beauty that we had dreamed. It was truly a wondrous time in our lives to be present for the awakening of that ancestral knowledge. Somehow we instinctively knew that the search to renew this ceremony would lead us to knowing more about ourselves and how we fit into these perplexing Native paradigms; we were deeply committed to uncovering our spiritual purpose and identity and to the renewal of our ceremonial lives. Although at times we struggled against nay-sayers, our spirits persisted, and I will never forget that.

During this search for personal identity and the deeper understanding of life and ceremony, the first and most significant dilemma that we faced was that of our own creation or evolution on Earth. To truly understand where we hoped to go in our quest for ceremonial life, we first must know where we come from. When we discussed this with our cultural advisors, we learned that there were many divergent opinions about the origin of Puhlik peoples. Essentially, Native people who were influenced by the Christian church would tell us that a single, omnipotent "god" (One-I a-ick, or, "the One above that holds us in his hands") "willed" us to be and, like magic, Auth (human beings) just appeared, along with other complex life forms and natural systems of the Earth. Other respected Native advisors referred to Indian legends and the wisdom of oral history and presented a very different understanding of how Auth came to be in the world. From such stories, we learned that human life is the product of the creative energies of the Earth along with the countless Wo-gay, Spirit Beings, who joined together with earthquake, lightning, thunder, water, and fire and gave life to humanity.

Within such legend, we also find that the Spirit Beings, including the spirits of plants and animals, combined their most dynamic and formidable qualities with the rich soil of Earth to form human life. The redwood tree gave Auth a strong heart; from the wisdom of oral history we now know that when building a canoe or constructing a home we must make sure that they each also have a strong redwood heart. Other trusted Native advisors advocate that humanity evolved or descended from the Wo-gay and that we still have some of their creative energies within our DNA. Still others suggest that during ancient noth-e-kon (a time before there was time), we emerged from the ocean. From the numerous stories found in oral history of the beginning of human life, we concluded that perhaps all of these contain key elements of our creation.

It is through oral history and ceremony that we as Auth understand that our creation happened here in our respective homelands. The mountains, rivers, and sacred rocks found within our homeland serve as monuments that now stand in testimony to the mythological world and corroborate the many components of our cosmology. Thus, nowhere else in the world can such a profound emotional and spiritual relationship exist other than within our homelands. We are spiritually connected to this place in what is now called Northern California, what we call home. As legends are shared, we understand that they contain many metaphors that reveal an intelligence of place and ecosystems where deep wisdom is present and can be found within our sacred homelands. As we have come to understand from the legends describing our creation, we too are peoples of the Earth, and this sacred wisdom can be found deeply rooted within our very own gene pool or DNA. We also know that the spirit peoples were instrumental in establishing ceremonies, philosophies, and what our teachers called Indian law and customs, or value systems and protocol—key teachings local tribal peoples still adhere to in contemporary time.

In terms of our creation, there exists a common understanding among all regional tribes that spirit peoples or spiritual beings were present on Earth, and that they played a significant role in bringing forth human life. The existence of a prehuman race of spirit beings that inhabited the Earth before humans is firmly situated within oral history, these spirit peoples are described among the Puhlik-lah as Wo-gay, the Hupa refer to them as the Kix-inay, Karuk call them Ikxaréeyav, and the Tolowa Deeni refer to them as Tr'vm-dan'-ne Me'-lash-ne. Some suggest that these spiritual beings were/are the same sentient beings for all our Tribal Nations.

The second and very pivotal issue that confronted us in our search for identity and the renewal of the Pecwan Wala-we ley ga was to resolve the question, to whom do we address our supplication when speaking with the fire? The response that we received from many of our advisors was simply that we talk with the "Creator," a single deity. However, based on oral history, the interpretations of stories, and research into the esoteric knowledge of the Puhlik-lah, we found no trace of a single monotheistic "God." In fact, the findings were quite the opposite. It is the understanding of the Puhlik-lah and perhaps other Tribal Nations that we are not monotheistic; we do not have only one God. Also, nowhere in our oral history it is suggested that we have evolved from a

Christian or Abrahamic theology; their story of creation differs significantly from Native cosmology. Lastly, our stories have no description of a migration across the Bering Strait, nor do they suggest that we are descendants from some lost Tribe of Israel.

However, with the invasion of Eurocentric thought and the oppression of Native spirituality, the need to establish greater conformity with Abrahamic theologies continued to promote the belief of a single God or Creator. Within Puhlik cosmology, there are three possible candidates for this single Creator. Perhaps the closest that can be likened to a single god is the energy or "spirit" found in the description for I'lah-lik-washaa, the creative energy that is all around us and links together all of life. This dynamic energy I'lah-lik-washaa is believed to be bound to the Earth and does not reside in a paradise called "heaven."

The other two candidates that could have been elevated to such a standing are two of many Wo-Gay. The first of these is Pue-lek-ue-kweyr-ek, known within legend for his creative energies. With his many accomplishments and heroic deeds, he would be best suited to carry the honored title of a "Creator." However, the horns on his back and heels and a name that is translated as "downward facing horns" infringe significantly upon elevating his statue for the role of "the Creator." As Christian theology would have it, anything with horns is considered to be devious or evil. This assertion was further reinforced by labels of heathenism and paganism against our Native relatives throughout the continent and the islands where Columbus happened to land in 1492. As we see in history and today, it is the extensions of this church-based rhetoric which fueled the Indian Wars and the internment of our own peoples in places like Fort Humboldt, Fort Seward, and Fort Gaston to later face slavery and exploitation.

The other candidate, although having many worthy accomplishments, is best known in legend for being a trickster and philander among multi-animal species. He is also known as a "womanizer" who only had to walk a short distance with a female and she would depart his company with child. His name is Wo-pek-ue-mew, or "cross the ocean widower." Because his name was more palatable with Christian theology, though, he has been preserved in legend as our "Creator."

So it is that despite the knowledge found within Puhlik-lah legends, many of our friends and families still adhered to the concept of a single deity, a "Creator God," and they continued to aggressively forward the need to compromise our spiritual understandings and thus better conform to an Abrahamic idealism. Still today, when a Puhlik person is asked to name their God, their response would be Wo-pek-ue-mew. To me, this element of conformity to our settler neighbors has been devastating to our peoples and our connection to our ancestors' lifeways. At the time of my mid-twenties, I was getting a glimpse into how this assertion would plague recovery of ceremonies and confuse the spiritual journeys of our peoples to this very day.

What we learned from our mythological inquiry has led us to believe that our supplication can be directed to those spirit beings that created the customs and ceremony that now instruct human behavior. Most noticeable of these beings are Puhlik-leh-ue kuar-ek, Wo-pek-eu-mew, Kupo low yo and May-gor mer; each of these Wo-gay played instrumental roles in the origin of life and ceremony. However, we are quite confident that humans that still speak with the fire must address our most important supplications to the creative energies of I'lah-lik-washaa.

The existence of the spirit peoples proved to further confuse prevailing Christian theology and, to this very day, many churches minimize or deny their existence. Those Native people who hold tightly to the percept of a single god or "all-mighty being" refer to the spirit beings as "Angels." However, through oral history we have come to believe that these spirit beings, although having certain creative powers, were/are very much like contemporary human beings. They can see and perceive the world, they have feeling and can laugh and cry, they are intelligent and have a consciousness much the same as we humans. Although such spirit beings may have human qualities and deficiencies, we also know that the Wo-gay, the Ikxaréeyav, and all the sentient beings were endowed with supernatural or creative energy, and in the noth-e-kon (mystic time), they—together with the Earth spirits, earthquake, thunder, water, fire, and the many animal spirits as well—conceived and brought about the balance and harmony that we enjoy on Earth today.

With the Earth spirits, the Wo-gay also established laws (Indian laws), customs, and ceremonies that were needed to maintain the harmony and balance of Mother Earth. As legend has described, the spirit peoples conceived and instructed humans on the process and protocols of elaborate ceremonies designed for the healing and renewing of the Earth. To know and better understand these spirit beings was not only fundamental to the recovery of ceremony but also to better appreciating the human purpose and how we fit into the spiritual world that we were rediscovering.

These ceremonies are ingrained into the hearts and souls of our peoples and reside within our blood memories and ancestral knowledge. They are expressed through focused and collective emotional energy. Some may refer to this expression as "prayer," but for many tribal peoples the word "prayer" conjures up a Christian process of supplication that involves sending one's desires to an "all-mighty god" that lives above. We have come to believe that during Earth Healing Ceremony our deeply held emotions and our love for the Earth are combined with the life-giving energies of I'lah-lik-washaa. As we learned more of the Earth-based theology, we have come to understand that the Earth is alive and has a spirit, and that humanity has a vital responsibility to help maintain such harmony. In fact, that is our primary purpose in life: we are Earth-healing and Earth-renewing peoples.

This mythological inquiry has also opened the doors (and opened our minds) to a completely different worldview; the concept of an Earth-based theology which now offers hope and direction to our quest for purpose and identity. Throughout the ten-day ceremonial engagement with Jump Dance, we continuously burn medicine root and "speak to the fire." In this way, we connect with the spirit of the Earth and our collective desires or "will" are expressed, causing renewed balance within self and the world. We give thanks and "pray," but not as lone acts equivalent to the world's mainstream religions. We give thanks and speak with the fire consistently throughout our time on Earth as a lifeway.

The Indian laws and customs that were established by the spirit beings and/or surmised by the Auth (human beings) in their astute observations of the natural world established a moral and ethical foundation steeped in generosity. Such laws mandate Indian lifeways that are based upon respect, responsibility, and reciprocity, and that are essential for healing and sustaining the world for the many generations to come. Through life and ceremony, these teachings have instilled within our peoples the important responsibility that mandates that we take from the natural world only what is needed for basic survival and give back an equal amount. Balance is secured and respect expressed through an offering of tobacco or medicine or through our good thoughts and deeply held emotions for what we have taken or received. This is a critically important role that we must fulfill; as Earth healing and Earth renewing peoples, this is our spiritual purpose and is most significant to the recovery of our ceremonies.

In the mid-1970s, concurrent with our search for ceremony and the sacred energies of the Earth, the Six Rivers National Forest Service launched a devastating and far-reaching blow to the spiritual lifeways of Native peoples throughout the United States. Their malicious plans to construct a logging road (known as the GO Road) between the two Northern California towns of Gasquet and Orleans would become an epic battle fought here within our homelands that would reach the U.S. Supreme Court. The plan would not only involve road construction, but also the implementation of a major timber harvesting plan, destroying the pristine qualities of sacred places in the Siskiyou Mountains used for Medicine Making purposes by Puhlik people for thousands of years. Because the sacred area that was targeted by the U.S. Forest Service was and continues to be indispensable to the efficacy of the Earth Healing Ceremony and central to the continuity of Puhlik-lah spiritual lifeways, the focus of our attention was deviated away from ceremony revitalization and toward stopping the road construction.

The GO Road case (Lyng v. Northwest Indian Cemetery Protection Association) would end with devastating impacts on the spiritual practices and religious freedoms of Native Peoples throughout the nation. Today, Native leaders have no recourse within the American judicial system to stop the desecration of places that are sacred to their spiritual lifeways. Suffice to say, battling the GO Road and preserving the spiritual life of the Puhlik people demanded a significant amount of time and resources from our small community. For many Tribal Nations, the decision in the GO Road case would represent a final act of cultural genocide. However, despite the ruling, we preserved a sliver of hope through the spiritual and religious practices of our Peoples.[1]

With the GO Road Case looming and a growing determination to fulfill what had come to be our ancestral legacy, the rebirth of the Wala-we ley ga, the need to expand our reach into local Native communities proved to be critical. Over the course of the next few years, we visited with many families and sought advice from cultural leaders on the significance of ceremony and place. However, most importantly, we took the time and visited sacred places in the high country: Doctor Rock, Elk Valley, Little Medicine Mountain, and of course Chimney Rock. Through contemplative thought, meditation, and speaking with the fire, we gained the strength of our convictions and reaffirmed our commitments to ceremony. Our conversations with communities became more focused on stopping the GO-Road and recovering the Wala-we ley ga.

Eight years after we unearthed the sweathouse and began asking our elders questions, we found ourselves back at Pecwan Village, again with pick and shovel, determined to remove the dirt and debris that had been accumulated in both the dance house and the old sweathouse. The community responded quickly and crews began splitting redwood planks and carrying them from far up Pecwan creek to be used to reconstruct the buildings for the sacred ceremony. The research and acquired knowledge of Wala-we ley ga here at Pecwan provided the confidence to see this Earth Healing Ceremony come to fruition.

As indicated earlier, there are two principal ceremonies for renewing and healing the Earth. The first is the Jump Dance Ceremony, which has been the focus of this writing. The other important ceremony is the Sraach a-pye-way, or White Deerskin Dance. With the Sraach a-pye-way, we as human beings connect with the spirits of the Earth (I'lah-lik-washaa) and we Renew the World. Throughout this ten-day ceremony we dance, sing, and speak with the fire to offer positive energy to help recreate a pristine world filled with an abundance of healthy living things and establish renewed harmony for the seasons to come. In the Sraach a-pye-way, we give thanks for all that sustains life and we celebrate the coming of new life and a new-year cycle.

Today, the Earth Healing Ceremonies still continue and have gained strength; now greater numbers of our people participate and understand the esoteric purposes of the Wala-we ley ga. As we grow in our ceremonies, we are healing our people and healing the world once again. With full knowledge that this healing process may take many generations, there is an increased optimism and a realization among the Puhlik-lah that we are a part of an important renaissance in thought and in time. We recognize that through this sacred process our cultural well-being and vitality as a people will be reachieved.

Endnotes

1. For more discussion on the Lyng V. NICPA (GO Road Case) refer to Chapters 9 and 10. – Ed.

CHAPTER 2

"More than a Boat": Bias, Institutional Frameworks, and Testimonial Injustice

Kishan Lara-Cooper

INDIGENOUS IDENTITY IS OFTEN INFLUENCED BY SINGLE NARRATIVES DEMONSTRATED IN TEXT-BOOKS, LITERATURE, MEDIA, AND SOCIAL INDICATORS. These imposed identities characterize Indigenous populations as having the highest rates of suicide, deaths due to violence, high school dropout, alcoholism, and child welfare cases. Social indicators highlight that even among health related issues, Indigenous people have the highest rates of diabetes and tuberculosis. Although these social indicators are critical to expose the need for support systems and services for Indigenous peoples, these forms of assessment paint a grueling and often depressing outlook for members of Indigenous communities. The purpose of this chapter is to emphasize the importance of Indigenous knowledge to healing. This chapter will discuss current challenges facing Indigenous youth, the causes of these challenges, and initial steps to healing.

Current Challenges Facing Indigenous Youth

Indigenous people make up 1.7% of the United States population[1]. In the 2010 census, 5.2 million people identified as American Indian/Alaska Native, and 2.9 million identified as American Indian/Alaska Native alone[2]. Thirty-two percent of the Indigenous population is under the age of 18, which indicates future growth of the population.

Despite the size of the population in relation to other peoples, Indigenous peoples experience the highest rates of health disparities, addiction, and violence. According to Indian Health Services, Indigenous people have the highest death rate in all of the following categories: heart disease, cancer, diabetes, stroke, liver disease, kidney disease, and influenza[3]. Alcoholism rates are 510% higher than the general population; Indigenous teens experience the highest rate of suicide, ten times the national norm; and violence accounts for 75% of deaths for Indigenous youth ages 12-20[4]. Indigenous peoples have a 229% higher rate of death in a car accident. While the number of fatal car accidents decreased by 2.2% throughout the rest of the nation in the last five years, the number of fatal accidents increased by 52.5% on reservations.[5] Indigenous adolescents have death rates two to five times the rate of Euro-American adolescence in the same age group[6]. Indigenous peoples have the highest proportion of those killed by police—a rate of 7.8 per million compared to the rate of 2.9 per million of Euro-American counterparts. Finally, high school dropout rates are double the national average and 50% higher than any other ethnic group in the State of California[7].

It is important to note that these statistics reflect more than numbers. These statistics affect our people: our parents, our siblings, our aunts, our uncles, our grandparents, and of course, our children. I remember when my son was born. I would gaze at him for hours and think of all the wonderful contributions that he would make to the world. Would he be a singer or dancer of our ceremonies? Would he be a protector? Would he be kind and generous? Would he be an advocate for our way of life? When a child is born, typically we think of their potential and we wish them a long and healthy life. Never do we wish for them to become a statistic, a victim to a violent crime, or a sufferer of an addiction or a disease. Yet, these are challenges that our children face. Furthermore, our children must survive through the loss and hardship of their family members who have fallen victim to statistics.

A few years ago, I helped to chaperone my nephew's tenth birthday party. He was thrilled to stay at a hotel, eat pizza, and swim with three of his friends. As the boys splashed in the pool, I was struck with the reminder of statistics that I had read earlier in the day: "1 out of every 10 become victims of violent crimes,[8] 1 of every 2 will drop out from high school,[9] and 1 of 4 will live in poverty."[10] What did this mean for these four boys? As I thought deeper about each child's situation, I realized that one of the boys was struggling with the divorce of his parents and another had lost his mother in a car accident two years earlier. It pained me to realize that these statistics were already manifesting in our children.

That night, around two in the morning, the third child's father arrived at the hotel. The child's mother had just passed away. I can still see the three boys huddled on the hotel room bed around their friend as he struggled to tie his shoes to leave with his father. The boy who had lost his mother two years earlier patted his back and said, "Don't worry, I know how you feel right now, but we are going to be okay."

The next morning, my nephew sat alongside me with a stressed look on his face and asked me, "How much longer do you think my mom has before she dies?" Thinking back to that moment, I feel like sobbing once again. It seems so unjust that a ten-year-old should have to worry about the loss of a parent, yet this is a fear of many Indigenous children. Often when we hear the statistics that our Indigenous people are facing, it is so overwhelming for *us* that we forget about the children who are witness to these atrocities.

In another experience, I watched a classroom full of third graders in our local community describe their "self-less acts" to each other as part of a classroom assignment. One child spoke of assisting in a ceremonial dance camp; another child spoke of helping her parents search for her missing brother, and every other child (one out of two) spoke of self-less acts related to loss and grief from within the last year. In many cases, Indigenous children have experienced so much loss that they are unable to fully grieve one loss before another occurs.

It is important to understand that these traumatic occurrences are not anomalies. Rather, they are evidence of intergenerational trauma and on-going oppression. These traumatic events further perpetuate health disparities, stress, depression, and anxiety, which continue the cycle. Furthermore, the statistics themselves provoke fear and negative thinking in Indigenous children. Likewise, Yellow Bird, a scholar in Indigenous people's health and neurodecolonization, argues that, "Unconstructive, negative thinking, feelings, and behaviors dampen and short circuit our brain's creativity and optimistic networks, and increase our susceptibility to stress, failure, complacency, and fear."[11]

Intergenerational Trauma and On-going Oppression

Research indicates that there is a direct correlation between historical experiences, such as genocide and boarding schools, and the current social indicators of Indigenous peoples. Likewise, these social indicators "have been theoretically and empirically linked to social, economic, cultural, or political inequalities and not an inherent Native trait or gene."[12] Trauma is "an experience that creates a lasting substantial, psychosocial, and somatic impact on a child."[13]

Intergenerational trauma is sometimes referred to as historical trauma, multigenerational trauma, or unresolved historical grief. Intergenerational trauma occurs from an overwhelmingly traumatic event on an individual or a shared group. For example, In the early 1940s, two brothers—one five years old and one seven years old—played on Requa Hill in Klamath, California. The boys were engaged in a tag game when they saw a flatbed truck making its way up the gravel road. At that time, these types of trucks would travel in highly populated Indigenous communities to kidnap children and take them to government-operated boarding schools. Having heard about these incidences, the eldest boy threw his little brother into the brush to hide. Unable to get away, the eldest boy was captured and taken in the truck to Chemauwa Institute in Oregon. When the truck was out of sight, the five-year-old crawled out of hiding and ran to tell his grandparents. The boys' grandparents were told by the boarding school that they had no parental rights as Indigenous children were considered wards of the State, and that they would see their grandson again when he was finished with his schooling. Ten years later, the eldest boy returned. He never spoke of his experience, but history would tell the story of the boarding school experience. Children at these institutions were stripped of regalia, given biblical names, beaten for speaking their Indigenous languages, and abused physically, sexually, and emotionally. Boarding schools operated on a military system. Children wore uniforms, and survived on small rations of food.

A few months after his return, this boy got into trouble and was sent to a Southern California prison. From his perspective, this institution was comfortable to him; in his words, "it was no different than boarding school." After release from prison, he married and divorced several times and fathered several children. His children fell victim to the same neglect and abuse that he had once endured.

Reversely, his younger brother grew up with the love and nurturing of his grandparents, and he likewise extended this love to his community, his family, and his grandchildren. Seventy-five years after the kidnapping, the younger brother's granddaughter asked him, "Why are you always joyful, loving, and happy, and Uncle is always cold, distant, and harsh?" The younger brother responded, "Because he gave his life up for me."[14]

In this example of the two brothers playing on Requa Hill, the eldest brother experienced trauma from this and subsequent events. In turn, his children and his grandchildren—who were not kidnapped and never attended boarding school—experienced intergenerational trauma, including acts of abuse and neglect as well as an absent and detached father. In addition, his children and grandchildren may have experienced a collective of historically traumatic events. Braveheart, a scholar in historical trauma, argues that, "…American Indians also have a pervasive sense of pain from what happened to their ancestors and [from] incomplete mourning of those losses… Closer examination of suicide studies [among Indigenous peoples] reveals implicit unresolved, fixated, or anticipatory grief about perceived abandonment as well as affiliated cultural disruption."[15]

Initial Steps to Healing: Pre-service and In-service Professionals

This section will identify three initial steps for pre-service (those going into the field) and in-service (those already in the field) professionals who work with Indigenous children, families, and communities to foster healing. Professionals in the field may have been exposed to terms such as *cultural sensitivity, mindfulness, decolonization, strengths-based approach*, or *diversity* and *equity*. These integral philosophies (and many more) begin with self-reflection. In order to create safe spaces for others, one must first explore what influences personal preferences, perceptions, assumptions, and realities. For example, one might ask herself, "What is important to teach my children?" to better understand personal values that influence thoughts of child-rearing best practices. Being aware of bias, shifting the paradigm of institutional frameworks, and creating spaces for testimonial justice are initial steps to healing. However, it is important to note that this is a topical list, and that in-depth pathways to healing should be further explored. For example, Yellow Bird's neurodecolonization equation, the White Bison Well-briety Movement, and Murphy-Shigematsu's mindfulness to heartfulness research are a few of these critical tools to healing.

Being Aware of Bias

The first step to creating a safe and nurturing environment for Indigenous children, families, and communities is being aware of personal bias and how one's perception of others is influenced by personal worldview and environmental surroundings. *Worldview* refers to a way of thinking and existing in the world that is influenced by our values, experiences, and beliefs. Each person has one. "A worldview consists of the principles we acquire to make sense of the world around us. Young people learn these principles, including values, traditions, and customs, from myths, legends, family, community, and examples set by community leaders."[16] It is also important to understand that each person has an *epistemology*, a "philosophy of knowledge"[17] or the way in which one makes sense of the world based on one's natural environment, surroundings, and view of the world. Although one's worldview and epistemology may constantly evolve, many deeply held beliefs are rooted in childhood experiences.

Within the first five years of a child's life, a self-concept, grounded in worldview and epistemology, is developed. As a matter of fact, bias is established during the infancy stage of development. At around three months of age, an infant will develop bias toward their home settings. For example, an infant may feel more comfortable with people that have a familiar sound, smell, touch, or appearance. What this means is that from a developmental perspective, it is nearly impossible to be non-bias. Although no individual person can completely eliminate her own bias, she can be aware that she has biases that influence her perceptions, expectations, and assumptions of others.

Teachers, social workers, and child advocates (to name a few) likely chose their career path in an effort to "help" people. Professionals in these fields often consider themselves to be "good" hearted people who want to ensure that children have "good" lives where they are "happy" and can be "successful." I have utilized quotes around these words because they are subjective words. For example, the use of the word "happy" is reflective of a person's worldview. Therefore, happiness to one may look very different to another. Despite the best of intentions, an individual's effort might actually have detrimental effects. For example:

> A man—let's call him Harry—was sitting in the front of a crowded conference room participating in a training when a fly landed on his ear. He brushed the fly away and continued to listen to participants' introductions. Once again, the fly landed on his ear; nonchalantly he brushed it away. Meanwhile, a woman sitting behind Harry rolled her papers into a cone and swatted the fly! Although she missed the fly, the coned papers left a red mark on the side of Harry's head. Startled, Harry clasped his hand to his ear. As the group nearest him chuckled, he sunk into his seat. A few introductions later, the woman introduced herself and proceeded to justify her actions by placing her hand on his shoulder and saying, "I saw that fly bothering you. I am a good person and I am in the business of helping people. So, I took care of it for you."

As you may notice. Harry was more affected by being hit with "good intention" than he was by the fly.

In a similar example, the Women's National Indian Association (WNIA) of 1879 "saw Indians as childlike, existing within a heathenistic culture that needed to be properly cleansed and replaced by the superior American culture."[18] Because of this world view, this group of "missionary minded"[19] women had no value for Indigenous knowledge or epistemology and "believed sincerely that it needed to be replaced for the good of the Indian."[20] Thus, "their efforts encouraged the U.S. government's assimilation policies designed to replace American Indian cultures, reduce the Indian land base through allotment and sale of reservation lands, and diminish the historic concept of Indian nations' sovereignty."[21]

As these examples illustrate, it is critical for professionals who work with children, families, and communities to understand how one's worldview and epistemology influence perceptions, assumptions, expectations, and interpretations of what is "right," "good," "correct," and "successful." Consequently, not only is it important to self-reflect on how worldview and epistemology influence personal perceptions, but it is also vital to understand that every human being with whom we interact holds values, beliefs, and experiences that undoubtedly influence their view of the world. In the story of the fly, the "caregiver" was bothered by the fly, while the "victim" wasn't even fully aware of the fly's presence.

In another example, a research study on giftedness among an Indigenous community in Northern California indicates that Indigenous language is an integral component of Indigenous thought, perception, and application of knowledge. Not only were speakers of Indigenous languages recognized as gifted, but Indigenous language was also identified as one of the most important things to teach to the community's children. [22] In contrast, a monolingual English-speaking professional working within this community might mistakenly characterize Indigenous language as insignificant or an unnecessary skill in today's society. As such, it is critical to be mindful of personal preference, assumptions, and expectations that influence our interactions and decision-making for others. These assessments are often reflections of our own bias.

According to Kang, a scholar in equality, diversity and inclusion, there are two types of bias: explicit bias (bias to which one is aware) and implicit bias (bias to which one is unaware).[23] A person is typically aware of her explicit bias and may choose to unveil this bias to others. Explicit bias that is unveiled to others tends to be non-threatening to a popular view. For example, the statement "my child is the smartest" is a typically accepted statement because society almost expects that a parent would feel this way. Furthermore, explicit bias may be exposed when a space subsists that nurtures similar thinking; for example, the statement, "It takes a special person to be a social worker; we are the greatest" to a room full of social workers can be shared explicitly because a space exists that supports this belief. Explicit bias that has been previously held privately might emerge when a space is generated that nurtures the bias. For example, an onlooker who observed the scenario of Harry and the fly may sit quietly and keep his bias private. However, once a space is created that supports his opinion about the scenario, he may be inclined to share his explicit bias.

Reversely, one might not be aware of her implicit bias. Mental associations may be so deeply rooted in previous environmental experiences that a person does not realize that it exists. As Banaji and Greenwald, authors of the *Blind Spot: Hidden Biases of Good People,* state, "…often these thoughts or feelings are reflected in our actions too…and they are at times completely at odds with our conscience intentions."[24]

Social mindbugs, an aspect of implicit bias, are "ingrained habits of thought that lead to errors in how we perceive, remember, reason, and make decisions."[25] They might show up through an exercise where all the vowels are missing from a paragraph yet one is able to read it, by remembering something that didn't occur because of an automatic association, or when predicting a person's personality or qualifications based on a facial image. Often, professionals in the fields who work with children and families, have such large caseloads that they rely on "quick readings" to assess their clientele. Consequently, social mindbugs influence these professionals' assumptions of the client and can give false illusions of the client's trustworthiness, competence, and character. Therefore a person classifies and interprets people and situations based on personal biases.

This type of monological thinking fulfills a human need to categorize and sort (a skill that is developed in middle childhood or school-age) through rapid intuitive thinking. This is referred to as *automatic processing,* whereby "we implicitly know something or feel a certain way."[26]

Numerous Implicit Association Tests (IAT) developed through Project Implicit[27] rely on the stored values, experiences, and beliefs (worldview) of participants in order to make categorizations. Results from nearly 700 million IATs indicate that:

> Most participants demonstrated implicit attitudes in favor of one social group over another…people are generally not "color" blind to race, gender, religion, social class, or other demographic characteristics. More important, participants systematically preferred socially privileged groups: YOUNG over OLD, WHITE over BLACK, LIGHT SKINNED over DARK SKINNED, OTHER PEOPLES over ARAB-MUSLIM, ABLED over DISABLED, THIN over OBESE, and STRAIGHT over GAY.[28]

How does this relate to professionals who work with children and families? Despite our desire to be objective, "open-minded," or a "good" person, we as human beings are influenced by our view of the world and the dominant narratives that construct our perceived identity of clients. It is our professional and humane responsibility to be cognizant of how these deeply rooted values, personal beliefs, and environmental experiences impact our "truth."

Another form of bias of which to be mindful is the cloning mechanism. In this circumstance, an individual may recognize a similar quality in another individual and will consequently assume that everything else about the individual is the same. For example, a teacher with a childhood history of being withdrawn from class due to illness may have a student that is withdrawn in the classroom. In turn, the teacher may address the student's behavior as if the student were ill. Similarly, cloning mechanisms can occur with those of the same age, gender, race, community, or occupation. In the story of the fly, the woman assumed that because of similarities with Harry (both of them were professionals attending the same training), his needs were the same as her needs.

Understanding that our worldview and epistemologies shape our interpretations, assumptions, and expectations of the children and families we serve is a critical first step in multilogical thinking. Multilogical thinking perpetuates awareness that each human has a worldview and an epistemology that has been established through their values, experiences, and beliefs since birth. Furthermore, awareness of implicit bias, explicit bias, social mindbugs, and the cloning mechanisms withheld in each of us creates an opportunity for self-growth and reflection.

Shifting the Paradigm of Institutional Frameworks

Institutions such as the child welfare system, judicial system, and educational system are built on frameworks influenced by historical, social, and economic interests. As professionals, it is important to research and be mindful of these influences, as well as how these interests continue to resonate in the genetic pools of institutions. For example, the educational system for Indigenous peoples was designed as an assimilation tool, meant to "Kill the Indian, save the man."[29] In this educational philosophy, constructed by Richard Henry Pratt in 1879, the values of Indigenous peoples were seen as insignificant, "heathen," and "savage."[30] Consequently, the tenets of colonial education were identified as key to the education and civilization of Indigenous children. These tenets include: 1) Native Americans are "savages" and have to be civilized, 2) Civilization requires Christian conversion, 3) Civilization also requires subordination of Native communities, frequently achieved through resettlement efforts, and 4) Native Americans have specific mental, moral, physical, or cultural deficiencies that require specific pedagogical practices.[31] Furthermore, parents were excluded from the educational systems, as interaction with parents was deemed as detrimental to the "civilization" process.

It is important to reflect on how these ideologies manifest themselves in educational systems of today. For example, in thinking about ways in which to solicit parent involvement in the school system, one must also think about what changes have occurred to shift the paradigm of education. At one time, the purpose of education was to exclude parents from the education of their children. What changes have been made to retract this policy? What has the educational system done to ensure that parent involvement is now welcomed? In another example, how has the educational system shifted from the deficit model or the assumption that something is wrong or missing? I am often asked, "How do we teach Indian children?" This question indicates that there are still remnants of the genetics of an education system that believes that "Indians" have deficiencies that require specific pedagogical methods.

Awareness of the historical influences of such institutions might explain why some clientele benefit and thrive from these institutional frameworks while other clientele continue to suffer and retrogress. Likewise, the authors of *The Role of Social Work in Advancing the Practice of Indigenous Education* state that, "The greatest obstacle to advancing Indigenous education may be the lack of acknowledgment and redress of its oppressive history. The removal of Indigenous children from their homes by the social work profession is part of that legacy."[32]

In order to address the alarming social indicators presented at the beginning of this chapter, institutional racism and on-going oppression must be addressed and a paradigm shift is needed. Furthermore, there is continued need for on-going self-reflection and assessment by professionals in the field. As a professional in the field, you might ask: *How do I benefit from the current institutional framework? Am I aware of my position of power within the system? Do I take extra steps to create safe spaces for my clients?*

Although it may not be solicited or desired, professionals who work with children and families inherit a position of power and authority within the current institutional framework. Yet professionals often expect clients to self-advocate, step out of their comfort zone, and initiate communication. These are difficult tasks to accomplish when you are not in a position of power. Furthermore, many professionals who acknowledge a need for a paradigm shift would like the formula delivered in a package to their front door. However, there is no blueprint for shifting the paradigm. Each community is unique and will require active participation, listening, brainstorming, reflecting, and exploring to foster change.

Healing through testimony

Norton, a California Indigenous historian, states that, "in the telling and in the listening, humanity meets."[33] This concept of bringing "meaning to the engagement between the storyteller and listener"[34] is critical in shifting the paradigm and initiating steps toward healing. In mainstream society, when an individual has experienced a traumatic event, opportunities are often provided for the person to talk about his experience. Support groups, vigils, community events, and mentorships are developed to support the healing process. Although the traumatic event is always a part of a person's life, these humane efforts assist the individual in movement toward healing. However, many Indigenous peoples have not been allocated this opportunity to share and heal from their pain. Often when an Indigenous person begins to speak of how he has been affected by the boarding school experience, genocide, or on-going institutional racism, he is silenced with statements such as, "that was a long time ago, get over it;" "that wasn't my fault, I didn't do it;" "stop wallowing in self-pity and make something of yourself;" or "you're too emotional." These responses are vile acts to humanity; dismissive of Indigenous experiences; and seeds of testimonial injustice.

Testimonial injustice[35] occurs when an individual or a group is omitted from a story because they are not deemed credible to share. Adichi, a novelist, argues that there is "danger in a single story" and through omitting narratives of marginalized groups, a construed picture of those groups is created. She states:

> So that is how to create a single story, show a people as one thing, as only one thing, over and over again, and that is what they become…But to insist on only these negative stories is to flatten my experience and to overlook the many other stories that formed me. The single story creates stereotypes, and the problem

with stereotypes is not that they are untrue, but that they are incomplete. They make one story become the only story.[36]

In response to the human desire to categorize, and a conditioned craving for concrete, single answers, society has established intuitive attitudes, thoughts, and perceptions of Indigenous identity. Deloria, an Indigenous scholar, refers to this automatic processing as "misplaced concreteness."[37] Relying solely on social indicators, statistics, or a single narrative to define Indigenous peoples creates a false, imposed, and misplaced sense of identity.

Due to testimonial injustice in textbooks, social media, newspapers, court systems, and educational systems, Indigenous communities are plagued with stereotypes. Furthermore, the Indigenous narrative is often omitted from United States and California history; Indigenous testimonies have been excluded from court proceedings that relate to Indigenous ceremonial sites, burial sites, water rights, and children's rights; Indigenous community concepts of giftedness have been omitted from standardized testing, academic State standards, and gifted education programs; and Indigenous experiences with colonialism are absent from pre-service and in-service professional development. These exclusions of testimony have led to a single story, a dominant narrative that has been executed on Indigenous children, families, and communities. Moreover, testimonial injustice has contributed to on-going oppression and institutional racism:

> The ignorance and prejudice toward Indigenous cultures by social workers was present for two reasons. First, social workers, like educators, were the products of a European American education system that disrespected or ignored Indigenous cultures while promoting its own history, heroes, language, and culture. Second, the education system did not (and still does not) equip students to understand how European American colonization oppressed the social, political, and economic lives of Indigenous peoples... to counter this reality, social workers and educators must seek out narratives of Indigenous peoples.[38]

Consequently, there is a need to solicit, create space, and actively listen to Indigenous narratives and testimonials.[39] For example, an Indigenous research project utilized testimonials to define giftedness from a community context. [40] The study included 250 Hupa, Yurok, and Karuk participants who reside on the Hoopa Valley Indian Reservation in Hoopa, California. Methods included in-depth interviews, survey, and focus groups. Participants were asked: 1) What do you identify as characteristics of giftedness? 2) What do you feel are the five most important things to teach to your children?

From testimonial, giftedness is defined as K'winya'nyan-ma awhiniw, "the way of the acorn eater (or, the human way)" to live in harmony with the world by valuing relationships with the human, natural, and spiritual realms of the world. Therefore, the community's definition of giftedness is constructed from the natural environment, including homeland, stories, songs, ceremony, and language. The testimonials identified important aspects to teach children as relationships with elders, community, self-respect, and for gathering sites, homeland, animals, water, and the environment; a spiritual connection to songs, ancestors, regalia, canoes, and the energies of the world; values of respect, responsibility, humility, a good heart, sincerity, generosity, and discipline; and cultural skills of basket-making, regalia-making, story-telling, fishing, hunting, gathering, and being a good listener. [41]

It is important to note that—despite depictions of imbalance, struggle, or loss of culture—this Indigenous community has deemed the above characteristics as components of giftedness that they wish to teach to children. Few, if any, of these characteristics appears on standardized tests, classroom assessments, or discussion boards for the local newspaper (where an excess of uninformed assessments appear). Yet, if the community were assessed on the increase of Indigenous language speakers, basket makers, regalia makers, singers, or dancers in the last twenty years, the community would excel. In turn, this excellence would undoubtedly impact the self-esteem, self-worth, and ultimately the self-actualization of Indigenous community members.

Initial Steps to Healing: "More Than a Boat"

Because of movements to shift the paradigm and create spaces for multiple narratives, educational systems, for example, have implemented activities that give children an opportunity to share their personal experiences, worldview, and epistemology with their classmates. The following example illustrates first steps to embracing testimonials of children, while also exposing a need for further self-reflection and institutional exploration:

> Ijo entered his first day of Kindergarten with excitement and nervousness about what the school year would bring. His teacher explained that they were going to have an assignment to get to know each other. "Each student will take home one of these paper bags," the teacher said with excitement, "and you will fill the bag with four items that are important to you."
>
> Ijo could not wait to get home to pick out his items. His mind was already thinking of all of the things that he might bring to share with his new friends. When he arrived home, he immediately ran to his room and began to select items. He pulled a baseball out of his toy box and placed it into his bag. He carefully selected a Spiderman figure from his superhero collection. He pulled out his step stool, crawled up to his shelf, and grabbed his auth wayatch (a Yurok dugout model canoe). He massaged the side of the canoe, whispered "aikuywee" (a special greeting), and placed it in his bag. Finally, he pulled a small trunk out of his closet, opened it, and selected an eagle feather. The eagle feather was not real. It had been made and hand-painted by his father so that Ijo could practice ceremonial dances at home.
>
> Ijo carefully placed the eagle feather in his bag and ran out to show his mother his selection. "What do you want to say about each item?" his mother asked. "I'm going to tell them I'm Nererner, Natinixwe, and Mvskoke. I love baseball. My dad and I play baseball in the backyard every day. I chose the Spiderman because I am going to be a superhero one day." Ijo spoke rapidly as he pulled each item out of the paper bag. "I'm taking this guy, [the canoe]. He has his own spiritual life and I take care of him and he takes care of me. This feather has his own life, too. He helps us in the dances to pray." As he spoke, his mother smiled with pride. She was overjoyed that, at five years old, her son had already established his own sense of identity and love for himself.
>
> "Will you go to school with me tomorrow and stand in the back?" Ijo asked. His mother nodded, knowing that, since he was new to a classroom environment, she had already planned to go to school with him all week anyway.
>
> The next day at school, Ijo was the first person asked to share.

He nervously walked in front of the class and quietly uttered his first words, "My name is Ijo and this is my baseball. I play baseball with my dad every day." The class watched silently. "I brought Spiderman because I'm going to be a superhero." The class began to make noise and get excited by the toy. Next, Ijo pulled the canoe out of his bag and said, "This is my auth wayach." Immediately a child hollered out, "That's not an auth wawa! That's a boat!" Ijo looked down at the canoe and mumbled, "Um, it's a canoe." "Whoa!" another child hollered, "this is deja vu!" Another child asks, "What does deja vu mean?"

The teacher, anxious to take advantage of the "teachable moment," responded, "Deja vu is when you experience something that you feel as if you have experienced before." One side of the classroom listened, engaged in the vocabulary lesson, while the other side of the room engaged in discussions about their summer vacations, paddling, and large boats.

Confused, Ijo put the canoe back into the paper bag, folded it closed, and said, "And that is all." He sat down in his seat and hung his head. When all the children ran off to recess, Ijo's mother, having had observed the entire incident, told Ijo, "You did a great job! How did you feel about your presentation?" "I didn't share my eagle feather," Ijo mumbled. "Why didn't you share your eagle feather?" Ijo looked into her eyes and shook his head, "They didn't deserve it."

At five years old, Ijo and his classmates are transitioning from early childhood to middle childhood, often referred to as "school-age." At this stage, children have typically established a self-concept that is based on their worldview. As such, the idea of this assignment was to create a home-to-school connection, whereby a safe space is created in the classroom that nurtures a child's self-concept and helps him to identify his space in the classroom. What wasn't understood by Ijo's peers or his teacher was that each presenter was sharing a gift, a piece of themselves, with the class. It was an opportunity to embrace multiple perspectives, interests, and worldviews.

Although with "good intention," the teacher seized the opportunity to teach an important vocabulary lesson. In so doing, he forgot about the lesson being given by the child. An auth we yoch, a traditional redwood Yurok dugout canoe, is made with a heart, lungs, kidneys, and nose. Yurok creation stories describe how the redwood became the keeper of the forest, and anything that is made of redwood has its own spiritual life. A caretaker of a canoe has a responsibility to nurture this life. Dismissing these lessons and referring to an auth we yoch as simply a mainstream interpretation of a boat minimizes its significance. At the initial dismissal by the students it could have been the opportunity for the teacher to be clear to Ijo and all the children that the purpose of sharing was to respect and learn more about each child's life and worldview. Consequently, by the second day of school, Ijo understood that what he treasured most was not valued in school.

During school age, children begin to evaluate themselves in comparison to their peers. This stage of development is referred to as self-esteem. Consequently, a kindergartner enters the classroom with a strong sense of self-identity but will typically experience a decline in self-esteem within the first year of school due to continual social comparisons with peers. Self-esteem will eventually increase as children learn to self-evaluate and cognitively regulate. However, Indigenous children are often faced with in-congruency between their personal values and beliefs and those of the mainstream classroom. In addition, they are in danger of falling into self-fulfilling prophecies. Deloria refers to this epidemic as the "schizophrenic nature" of education, whereby children are constantly trying to meet the expectations from mainstream education as well as from their home and community. Although a typical struggle for Indigenous children, this is not the norm for children whose philosophies and worldviews are constantly validated in the educational system. This inequity resonates from the genetic pool and historical legacy of educational systems for Indigenous people. From these experiences, children like Ijo might intentionally separate their home life from the understood expectations of the classroom.

Social indicators, explicit and implicit bias, and institutional frameworks often perpetuate stereotypes and generalizations of Indigenous communities. Perhaps, in these cases, the assessors (professionals) are unaware of the "eagle feather" tucked away in the bag, and so an effort is never made to listen to and observe the values and beliefs (i.e., worldview and epistemology) from a community context. Perhaps the assessors got a glimpse of the auth weyoch, yet label it a "boat." When this happens, an opportunity may have been created to listen, but the treasure is misinterpreted and minimized through the assessor's own perception. Or perhaps, the assessor becomes excited over the Spiderman figure and, through the cloning mechanism, walks away thinking, "we are all the same." Consequently, it is critical to be aware of multiple views of excellence in and out of the classroom.

Initial Steps to Healing: From a Community Context

In attending a ceremony of Northern California Indigenous peoples, you might be told, "Be aware of what you say, think, and feel at ceremony, because every word that is spoken is a wish for yourself." Likewise, Yellow Bird argues that, "...creative, healthy, decolonized thinking, actions, and feelings, positively shape and empower important neural circuits in our brain, which in turn provide us with personal resources, strengths, and abilities that we need to overcome colonialism."[42] Yellow Bird's neurodecolonization research suggests that ceremony and culture can heal the body from the effects of intergenerational trauma and on-going oppression. Furthermore, a study on Indigenous youth found that, "...cultural affinity promotes self-esteem and that cultural identity, combined with high self-esteem, is a protective factor against alcohol and substance abuse."[43]

When a child experiences trauma, shrinkages of the white matter in the brain occur. These shrinkages can be expressed in multiple ways; for example, a person's emotional regulation, attention span, or memory may be affected by traumatic events. The brain, however, is malleable. This means that the brain can heal. Healing occurs when the brain is stimulated. According to Yellow Bird, stimulation transpires when an Indigenous person is engaged in regalia-making, basket-making, singing, and ceremony. At this moment, a person has a sense of well-being, the temporal parietal junction of the brain becomes activated, and the individual transcends to a level of happiness, joy, and optimism.[44] In other words, the act of participating in cultural activities stimulates the brain and releases feelings of positivity which can lead to healing. An example of this transcendence can be depicted in the following journal description from a contemporary Indigenous California woman:

> The sun has dipped over the horizon. The smell of Majache xolen (medicine root) from the small fire within the dance pit still lingers in the air. Only moments ago the medicine woman performed the ritual of her healing. A hundred or more family

members huddle together on benches surrounding the dance pit. A light chatter of greetings, well wishes, and sighs of the work week slowly began to slip away. At some time, the illumination from the pit becomes the center of the world, and the dancers file in—circling the perimeter of the dance house. The heavy song (the first prayer) begins and for an instant—I am breathless. The prayer seems to swirl into the darkness above and my soul is taken with it. Just as quickly, the men in unison begin a deep guttural chant. My body is grounded with new enlightenment. Throughout the song, I am paralyzed in fear it will stop. A brief rest and the song begins again. I am ascended even higher into the darkness. Only when the men back up the song with the heavy guttural chant does my mind slam to the ground and become one with the heartbeat of the world. Three rounds, I succumb. This is where the healing has taken place within me. I wrap myself tightly in blankets to hold on to this feeling of *xoji doni*—what is pure.[45]

This journal entry reflects the woman's feelings of transcendence at a Brush Dance ceremony. Although the ceremony is for the healing of a sick child. Many participants and on-lookers benefit from the healing energies of song, dance, and prayer. The engagement in deep levels of mindfulness, meditation, and repetition through ceremony, song, and language activate a sense of well-being. Yellow Bird contends that healing "requires going back to what we know."[46] In other words, the remedy to intergenerational trauma is within Indigenous knowledge.

For Indigenous families that are out of balance due to trauma, oppression, and colonialism, it is important to "reweave the social fabric and recapture the old ways."[47] In re-centering and reclaiming Indigenous knowledge, children build an anchor in their home culture that gives them the strength to cope with marginalization by mainstream society. Ijo, for example, had a strong enough foundation in his Indigenous identity from his experience with culture, ceremony, language, and family relationships that he was able to protect his eagle feather and state, "They didn't deserve it."

Perry, a senior fellow of the Child Trauma Academy and a leading practitioner of children's mental health, states that key aspects of healthy child development already exist in healthy Indigenous cultures. For example, Indigenous cultures are wealthy in relationships with grandparents, extended family, and community. These communal interactions with children help to nurture physical, social, and emotional health. The implications from research indicate that the tool to healing rests within the epistemology of Indigenous communities. Had it not been for colonialism, testimonial injustice, institutional frameworks, and bias, Indigenous knowledge might have been validated sooner.

Summary

Social indicators of Indigenous peoples specify alarming rates of suicide, alcoholism, deaths due to violence, and health disparities. There is a direct correlation between the current struggles of Indigenous families and historical and on-going trauma. Initial steps for professionals in the healing process are 1) becoming aware of bias, 2) shifting the paradigm of institutional frameworks, and 3) seeking testimonial justice. From a community context, the tools to healing rest within Indigenous knowledge.

Endnotes

1. 2010 Census. "The American Indian and Alaska Native Population." *Census Bur*eau. Accessed October 3, 2017. https://www.census.gov/prod/cen2010/briefs/c2010br-10.pdf.

2. Ibid.

3. Indian Health Services. "2009-2011 Health Disparities Fact Sheet." *Indian Health Services.* Accessed October 1, 2018. http://ihs.gov/newsroom/factsheets/disparities.

4. Aspen Institute. "Fast Facts on Native American Youth." *Aspen Institute.* Accessed October 1, 2018. http://assets.aspeninstitute.org.

5. National Congress of American Indians. "2018 Demographics." *National Congress of American Indians.* Accessed September 21, 2017. http://ncai.org.

6. Aspen Institute. "Fast Facts on Native American Youth." *Aspen Institute.* Accessed October 1, 2018. http://assets.aspeninstitute.org.

7. Ibid.

8. National Congress of American Indians. "2018 Demographics." *National Congress of American Indians.* Accessed September 21, 2017. http://ncai.org.

9. Aspen Institute. "Fast Facts on Native American Youth." *Aspen Institute.* Accessed October 1, 2018. http://assets.aspeninstitute.org.

10. Ibid.

11. Michael Yellow Bird. *Decolonizing the Mind: Healing through Neurodecolonization and Mindfulness.* Produced by Cheryl Easter and Neil Ruckman, 2013. Accessed September 27, 2018. Vimeo.com/86995336.

12. Karina Walters, Selina Mohammed, Teresa Evans-Campbell, Ramona Beltran, David Chaex, and Bonnie Duran. *Bodies Don't Just tell Stories, they tell histories: Embodiment of historical trauma among American Indians and Alaska Natives.* US Library of Medicine National Health Institute, 2011.

13. Cathy Malchiodi. Creative Interventions with Traumatized Children. (New York: Guiford Press, 2015).

14. Walt Lara. Personal Interview, August 7, 2005.

15. Maria Yellowhorse Braveheart and Lemyra M. DeBruyn "The American Indian Holocaust: Healing Historical Unresolved Grief," *American Indian and Alaska Native Mental Health*, 8, no. 2 (1998), 56.

16. Angayaqaq Oscar Kawagley. *Yupiaq Worldview: A Pathway to Ecology and Spirit.* (Long Grove: Illinois, 2003), 7.

17. Manulani Meyer. *Ho'oulu our Time of Becoming: Hawaiian Epistemology and Early Writing.* (Honolulu, HI: Native Books, 2003).

18. Valerie Mathes. "Nineteenth Century Women and Reform: The Women's National Indian Association." *American Indian Quarterly* 14, no. 1 (1990): 1-18.

19. Ibid, 3.

20. Ibid, 3.

21. Margaret Connell Szasz. "Foreward." *Women's National Indian Association: A History,* ed. Valerie Sherer Mathes. (Albuquerque, NM: University of New Mexico Press, 2015), ix.

22. Kishan Lara. *Concepts of Giftedness on the Hoopa Valley Indian Reservation.* Unpublished Dissertation. (Tempe, AZ: Arizona State University, 2009).

23. Jerry Kang. "Immaculate Perception." *Ted Talkx.* Filmed in San Diego, California. Accessed August 10, 2017. https://www.youtube.com/watch?v=9VGbwNI6Ssk.

24. Mahzarin R. Banaji and Anthony G. Greenwald. *Blind Spot: Hidden Biases of Good People.* (New York, Delacorte Press, 2013), 55.

25. Ibid, 4.

26. Ibid, 55.

27. Project Implicit is operated through Harvard University, University of Washington, and the University of Virginia.

28. Jerry Kang and Kristin Lane. "Screening through Colorblindedness: Implicit Bias and the Law." *UCLA Law Review* 58, (2010), 474.

29. John Reyner and Jeanne Eder. *American Indian Education: A History.* (Norman: University of Oklahoma Press, 2000).

30. Terms used by educational systems.

31. Tsianina Lomawaima. "The Unnatural History of American Indian Education," ed. Karen Swisher and John Tippeconnic *Next Steps: Research and Practice to Advance Indian Education.* (Charleston, West Virginia: Clearinghouse on Rural Education and Small Schools, 1999), 1-32.

32. Michael Yellow Bird and Venida Chanault. "The Role of Social Work in Advancing the Practice of Indigenous Education: Obstacles and Promises in Empowerment Oriented Social Work Practice" ed. Karen Swisher and John Tippeconnic *Next Steps: Research and Practice to Advance Indian Education.* (Charleston, West Virginia: Clearinghouse on Rural Education and Small Schools, 1999), 201-238.

33. Jack Norton. *Genocide in Northwestern California: When Our Worlds*

Cried. (San Franciso, CA: Indian Historian Press, 1979).

34. Michael Yellow Bird and Venida Chanault. "The Role of Social Work in Advancing the Practice of Indigenous Education: Obstacles and Promises in Empowerment Oriented Social Work Practice" ed. Karen Swisher and John Tippeconnic *Next Steps: Research and Practice to Advance Indian Education.* (Charleston, West Virginia: Clearinghouse on Rural Education and Small Schools, 1999), 201-238.

35. Miranda Fricker. *Epistemic Injustice: Power and Ethics of Knowing.* (New York, Oxford University Press, 2007).

36. Chimamanda Ngozi Adichie. *The Danger of a Single Story.* (National Geographic Learning, 2016) 85.

37. Vine DeLoria and Daniel Wildcat. *Power and Place: Indian Education in America.* (Colorado: Fulcrum Resources. 2001).

38. Michael Yellow Bird and Venida Chanault. "The Role of Social Work in Advancing the Practice of Indigenous Education: Obstacles and Promises in Empowerment Oriented Social Work Practice" ed. Karen Swisher and John Tippeconnic *Next Steps: Research and Practice to Advance Indian Education.* (Charleston, West Virginia: Clearinghouse on Rural Education and Small Schools, 1999), 201-238.

39. Linda Tuhiwai Smith. *Decolonizing Methodologies: Research and Indigenous Peoples.* (London: ZED Books, 1999).

40. Kishan Lara-Cooper. "K'winya'nya:nma-awhiniw: Creating a Space for Indigenous Knowledge in the Classroom." *Journal of American Indian Education* 53, no. 1, (2014): 3-20.

41. Kishan Lara. *Concepts of Giftedness on the Hoopa Valley Indian Reservation.* Unpublished Dissertation. (Tempe, AZ: Arizona State University, 2009).

42. Michael Yellow Bird. *Decolonizing the Mind: Healing through Neurodecolonization and Mindfulness.* Produced by Cheryl Easter and Neil Ruckman, 2013. Accessed September 27, 2018. Vimeo. com/86995336.

43. Mick Adams, Peter Mataira, Shayne Walker, Michael Hart, Neil Drew, and Jess John Fleay. "Cultural Identity and Practices Associated with the Health and Well-being of Indigenous Males." *Journal of Indigenous Studies and First Nations and First People's Cultures* 1, no. 1, (2017): 42-61.

44. Michael Yellow Bird. *Decolonizing the Mind: Healing through Neurodecolonization and Mindfulness.* Produced by Cheryl Easter and Neil Ruckman, 2013. Accessed September 27, 2018.

Vimeo.com/86995336.

45. Callie Lara. Journal Entry, July 17, 2017.

46. Michael Yellow Bird. *Decolonizing the Mind: Healing through Neurodecolonization and Mindfulness*. Produced by Cheryl Easter and Neil Ruckman, 2013. Accessed September 27, 2018. Vimeo.com/86995336.

47. Bruce Perry, *What We Have Always Known: A Program Presenting Key Parenting Skills of the Native Am*erican Culture. (The Child Trauma Academy, 2003).

CHAPTER 3

Xo'ch Na:nahsde'tł'-te Survivance, Resilience and Unbroken Traditions in Northwest California

Cutcha Risling Baldy & Kayla Begay

Na:yisxun-te 'ułkyowe: -ding ninis'a:n me:q'. 'Ah-ne'in do:-
na:xohsdileh-te 'aht'ing ning'e:tł' xo'ch na:nahsde'tł'-te
Nais-xun-te ul-kyo-we-din nin-nis-an meuk a-ne-en do-na-
xos-dil-le-te a-tin nin-el xotc
Na-nas-del-te.

There will be sunshine everywhere in the world. Clouds that used to be will be no more. Everything that is good will become.[1]

IN HIS BOOK, CENTERING IN TWO WORLDS, HUPA SCHOLAR JACK NORTON SHARES A STORY ABOUT A TIME WHEN A DARK CLOUD MOVED OVER THE HOOPA VALLEY, BRING-ING "SICKNESS AND POOR HEALTH" TO THE WORLD.[2] According to Norton, the K'ixinay, realizing the world has become unbalanced, respond by providing the people with songs and the Jump Dance.[3] Because of this, "on the tenth day, the cloud had disappeared."[4]

Through ceremonies the world had been put back into order. Stories of surviving dark, destructive times, and of the consistent resistance to this attempted destruction, demonstrate the power of culture, ceremonies and Indigenous knowledge. These types of stories—oral traditions that build California Indian culture—will guide Northwest California Indian people as they navigate their worlds.

Ongoing spiritual and cultural resistance of Native American peoples to an unbalanced world is foundational to Northwest California tribes. The Hupa, Yurok, Karuk, Wiyot, and Tolowa lived in spiritually balanced relationships with their lands, waters, and more-than-human relatives.[5] For many of the tribes in Northwest California, their First Peoples are spiritual beings that are a part of their everyday world.[6] After the First Peoples prepare the world for humans, they either leave the earth, or go into the rocks, rivers, trees, animals, plants, mountains and other parts of the earth. Essentially, First People imbue the world with spirit and frame the world not as "inanimate," but instead as being populated with humans and, as Métis anthropologist Zoe Todd conceptualizes, "more-than-human beings."[7] In addition, some of these spiritual beings exist in the afterworld that begins across the ocean. This grounds Northwest California Indian people in a space that is embodied by culture and spirituality. As Karuk storyteller Julian Lang writes about Karuk First Peoples, "It is encouraging to know that our Ikxaréeyavs rarely recede into oblivion. After all, are there not yet rattlesnakes? Or frogs, eels, mountains, creeks, trees, and sacred ceremonies?"[8]

To understand the ongoing efforts of Northwest California tribes to maintain and reclaim relationships to land, language, culture, and ceremony, we must understand their histories of survivance, resilience, and unbroken traditions. Survivance, a term most thoroughly explored by Anishinaabe writer and scholar Gerald Vizenor, is an important framework for understanding Native peoples not as passive victims in history, but instead as active, present, and continuing. Vizenor argues that Native histories are not mere reactions to colonization; they are "renunciations of dominance, detractions, obtrusions, the unbearable sentiments of tragedy, and the legacy of victimry."[9]

This chapter explores the history of Northwest California by centering relationships to land in order to understand histories of survivance and continued fights for sovereignty and self-determination. The chapter reflects a language of history grounded in Native epistemologies whereby the land knows us, and our languages orient us to the land.

We maintain that contemporary Northwest California activism and cultural revivification are grounded in ongoing connections to land that center systems of "recognition of relatives." Hunkpapa Lakota author, theologian, activist, and lawyer Vine Deloria, Jr. notes that most Indian people hear, "We are all relatives" throughout their lives as "they attend or perform ceremonies" or as an ongoing part of everyday life.[10] But he also maintains that we can use this understanding of the world as a framework and tool for investigation to engage Indigenous philosophy, knowledge, and history. Deloria notes that, "All relationships are historical" and further argues that, "As the universe was known by the Indians to be alive, it followed that all entities had some memory and enjoyed the experience of the passage of time."[11] In fact, all entities have, hold, and write history. The interrelationship between Native peoples and their landscapes builds the history of the region now known as California, long before the first non-Native explorer or settler invaded the land. History, therefore, is written on the landscape and is embodied in stories as well as in the ongoing presence of an interrelationship with sites that build these stories. Zoe Todd calls this a "storied landscape." The history of the Northwest California region is a storied landscape of survivance, resilience, and, most importantly, continued revitalization and revivification.

For over a century, Northwest California groups have been the subject of scholarly research in fields such as Anthropology, Linguistics, and History. The nineteenth century included an influx of ethnographers attempting to document what they thought was a "dying" culture and history of Native peoples in California. Scholars like Alfred Kroeber, Pliny Earle Goddard, Edward Sapir, and T.T. Waterman were hoping to recreate what they considered the "real" Native culture that existed before 1849 and the attempted genocide and widespread destruction caused by the Gold Rush in California. These types of ethnographies framed Native peoples and their cultures as being in the past and not as part of a vibrant present or future. These ethnographies were widely popular at the time, and continue to be some of the most cited works on California Indian culture.

The most popular recent histories of California Indian peoples focus on the attempted genocide at the hands of white settlers during the Gold Rush. In the past few years, two lengthy texts have been published by leading scholarly presses exploring the attempted extermination and near genocide of Native peoples in California. Brendan Lindsay's

Murder State was published in 2012, followed by Benjamin Madley's *An American Genocide* in 2016. Both texts received widespread acclaim, with Madley's book being featured in the *New York Times* and *Los Angeles Times*. Despite histories like these, the fantastical legend of a prosperous Gold Rush that built the State of California is deeply embedded in school curricula. Rarely does the school curriculum touch upon the depraved violence and attempted annihilation of Indigenous peoples of California, which resulted in "brutality, savagery and filthiness" that was "the worst that was to be found in the Frontier phenomenon."[12] But in 1979, Hupa scholar Jack Norton wrote *Genocide in Northwest California,* where he set out to "document the historical evidence, the words and actions of the American murderers, who were ever present in northwestern California."[13] At the time, Norton's work was met with skepticism and "derision."[14] Norton writes that "...some public-school districts would not allow the book in their libraries."[15]

Since Norton's book in 1979, several articles and lengthy books have been published exploring the attempted genocide of California Indians. In 2016, Ben Madley published, to much fanfare, his book *An American Genocide: The United States and the California Indian Catastrophe.* Madley's book was endorsed by California Governor Jerry Brown who stated:

> California history tells us much about the gold rush and the mass migration it inspired, but very little of the mass destruction of its native peoples. Benjamin Madley corrects the record with his gripping story of what really happened: the actual genocide of a vibrant civilization thousands of years in the making.[16]

While these explorations of the brutal, disquieting history of California are important for intervening on the sanitized history often taught in schools, references only to our genocide, our victimization at the hands of egregious laws and depraved settlers, frame our peoples as passive victims who perished at the hands of settlers, thereby erasing our continued presence on this land. Gov. Brown's statement above, seemingly final in its conclusion that our vibrant civilizations perished because of genocide, does not center our histories of ongoing resistance, activism, political interventions, and continued fights for our land, water, fish, and cultures. It is only through centering our ongoing activism, our resistance, and our cultures that we center not our deaths, but our lives and our futures. Survivance teaches us to recognize the ongoing relationships we have maintained to our lands, our cultures, and our histories.

This chapter necessarily examines points of disruption, pressures of assimilation, and ongoing settler colonialism that built the state of California, and the attempts in the larger U.S. to sever Native ties to land, as being met with resistance that laid the foundation for future enactment of survivance and activism. Our activism is highlighted as central to how we navigated the changing world. These are the decolonial skills embedded in our oldest stories. How we continue to enact survivance—to sing the songs, dance the dances, tell the stories, and push against the dark cloud that settled over us—is how we understand our histories as much older and more complex than the attempted genocide of us, and is also informative of how we continue to resist and how we will build our futures.

Time Immemorial

Since time immemorial, distinct peoples with unique languages, cultures, and philosophies have shaped and been shaped from the land that is known today as Northwest California. Diversity between language families and the variations within languages especially define existence and tribal identities in an area where much is shared culturally. Languages and language practices also encode tribes' original instructions and views on being on the land.

Wiyot, Yurok, Hupa, Tolowa, Wailaki, Nongatl, Sinkyone, Lassik, Wintu, Chimariko, Karuk, and Shasta peoples came into existence in conversation with the land, with non-humans, and with each other. These inter-relationships include relationships with salmon, deer, acorns, other first-foods and animals that human people rely on for medicines, teachings, and the important roles carried on the land.

Oral traditions in each tribe speak of a time before humans, of the world as it was being prepared by non-humans for human people. Because of this, respect, reciprocity, and balance is emphasized in ceremony and cultural traditions that protect these relationships between human and non-humans. In Karuk, the time before is pikváhahirak,[17] and in Hupa, it is ch'ixolchwe-dung.[18] In the time after, in Yurok, 'Woo-gey[19] are spoken about as having mostly left this world, and noohl yuenoyohl,[20] or just before human people were to be around. Creation in this way took place in collaboration, with many helpers and centers of the world. As Bauer writes, "Creation narratives were not inert historical sources and interpretations. Rather they are living understandings of what happened in the past."[21] Though having suffered assaults linguistically and culturally, these narratives have structured law and morality in social, political, economic, and cultural practices.

The land known as California represents one of the most linguistically diverse language areas in North America, with at least six unrelated classificatory groupings representative of language families that span the continent. Up to a dozen languages—depending on definitions of *language* versus *dialect*—were spoken in Northwestern California.[22] These larger language families are recognized today as Algic (Wiyot, Yurok), Dene/Athabaskan (Tolowa, Hupa, Nongatl, Lassik, Sinkyone, Wailaki), Penutian (Wintu), and Hokan families (Chimariko, Karuk, Shasta). The most tenuous of these linguistic relationships are between Hokan languages comprised of isolates and small language families that are proposed to be very distantly related, share some structural similarities, and represent some of the oldest language history in Northern California. Two small language families Yukian and Chumashan are considered to have no close or distant relatives.

Many tribal relatives, however, have their own ways of describing *relatedness* as well as *distinctness*. For Hupa-speaking peoples, important village and political groupings have names along with larger geographic ethnonyms that include Na:tini-xwe (Hoopa Valley People), Tse:ning-xwe (South Fork People), and Xwiyłq'it-xwe (Redwood Creek People), referring to themselves along with non-Hupa speaking language relatives such as Tolowa as Dining'xine:wh or Dene speaking peoples, who called themselves similarly as Dee-ni', having more closely relative linguistic relatives in Oregon. Karuk-speaking peoples speak of themselves according to principle villages, including Panámniik,[23] Ka'tim'iin,[24] Ameekyáaraam,[25] and as Karuk-arara.[26][27] Yurok-speaking peoples refer to themselves by villages—sometimes village networks—but also by larger geographic ethnonyms including Pue-leek-la,[28] Pe-cheek-la,[29] and Ner-'er-nerh.[30] Wiyot people call themselves according to three groups: Patawat in the north, Wiki around Humboldt Bay, and Wiyat to the south along the lower Eel River.[31] Dene/Athabaskan speaking peoples, further south along the Eel and Van Duzen rivers, share a larger term—Nung-kahł—along with numerous village names and geographic-based terms ending in "Keyah" that do not always fit neatly into the four anglicized terms Nongatl, Sinkyone, Lassik and Wailaki as introduced by Kroeber and Goddard, but are somewhat recognized and used more by Merriam. Many modern tribal designations in the area come from treaty negotiations or later descriptions by anthropologists.

In describing the land, the peoples along the Klamath and Trinity Rivers, Humboldt Bay, Eel River, and surrounding regions share in directional systems that orient themselves to the land rather than the land to the people. Important directions include upriver/down the coast, downriver/up the coast, uphill (away from the river/water), downhill (toward the river/water). Less important are relative directions based on orientation of the body. For instance, Yurok Elder Florence Shaughnessy once clarified that in order to turn on the burner of a gas stove, "It's like this: you turn it down by turning the knob downriver, and up upriver," rather than using English-egocentric left or right.[32]

These kinds of cultural similarities lead scholars to argue that Northwestern California peoples share identical culture across language boundaries. Sapir argues, "It is difficult to say what elements in their combined culture belong in origin to this tribe or that, so much at one are they in communal action, feeling, and thought.[33] Kroeber also writes that Yurok peoples are "surrounded by people speaking diverse languages but following the same remarkable civilization."[34] While there is good evidence for Northwestern California as a distinct language and culture area, sharing many areal features across languages, many of the features that occur in Northern California extend up the Pacific coast and suggest that Northwestern California can also be understood as a peripheral part of the better-supported Northwest Coast linguistic area.[35]

Variation existed and exists both within and across linguistic groups. Ceremonies like those for World Renewal have many local variations that pattern with distinct peoples and geographies, regardless of linguistic boundaries.[36] Different tribal groups came together, however, to observe important high ceremonies at their various centers of the world. Tribes in Northwest California locate centers of their worlds in their respective lands, but also come together in other ceremonial places of great significance. One of the largest on the coast in Yurok territory was called 'O Pyuue-weg, *Where They Dance,* at Big Lagoon.[37] According to a Hupa story recorded by Pliny Earle Goddard, it was at Big Lagoon that there was "placed a sweat-house and a house in which the people should dance. 'Here' he said 'they will dance if anything goes wrong with the ocean. If the water rises up they will dance here and it will settle down again.'"[38] Yurok elders in the 1970s continued to describe 'O Pyuue-weg as a "ceremonial ground." 'O Pyuue-weg is a starting place for the Jump Dance for people from 'O Pyuue-weg (and Peen-pay), but for the Yurok the dance is a traveling dance where they meet up with other coastal villages at Saypoola Ha'ag.[39] The Yurok Jump Dance also starts at Chapekw at the same time as 'O Pyuue-weg. Other coastal centers and ceremony also focused on the ocean, while inland, high ceremonies that brought downriver and coastal guests focused to the east, the mountains, and Mt. Shasta. It would be non-Indigenous people—known as Yima:n'dil[40] (Hupa), Apxantínihich[41] '(Karuk),' 'Woo-gey[42] (Yurok) mistaken for returning First Peoples, or Ch'indin[43] (Wailaki) "that left the site of creation" according to Wailaki oral tradition[44]—that would bring the biggest disturbances to these centers.

Early Contact: 1700 to 1800s

Scholars have noted that settler establishment in the region happened relatively late in the 1800s. Though Juan Rodriguez Cabrillo claimed lands for Spain in California in 1542—and may have sailed into Humboldt Bay at some point—it wasn't until June of 1775 that, conclusively, two Spanish ships under the command of Don Bruno de Hezeta sailed into Trinidad Bay and made records of their incursion. They entered the Yurok Village of Chuerey (Tsurai–Trinidad, CA) which they described as peaceful, but also noted that residents were reluctant to provide the Spanish with Yurok women.[45] Sexual aggression against native women was often among the first recorded acts by the Spanish in encountering native peoples in Northern California, and though they were there to trade, they also threatened the village with whippings, kidnapping, and seizure of property.[46] Their departure on June 19, 1775 was welcomed.

Other early expeditions include an 1802 expedition lead by American William Shaler, who fired cannon shots against rocks in Trinidad Bay to intimidate Yurok people.[47] In 1806, the ship *O'Cain* led by Captain Jonathan Winship, Jr. sailed into what would become known as Humboldt Bay and along the coast, generally to hunt sea otter. E. H Howard and H. H. Buhne were the first recorded white men to enter

Humboldt Bay in April 1850, naming the bay as well as a settlement Humboldt City after German scientist Alexander von Humboldt a site today known as King Salmon.[48]

To the south, Russian fur traders aboard American ships established a settlement from 1812-1842 called Fort Ross, in what is now Sonoma County and historic Kashaya Pomo territory. American and British fur trappers in the late 1820s made their way inland, exhausting the fur trade in the region by the 1840s and spreading diseases. Jedediah Smith, in 1826, is regarded as one of the first Euro-Americans to have made the trip overland up the Sacramento, turning northwest to enter Hupa territory and later Yurok territory toward the coast. Peter Skene Ogden led a group of British trappers in late 1826 and moved along the upper Klamath River and Karuk territory, while Francois Payette, in early 1827, led ten of these men southwest to Yurok territory. Major P.B. Reading found gold in 1848 in the upper Trinity River, and by 1849, gold seekers made up most trespassers into the region. By spring 1850, shiploads left San Francisco for the bays of Northwestern California, with settlers establishing Trinidad, Humboldt City, Eureka, Bucksport, and Union (later called Arcata).

Lucy Young, Lassik/Wailaki estimated to have been born in 1846, relayed almost 100 years later that her grandfather dreamt about the coming of white settlers when she was a young child, telling her "You young people are gonta see this"[49] Young noted that, "Every day he would dream and say this," but that, "long time you gonta live, my child, you live long time in this world." Many later informants for documentation of culture and language were children at the time of white establishment in Northwestern California, having survived the horrific turning of the world out of balance.

The Gold Rush & California Genocide

During the 1849 Gold Rush, thousands invaded Northwest California in hopes of striking it rich. California Indians often refer to this period as "the end of the world," where indiscriminate massacres, murders, kidnappings, and removal were commonplace. Scholar Sherburne Cook estimates that the deaths of California Indians between 1770 and 1900 amounted to over 90 percent of the original population. Hupa historian Byron Nelson writes that, during the Gold Rush, Indian people faced numerous challenges including the "…kind of violence the area had never known."[50] Horrific incidents of violence run rampant throughout the historical record and include indiscriminate massacres, assaults, and kidnapping of Native women and children.

The 1860 massacre of the Wiyot people on Tuluwat Island in Humboldt County has become an infamous example of the depravity of settlers during the Gold Rush. Most often referred to as the "Indian Island Massacre," the massacre targeted Wiyot people while they were holding a World Renewal Ceremony. It was "The most heinous massacre," writes historian Tony Platt, "a coordinated affair carried out on Indian Island and at other locations by some of the county's leading landowners and businessmen on February 25, 1860, [resulting] in the murder of as many as two hundred innocent Wiyot people. Mostly women, children, and elderly were hacked to death…"[51] The tragedy of a massacre led by everyday Humboldt County citizens against a peaceful group of Native people who were in ceremony would become a defining part of Humboldt County history. However, Wiyot history would not focus on the Wiyot as merely victims of a massacre, but instead would demonstrate their ongoing survivance and resilience. At the heart of their ongoing resistance was the determination to revitalize their World Renewal Ceremonies, and in 2014 they would hold a World Renewal Ceremony on Tuluwat (Indian Island).

Ongoing resistance throughout the Gold Rush is an important part of California Indian history. Leading scholar Jack Forbes notes that, "Many native groups, from the Klamath River to the Colorado River, offered notable resistance during the early 1850s," and describes how "In all of these wars the Indian people exhibited great bravery in the defense of their homes, or in their efforts to insure a food supply for survival…"[52]

The systemic violence of the Gold Rush was also government funded and supported, as the newly formed State of California legalized the enslavement, killing, and kidnapping of California Indian people. On April 22, 1850, the California legislature passed "An Act for the Government and Protection of Indians." The Act authorized the arrest of Indian people for "loitering and strolling about," which required they appear before the Justice of the Peace. "If a convicted Indian was punished by paying a fine, any white person, with the consent of the Justice, could give bond for the Indian's fine and costs. In return, the Indian was 'compelled to work until his fine was discharged or cancelled.'"[53] The

Act further stated that, "Any person could go before the Justice of the Peace to obtain Indian children for indenture."[54] Anthropologists Robert Heizer and Alan Almquist note that between the years of 1860 and 1863, a majority of the people indentured in Humboldt County were children between the ages of seven and twelve.[55] Alongside the Act for the Government and Protection of Indians, the California Legislature enacted two laws: An Act Concerning Volunteer or Independent Companies and An Act Concerning the Organization of the Militia.[56] Under these laws, California approved an extermination policy that would pay for the killing of Native people. In 1849, the first year of this legalized genocide, the State of California paid close to $1 million for the killing of California Indian people.

California Indian people were faced not only with the destruction of their people and cultures, but also with the continuing destruction of and separation from their land. Brendan Lindsay notes that while the legend of the Gold Rush that has been maintained in contemporary history is focused on gold as the driving force during this historical period, the actual goal was "getting lands owned by the Indigenous peoples of California into the hands of Euro-American settlers."[57] Land would prove to be far more profitable for settlers than gold, and would be at the heart of continued struggles as settlers attempted to wrest the land from the rightful Indian owners.

The 18 Unratified Treaties & Ongoing Land Struggles

By the 1800s, the Supreme Court, along with Congress, had established that Indian land titles could only be negotiated and enforced by the federal government. Treaties had been established with Indian tribes throughout the United States, in many cases resulting in the removal or relocation of Native people to lands further west. With the establishment of the state of California there was no longer a way to push Native people west or negotiate removal to other territories.[58] Because of the ongoing violence, three commissioners were sent from Washington D.C. to California to negotiate treaties and peaceful transfer of lands.[59] Between March 19, 1851 and January 7, 1852, the three commissioners met with hundreds of California Indian people and established eighteen treaties after several complicated and sometimes strained negotiations. Treaties would define "tracts of land within the state...assigned the

Indians for their sole occupancy and use 'forever.' ...The Indians, in turn, ...placed themselves under the protection of the United States, and agreed to keep the peace."[60]

In total, eighteen treaties were signed with various tribes, setting aside millions of acres of land in California. It is estimated that the land guaranteed in these treaties would have amounted to 7,488,000 acres, or 7.5% of the state.[61] The treaties were sent to Congress and were never ratified. Congress, seemingly responding to the outcry from settlers in California, put the treaties under an injunction of secrecy and did not inform the Native tribes that the treaties were null and void.[62] Many of the Native peoples in Northwest California had already begun to live on their designated lands as were agreed to in the treaties. When it was finally revealed that the treaties were null and void, California Indians tribes were then subject to removal and relocation. The result of the unratified treaties of California would continue to wreak havoc on Native tribes for hundreds of years.

Reservations & Ongoing Resistance

The reservation system in California, much like reservations throughout the United States, was meant to assimilate Native people and encourage their incorporation into mainstream American society by changing their tribal communal lifestyle to one that was run by the Federal government. In 1871, H. L. Knight, a lawyer from Eureka, California, commented that in Northern California, "If the Reservation was a plantation, the Indians were the most degraded slaves. I found them poor, miserable, vicious, degraded, dirty, naked, diseased, and ill-fed."[63] Government agents, also called "Indian agents," were appointed by the federal government to keep a watchful eye on Indian people. Throughout, United States missionaries had been assigned to the reservations in hopes of converting Native people to Christianity. In 1882, the Department of Interior ordered the end to all "heathenish dances" and ceremonies due to their "great hindrance to civilization."[64] Two years later, the Bureau of Indian Affairs passed policies to imprison Natives who participated in cultural ceremonies.[65]

Despite the continued attempts to instill fear or to outlaw ceremonies, tribes throughout Northwest California continued to come together for ceremonies. These acts of survivance showcased how tribes were fighting back against a system designed to negate and destroy their cultural systems. Hupa historian Byron Nelson writes that, "Almost everyone in the valley attended the traditional White Deerskin Dance in August 1875."[66] In 1864, Superintendent Frank Kyselka wrote that he found the "tenacity with which the majority of Indians" held on to traditional beliefs in Northwest California "very discouraging."[67] Yurok writer Lucy Thompson noted that, "In the fall of 1876 I counted upwards of three thousands Indians there at a White Deerskin Dance. There were five different languages spoken among them: the lower Klamath, upper Klamath, Hoopa, Smith River and Mad River. Some of them could speak two and some three, while others could speak only one."[68]

There had been many changes in Northwest California over these years, and the consistent attempts by outsiders to "domesticate or exterminate" Native people had proved futile. Native peoples continued to maintain ties to their First People, culture, ceremonies, and land, and they had survived one of the most violent times in their recent history. Their insistence on cultural continuity and resistance would be important to the ongoing negotiations they would continue to face throughout contemporary history.

Assimilation

During the late 1800s, the federal government refocused Indian policy to reflect what they believed was a more humanistic approach to the "Indian problem" by targeting for breakup any village and communal living that was not already affected by Gold Rush violence. The Dawes Act of 1887 resulted in reservation lands being privatized, with individual parcels allotted to Yurok Indians prior to national policy in 1883 and 1884 by Agent Porter as a deterrent to non-Indian claims.[69] This was largely unsuccessful, however, and many claimed Yurok lands. In addition, "surplus lands" created by the Dawes Act National Policy were also sold to non-Indian homesteaders, who were thought of as examples for Indian neighbors to emulate. Though Indians locally participated fully in developing agricultural economies, those in and around the Hoopa Valley, for instance, would not give up their cultural beliefs or practices, and many of them continued to live in their traditional village sites well into the 1930s. These cultural practices included cultural burning that was the ire of superintendents and Forest Service personnel, who sought a crackdown on as many as 102 intentionally lit fires in Hoopa between 1927 and 1930.

A Hoopa Boarding School operated from 1893 through 1932, located at the former site of Fort Gaston in Hoopa which had been closed in 1892. The school started its first year with only 38 students, but by the start of the next school year had increased enrollment to 147 students. Lieutenant Gordon Winslow declared that only children who attended the school would be receiving clothing with their rations.[70] Hupas objected to proposals by Indian Agents that their children leave the valley, and surrounding tribe's children were also brought to Hoopa. Another on-reservation site, Round Valley Indian boarding school, functioned similarly, as did later off-reservation schools at institutions such as Sherman Indian High School in Riverside, California.

Students at the Hoopa site as well as at the Round Valley Indian Boarding School were subject to the same types of treatment and curriculum that was employed at other schools throughout the United States during this period. Students were made to cut their hair, and, despite proximity to family in location:

> All pupils were required to reside at the school with home visits limited to once or twice a month. The children adhered to a quasi-military regimen that included drilling, calisthenics, unquestioned obedience, and severe punishment for infractions. They were also obliged to perform heavy chores vital to the maintenance of the residents and the operation of the physical plant. Instruction was in English and conversing in an Indian language was strictly forbidden. In addition to the three R's and occasional activities such as singing, games and holiday programs there was vocational trainings for the boys in agricultural techniques and in trades such as blacksmithing and carpentry, and practice in domestic skills for the girls.[71]

The Hupa word Xontah-Chwa:xołwil (*house-it's dark*) was used to describe the basement of the boarding school in Hoopa as dark and without light, reflecting the treatment of children should they be found speaking Hupa, Yurok, Karuk, or other languages, or practicing/playing aspects of culture and ceremony. Students with this punishment would be left in the basement for days at a time.[72] The word later became the Hupa word for jail.

A common problem for boarding school was the tendency of children to run away, a form of resistance of many of Indian children and their parents against the attempts to assimilate their children. The Superintendents of the schools were sure that the influence of the school would finally assimilate Indian people. Kyselka's term as Hoopa's Superintendent from 1901-1908 included a limited number of visits by children to their families as well as his encouragement of children to leave their family and attend boarding school off the reservation. "In his first three years at Hoopa, he sent sixty-two students to those schools."[73] Some returned, having run away, while others later joined war-time efforts or the military in WWI and WWII. In 1932, the Hoopa Boarding School became a public school. The curriculum at the school changed to match the offerings of local public schools.

Land Claims Commission

In the early 1900s, the 18 Unratified Treaties of California were rediscovered after they had been hidden away in secret in Senate archives for fifty years. Reformers and advocates for Indians petitioned Congress to appropriate money to provide land for homeless Indians, and Congress appropriated money to purchase 9,000 acres for 50 separate Rancherias, including some in Northern California. Many Rancherias would later petition for federal recognition. These include Bear River Rohnerville Rancheria, Blue Lake Rancheria, Big Lagoon Rancheria, Trinidad Rancheria, Smith River Rancheria, Elk Valley Rancheria, Table Bluff Rancheria, and Resighini Rancheria.

With the rediscovery of the unratified treaties, passage of The California Indians Jurisdictional Act in 1928 authorized California's attorney general to sue the federal government on behalf of California tribes whose lands were stolen. Plaintiffs' claims were consolidated, and any descendent of living Indians from July 1, 1852 were considered. Settling in 1944, payments were made from the 1950s through the 1970s. The 1928 claims settlement subtracted administrative costs. A second land claims case was authorized in 1946, appealed, and not decided on until 1963. California Indians were treated in payment as one unit, and received checks for $633, with many not understanding what the money was for or what it meant to receive payment for stolen lands and "settle" their aboriginal title claims.

Kroeber testified against some of his own former students in the second land claims case, arguing for the tribes using land use and linguistic evidence.[74] Revised versions of Kroeber's maps were used, although he questioned the use of the term *tribe*. Since the 1920s, he had used the term *tribelet* to describe the social structure of the majority of California Indian groups, a term that undermined later usage of the term *tribe* for California Indians going through the Federal Acknowledgment process.[75] Less-than-accurate territory maps also caused problems between tribes that, though treated as a unit in payment for land claims, could have been helped individually with more accurate mapping of tribal territories. These inaccurate territory maps also produced situations in which expansion of one meant encroachment and loss for another.

In 1953, in yet another attempt to assimilate Indians, the California Rancheria Act called for termination of federal trusteeship of Rancherias in California, and 46 were terminated. An updated Dawes Act, including private ownership of tribal lands, was offered to California Indians in exchange for their tribal status. Difficulties in interpreting federal agents' proposals caused confusion around the act, and many California Indians seeking individual lands found they lost their status as tribes.[76] Restoration of 31 Rancherias has since occurred. Blue Lake, Rohnerville, Quartz Valley, and Smith River Rancherias were restored in 1983. Table Bluff Rancheria was restored in 1981.

From Relocation to Revivification

In the 1950s, the federal government set forth a policy of relocation, moving countless numbers of Native people into urban areas. The relocation program included several cities in California. Winnebago anthropologist Renya Ramirez notes that, "Many Indians participated in the Federal Relocation Program because their reservations suffered from much economic hardship and they needed employment."[77] This was as a direct result of historic policies that stripped Native people of land and access to resources. Government program leaders believed that if Native people were removed from their lands and relocated to urban centers, they would quickly assimilate and lose their ties to their aboriginal lands. In her book, *Native Hubs,* Ramirez explores how "Indians' movement into the cities has increased the possibility for gathering and politically organizing, rather than causing Native Americans to assimilate and lose a sense of their Native identities."[78] Out of the relocation program came a building of partnerships and ideas across tribes. In many ways, these partnerships supported activist movements as Native people found common ground at the continuing issues that were still facing their communities and cultures.

The 1970s ushered in a renewed and urgent sense of activism. The occupation of Alcatraz, ongoing efforts by the American Indian Movement, the establishment of Native American Studies departments across the country, and the founding of the first tribal college in California—DQ University—invigorated Native peoples throughout the state and beyond. The national news often featured stories about Native activism, headlines focused on the contemporary Native experience, and for the first time Native people were moving beyond the imagined stereotype of a stoic, passive Indian into a vibrant contemporary political presence. In the Northwest California region, organizations like the Northwest Indian Cemetery Protection Association (NICPA) gained local and national prominence as they worked to intervene on legislation and policies that affected Native lands and cultures. NICPA worked tirelessly to stop the desecration of graves and sacred sites, and through local activism and partnerships helped guarantee access to state parks and land for use in continued ceremonies.[79]

Northwest California tribes and tribal organizations have also continued their activism and protection of their more-than-human relatives and lands throughout the past 30 years. In 1978, when the state of California imposed a ban on sports and Indian fishing on the mouth of the Klamath River, the Yurok responded swiftly. The ban on fishing had gone into effect during the height of a fall run, and when local Yurok fisherman continued to fish, federal agents—along with Sheriff's deputies and the Coast Guard—responded with violent raids and arrests.[80] Days later, federal agents showed up heavily armed and encountered twenty boatloads of Yurok Indians. Though the Indians were unarmed, they were met with violence, with some Yurok people reporting they were held underwater.[81] The Yurok responded by engaging in "protest fishing," with numerous Native people coming to the Klamath, some not even using nets, but still providing resistance to the fishing moratorium. In several instances, Yurok people utilized their ceremonial and cultural practices to help maintain the strength and persistence they would need to fight the fish wars. Former Yurok Chair and Vice-Chair Susan Masten relayed the story of her grandmother, who was hanging on to a net that was being pulled on by federal agents. Masten's grandmother "stood up and she began to sing a prayer song in Yurok....She was holding her arms up singing and all the birds in the area came and began to circle around up above." Masten adds, "It was a very powerful moment that here's this little woman who is so small in stature but so big in her medicine..."[82]

Conclusion

While previously written histories have framed Native cultures as "dying" or "vanishing," in Northwest California, culture has been an ever-present foundation for our resistance. This activism and survivance continues with the revitalization and revivification of ceremonies as located spaces of decolonization. While many women's coming-of-age ceremonies had not been commonly practiced for numerous years, "with some anthropologists and ethnographers going so far as to call it extinct[, this] does not mean [it] did not remain part of our cultural imagination."[83] As Hupa elder Callie Lara explains "All those pieces that people had— the songs, the medicine, the sticks, the dresses—it all started coming together and it was like we didn't ever forget."[84] The revitalization of women's coming-of-age ceremonies has been particularly vibrant in Northwest California, where the Karuk, Hupa, Yurok, and Wiyot have all revived this ceremonial practice in the past few decades. These ceremonies are meaningful forms of Indigenous narrative that help Native peoples enact decolonization and, as Cutcha Risling Baldy explains "(re)write, (re)right and (re)rite histories."[85]

The act of making what was once thought of as intangible into the tangible again is an important assertion of self-determination that centers our own stories of activism, resistance, and survivance. The historical movements of assimilative and genocidal policies of California have, at every turn, been combatted by our ties to land and culture. The disruption experienced in the nearly last two centuries since the arrival of Euro-American settlers and settler-colonialism has been but a short time in Northwest California tribal history compared to the length of time and depth of tribal relationships with the land. And it is our stories and histories that have and will continue to frame our futures.

Endnotes

1.   Pliny Earle Goddard. *Hupa texts* (Berkeley, CA: The University Press, 1904), 228. With additional translation provided by Kayla Begay, December 3, 2017. There are two Hupa written translations offered in this opening. The first is by Kayla Begay. The second is a direct written quote from Pliny Goddard from Hupa texts. The lines reflect the same line as translated in English. In this translation we have italicized the English translation of the Hupa story. While this is not common practice in many academic disciplines, in Native American Studies we work to not treat Indigenous languages as foreign by delineating them with italics which some scholars argue "others" Indigenous languages.

2.   There are two ways to spell Hupa/Hoopa depending on context. Hupa is used to refer to the people while Hoopa is used to refer to the place. The tribe is known as the Hoopa Valley Tribe. This is common practice when writing about and referencing the Hupa people or the Hoopa Valley.

3.   K'ixinay [='the ones who escape, the ones who are safe'] immortals, spirits, "angels" (The people who inhabited this world before human beings arrived to claim it. They had no fire, and didn't know death. They now live in Heaven—a world across the eastern ocean, beyond the sky— and are prayed to. Equivalent to Yurok 'Woo-gey, Karuk Ikxareeyav.) xay-ch'idilye • Jump Dance [literally, *winter-religious dance*] • compound noun • *Semantic domain: ceremonies.*

4.   Jack Norton, *Centering in Two Worlds: Essays on Native Northwestern California, Culture and Spirituality* (Hemet, CA: Center for the Affirmation of Responsible Education, 2007), 180.

5.   The term "more-than-human relatives" is adopted from Zoe Todd's work on the complex relationships between Indigenous peoples and the other beings that inhabit the world including animals, rocks, rivers, trees, and other parts of our world that are often referred to as "objects" or "resources" in a contemporary context. Todd's insistence at referring to these beings as "more-than-human" instead of "less-than" or "other-than" is an important epistemological framework to demonstrate how Indigenous peoples worldview understands the interrelationship and relativity of all beings.

6.   The Hupa refer to their First People as K'ixinay, the Yurok as 'Woo-gey, and the Karuk as Ikxareeyav.

7.   Zoe Todd. "From a Fishy Place: Examining Canadian State Law Applied in the Daniels Decision from the Perspective of Métis Legal

Orders." *TOPIA: Canadian Journal of Cultural Studies* 36 (2016), 231.

8. Julian Lang, *Ararapikva* (Berkeley, CA: Heyday Books, 1994), 25.

9. Gerald Vizenor, Survivance: Narratives of Native Presence (Lincoln, NE: University of Nebraska, 2008), 1.

10. Vine Deloria, Jr., *Spirit and Reason*, (Golden, CO: Fulcrum Publishing, 1999), 34.

11. Ibid., 53-54.

12. Jack Norton, *Genocide in Northwest California* (San Francisco, CA: The Indian Historian Press, 1979), 58.

13. Ibid., xv.

14. Ibid.

15. Ibid., xvii.

16. Jessica Wolf, "Revealing the history of genocide against California Native Americans" UCLA Newsroom, August 15, 2017. http://newsroom.ucla.edu/stories/revealing-the-history-of-genocide-against-californias-native-americans.

17. "story-where"

18. '(world)being made-when (in the past)'

19. the First (Immortal) People

20. "transformed long ago"

21. William J Bauer Jr, *California through Native eyes: reclaiming history*, (Seattle, WA: University of Washington Press, 2016), 10

22. Conathan, Lisa. "Recovering sociolinguistic context from early sources: The case of Northwestern California." *Anthropological linguistics* (2006): 211.

23. The Flat Place–Orleans

24. Upriver Edge Falls

25. Salmon Making Place-Village near Ike's Fall

26. Upriver people

27. Ararahih'urípih: A Dictionary and Text Corpus of the Karuk Language, http://linguistics.berkeley.edu/~karuk/index.php.

28. (Down) River Yurok People

29. (Up) River Yurok People

30. *Constitution of the Yurok Tribe.* Yurok Tribe, 1993, 1.

31. Victor Golla, *California Indian Languages*, (Berkeley, CA: University of California Press, 2011), 62.

32. Leanne Hinton, *Flutes of Fire: Essays on California Indian Languages*, (Berkeley, CA: Heyday Books, 1994), 53.

33. Edward Sapir, "Language: An introduction to the study of speech, "

(New York: Harcout, Brace & Company 1921), 228-29

34. Alfred Louis Kroeber, *Yurok myths* (Berkeley, CA: Univ of California Press, 1978), 1.

35. Haney

36. Alfred Louis Kroeber and Edward Winslow Gifford. *World renewal: a cult system of Native Northwest California*. Kraus Reprint Company, 1949.

37. Platt, 14.

38. Goddard, 132.

39. With the guidance of testimonials from Nererner elders (that were never recorded by Pliny Goddard), this ceremony was revitalized after a 130 year absence in 2011. This first fire and prayer for this Nererner ceremony begins at the village of Chapekw at Stone Lagoon. Once the first fire is built, the coals will be shared with the villages of Chotchkwee, Peenpay, and 'O pyuue-weg. The 10 day ceremony is a traveling ceremony that culminates with all 4 villages at Meyweehl O'leguehl and includes the dance for protection from tsunamis at Hewon Keta above Stone Lagoon.-Ed.

40. "(from) across they go around"

41. "flat-hats"

42. Lost 'Woo-gey

43. white skin people associated with death

44. Bauer Jr, 16.

45. John E. Mills, *The four ages of Tsurai: a documentary history of the Indian village on Trinidad Bay* (Berkley, CA: University of California Press, 1952).

46. Antonia I Castañeda, "Engendering the History of Alta California, 1769-1848: Gender, Sexuality, and the Family." *California History* 76, no. 2/3 (1997): 230-259.

47. Jack, J. Norton, and T. Hunnicutt. "A Teacher's Source Book on Genocide: The Native Experience in Northern California." *The Bridge Gulch Massacre* (1852).

48. Jamie L. Bush, "Exploring and settling Humboldt Bay." PhD diss., Humboldt State University, 2005.

49. Edith VA Murphey, and Lucy Young. "Out of the Past: A True Indian Story Told by Lucy Young, of Round Valley Indian Reservation." *Calif Hist QJ Calif Hist Soc* 20, no. 4 (1941): 349-364.

50. Byron Nelson, Our Home Forever: The Hupa Indians of Northern California (Salt Lake City, UT: The Howe Bros., 1978), 45.

51. Platt, 53.
52. Jack Forbes, Native Americans of California and Nevada (Happy Camp, CA: Naturegraph Publishers, 1993), 75
53. Ibid., 10-11.
54. Ibid.
55. Robert F. Heizer, and Alan J. Almquist, *The other Californians: Prejudice and discrimination under Spain, Mexico, and the United States to 1920*, (Berkeley, CA: Univ of California Press, 1977), 53-57.
56. Johnston-Dodds, 17.
57. Lindsay, 2.
58. Heizer and Almquist, 68.
59. Ibid.
60. Ibid., 69.
61. Sara Larus Tolley, *Quest for Tribal Acknowledgment: California's Honey Lake Maidus*, (Norman, OK: University of Oklahoma Press, 2006), 22.
62. William B. Secrest, *When the great spirit died: The destruction of the California Indians, 1850-1860*, (Fresno, CA: Quill Driver Books, 2003).
63. Goddard *Life and Culture*, 10.
64. Sharon O'brien, *American Indian tribal governments*. Vol. 192, (Norman, OK: University of Oklahoma Press, 1993), 28
65. Ibid.
66. Nelson, 108.
67. Ibid., 146.
68. Lucy Thompson, *To the American Indian: reminiscences of a Yurok woman*, (Berkeley, CA: Heyday, 1916), 2.
69. Nelson, 119.
70. Nelson 118.
71. John H.Bushnell, "From American Indian to Indian American: the changing identity of the Hupa." *American Anthropologist* 70, no. 6 (1968): 1110-1111.
72. Personal Communication with 'e:wa:k Jimmy Jackson, 2002, later corroborated in 2017 by personal communication with Hupa language advocates Danny Ammon and Gordon Bussell. *A Boarding School Experience* By Winnie Baldy George As told to Laura Lee George, reprinted in *Our People Speak: An anthology of Indian Writing*. Published by students at Humboldt State University with the cooperation of Indian Teacher Education and Preparation Program and the Redwood Writing Project. Summer 1982.
73. Nelson, 146.

74. Omer Call Stewart, Kroeber and the Indian Claims Commission Cases. California Indian Library Collections Project, 1989, 185.

75. Tolley, 78.

76. Ibid., xiii.

77. Renya Ramirez, Native Hubs: Culture, Community, and Belonging in Silicon Valley and Beyond (Durham, NC: Duke University Press, 2007), 46- 47.

78. Ibid., 2.

79. Platt, 148-149.

80. Kaitlin Reed, "We Are Salmon People: Constructing Yurok Sovereignty in the Klamath Basin," 2014, 14.

81. We're all Gonna Die Right Here': Talking About the Klamath Salmon Wars, KCET, October 16, 2016 https://www.kcet.org/shows/tending-the-wild/were-all-gonna-die-right-here-talking-about-the-klamath-salmon-wars.

82. Ibid.

83. Cutcha Risling Baldy "Water is Life: The Flower Dance Ceremony" *News from Native California*, Volume 30, Issue 3, Spring 2017.

84. Les W Field, *Abalone tales: collaborative explorations of sovereignty and identity in Native California*. (Durham, NC: Duke University Press, 2009), 121.

85. Cutcha Risling Baldy, We Are Dancing For You: Native Feminisms and the Revitalization of Women's Coming-of-Age Ceremonies, (Seattle, WA: University of Washington Press, 2018).

CHAPTER 4

American Indian Mental Health in Northwest California: A Call for Structural Interventions

Dr. Virgil Moorehead Jr.

IN A SPAN OF ONLY 30 TO 40 YEARS, FROM THE MID-19TH TO THE EARLY 20TH CENTURY, NORTHWEST CALIFORNIA INDIANS EXPERIENCED REMARKABLE LOSSES. During this period, the settler-colonial policies throughout California were designed to erase Indian cultures and exterminate the tribal nations.[1] In his book *American Genocide: California Indians*, Benjamin Madley conservatively estimates that from 1846 to 1873, 9,000 to 16,000 California Indians were killed by Euro-American settlers, state vigilantes, militiamen, and federal soldiers.[2] Violent repression and diseases transmitted from European American settlers plunged the California Indian population from approximately 150,000 to 30,000 by the end of the 1860s.[3] The Yurok population of the Klamath River was reduced to roughly 700 by the end of the 19th century, a 75 percent reduction from pre-European contact.[4]

This chapter will briefly describe the genocidal history in Northwest California, highlighting the interconnection of four incidents that were devastating to Indians: the Indian Island Massacre, the Gold Rush, California Indian slavery, and the U.S. government-sponsored boarding schools. The initial goal of the chapter is to deepen our understanding of the genocidal practices that arose from greed, exploitation, and racism, and led to the devastation of many Indian communities. After discussing American Indian peoples' formidable response to these events, as well as the distressing consequences of colonial violence, this chapter will explore how the U.S. mental health field has sought to assist American Indians in ameliorating elevated rates of suffering in their communities. After examining the positive and negative effects of a burgeoning American Indian mental health field, the discussion will advocate expanding the field to increase the emphasis on structural interventions. As used in this chapter, *structural interventions* refers to changing the context in which mental health is produced. This context includes the economic, social, and political environments that form and constrain individual, community, and societal mental health outcomes.

The Multidimensional Dynamics of European Colonization in Northwest California

The events described in this section have been selected to demonstrate the similarities between current struggles in Northwest California Indian communities, and those faced by Indians in the mid-19th and early 20th century. A substantial part of the chapter discusses the violent history in Northwest California, because one must be aware of the complicated dynamics of European colonization in order to shape the U.S. mental health field to positively impact contemporary Indian children. More specifically, a description of the history in Northwest California is important to understand because distinct patterns in this history persist in today's sociopolitical climate. Understanding these patterns, including the ways colonial violence is multifaceted, offers solutions to overcoming the social ills faced by contemporary Indian communities. While many factors are related to colonial domination (e.g. religion, gender, racism, and land exploitation), the primary focus of the chapter will be on economic factors influencing the health of Indian families, because these factors continue to severely impact Indian children.

Beginning in 1883, renowned historian of the American West

Hubert Howe Bancroft called the killings of California Indians during the mid-19th century one of the "last hunts" of North American civilization, and "the basest and most brutal of them all."[5] Nearly 30 years later, when discussing the history of Northern California Coastal Indians, noted archaeologist of the Wiyot people Llewellyn Loud stated, "to a member of the present generation, learning only a few isolated facts of the early history, it may seem that Humboldt County is preeminently disgraced by a blot of greater foulness than was ever attached to any other locality."[6] Disease, dislocation, and starvation caused many of these deaths; however, abduction, indentured slavery, homicides, military campaigns, and massacres also eliminated thousands of lives. Throughout the 1850s and 1860s, the State of California authorized paying volunteer groups thousands of dollars to suppress what they felt were violent raids by Indians against their livestock. In fact, the newly formed California government financed 24 state militia campaigns that killed thousands of California Indians and inspired numerous vigilante killings.[7] Well-documented examples from the Euro-American colonization of California described coordinated homicides by settlers and volunteer militia with government support—qualifying these actions as genocide.[8]

Economic Interests and Genocidal Practices in Northwest California

One of the most well-known examples of genocidal practices illustrating the systematic slaughter of Northern California Indians occurred on February 26, 1860. More than 200 Wiyot men, women, and children were massacred along the shores of Humboldt Bay. While engaged in a world renewal ceremony, they were killed by a handful of Euro-Americans armed with axes, hatchets, and knives.[9] The massacre was carried out in the early morning by European immigrants who recently settled in the area. Only a few Wiyot survived. While the massacre appeared to be unprovoked and the victims were largely women and children, following the slaughter, throughout the Humboldt Bay area, the response to the killings was largely muted. In fact, when Bret Harte, assistant editor of *Northern California*, editorialized against the massacre, his life was threatened and he was forced to flee the area.[10]

In considering the Indian Island and other massacres around that time, many critical questions emerge. What drove these Euro-Americans to slaughter a group of unarmed Indians? Why was the surrounding community not outraged, but silent? It is tempting to diminish the massacre to a small, isolated group of white men who slaughtered hundreds of women and children; however, this would be far too short-sighted. Instead, to adequately address these issues, we must situate the conflict in broader sociopolitical contexts. The answers to these questions can be found in the larger economic and social forces that altered the United States during the second half of the 19th century. In this sense, the Indian Island Massacre serves as a window into the violence of the Western United States that accompanied the Reconstruction Era, the colonization of California Indians, and the expansion of capitalism. The national factors that influenced the massacre and the many ecological changes that followed were largely economic and ideological, such as clashes over the meaning of place and how to live with the land.[11] As Hupa/Cherokee historian Jack Norton describes in his book, *Genocide in Northwestern California: When Our Worlds Cried*, the men who committed the massacre were unemployed and hoped to be reimbursed by the State of California. Norton concludes that money was a primary motivation behind many of the killings of Indians in Northwest California. Benjamin Madley also discovered in his research on the California Indian Genocide that feelings of racial superiority justified the killing of Indians, and greed supplied the sense of urgency. Perhaps Karuk artist Brian Tripp captured it best when he described the history of Humboldt County: "this place is a colony of Wall Street."[12] Like Norton and Madley, Tripp identifies the strong economic factors that shaped the history of Northwestern California.

One cannot accurately understand the killings and silence regarding the massacre without further contextualizing California's history during the previous decade. The "end of Indian time," as some Northwestern California Indians call this period, began in the late 1840s when the Gold Rush forever altered the area's history. Genocidal practices began during the gold mining expeditions. White settlers left wives and families, abandoned professions, and hurried to the mines and river beds of Northern California in a largely ill-advised frenzy in order to pursue, at any cost, a chance at fortune. Many of the supposed gold fields in California's "northern" gold rush lay in or near the ancestral lands of tribes such as the Yuroks. Gold discovered at Sutter's Mill in Coloma in 1848, and later the same year in Trinity County's Trinity River, set the stage for conflict between Indians, settlers, and gold seekers who flooded into the region and eventually the Northern California coast. Ultimately, Gold Rush fever led to much of the great population decline and cultural destruction of Northern California Indians.[13]

While the Gold Rush miners and European settlers caused significant destruction to Northwestern California Indians during the mid-19th and early 20th centuries, the state and federal governments also played a major role in negatively impacting Indian communities. Beginning in 1846, at least 20,000 California Indians worked in various forms of bondage under state government rule.[14] The newly formed State of California established statutes and selective enforcement that enabled and reinforced a statewide Indian slave trade. For example, Hupa children were kidnapped and sold for up to $250 each.[15] State officials made slavery possible via statutes such as the Act for the Government and Protection of Indians. Signed into law by Governor Peter Burnett on April 22, 1852, this statute codified a caste system based on a series of inequalities. Under this statute, any white person could appear before a state official to obtain an Indian child as a slave, if the court justice determined that no compulsory means were used to obtain the child. However, these "compulsory means" were very loosely defined, and allowed many whites to enslave Indian children.[16] Furthermore, following increased demand for California labor due to population surges, kidnappings of Indian children occurred and were largely legalized based on these oppressive laws. Consequently, American Indian communities were severely impacted by the kidnapping of Indian children.

Enduring Economic Influences: Indian Boarding Schools

When extermination was no longer an economically or politically viable tactic in the U.S., an era of assimilation to Euro-American colonial doctrine was ushered in, resulting in the creation of Indian boarding schools. Between 1879 and 1930, the U.S. Bureau of Indian Affairs maintained a large system of on-reservation and off-reservation boarding schools for Indian children, including a boarding school on the Hoopa Valley Reservation. In 1932, the Hoopa Boarding School was one of the first schools to transform into a day school.[17] The ultimate goal of these schools was to assimilate Indian children into the

Euro-American ways of life. Children were taken from their families and homeland, forbidden to speak their native languages, and stripped of their clothing and regalia. An important theme omitted from many historian, ethnographer, and educator descriptions is the role of what anthropologist Alice Littlefield refers to as "proletarianization."

Like the Gold Rush and implementation of slavery, the federal government boarding schools had deep economic interests. These boarding schools strongly emphasized transforming previously independent Indians who were farmers, hunters, and gatherers into wage laborers. Littlefield argues that white-run Indian schools served as instruments for "imposing the behavioral routines…necessary for adapting to an industrial economy."[18] Government officials reasoned that by isolating Indian children from the influences of their parents and sending them to boarding schools and/or farming families in the summer to work through an "outing program," they could cultivate and inculcate new desires. These desires included motivating Indian children to work for the money needed to acquire material possessions, or to become better workers for Euro-American owners in the cash economy, separate from the influence of their own culture. Winnie Baldy George described her experiences at the Hupa boarding school: "…if you went to school in the morning, well you had to work that afternoon…they put you in the kitchen or they put you in the laundry or sewing room and all that."[19]

Previously, Native cultures such as the Hupa lived off the land and embodied ways of engaging work that were consistent with their eco-friendly and village based belief systems. While many Northwest California Indians engaged in trade with nearby tribes, virtually all of the material needs of the tribe were met by resources immediately at hand. It can be argued that as part of the assimilation process, boarding schools aimed to turn Indians from their village based lifestyles into wage laborers in order to meet the needs of powerful business elites and governmental interests. In other words, the boarding school experience facilitated the process of proletarianization by imposing the behavioral routines, patterns of social interaction, and personal dispositions necessary for adapting to the industrial economy.

Improbable Thriving and Current Mental Health Consequences

While yet to be described, an important element for understanding the history of Indian people in Northwest California is Indians' response to the genocidal acts waged against them. Far too often, including in contemporary mental health theories and practices, Indian people are portrayed as docile, subservient to the needs of an expanding capitalist economy and the U.S. government's settler colonial (i.e., extermination of Indians for land) interests. This representation is far from the truth and must be contested. Despite extreme hardship, the Indian people of Northwest California survived. In the 20th century, a dramatic revitalization of North American Indian populations occurred, moving from beyond mere survival to the possibility of prospering. These Indian nations employed substantial measures to maintain their traditional ceremonies, languages, and epistemologies. For example, many Northwest California Indians understood that capitalism was not going anywhere, so they participated in the local industrial/capitalist economy in complex ways. They labored on Pacific Coast bulb farms and worked in fisheries and lumber companies during the late 19th and mid-20th centuries.[20] More recently, tribes have built casinos, restaurants, timber industries, hotels, and numerous other enterprises for economic sustainability. In these ways, Northwest California Indians creatively adapted to Euro-American settler policies and the relentless pressures of the capitalist economic system.

This determination and adaptation have led to a strong resurgence of cultural practices and an increase in each tribe's population in the last four decades. A visit to Northern California in the last 30 years would reveal a remarkable story of resilience and cultural revitalization. Following years of inactivity, the Flower Dance ceremony honoring a young woman's coming of age is thriving again among the Yurok, Hupa, Karuk, and other Northern California tribes. The Brush Dance (a healing ceremony for ill children), as well as the Deerskin Dance and the Jump Dance renewal ceremonies, are practiced during the summer, with scores of people in attendance. The Hupa, Yurok, Karuk, Tolowa, and Wiyot nations are also taking practical steps to restore their languages. Teachers are learning basic Hupa in order to teach it in elementary and high schools, and public-school instructors in Humboldt and Del Norte Counties are teaching the Yurok language. Throughout the last half-century, the Wiyot people of Humboldt Bay have also fought tirelessly to ensure that the victims of the Indian Island Massacre are not forgotten. To this end, the Wiyots have sought to regain Tuluwat (i.e, Indian Island), and in 2017, after decades of persistence, the Eureka City Council agreed to return Indian Island to them. Undoubtedly, the political activism, economic experimentation, and cultural renaissance of Northwest California Indians have led to the resurgence of these communities.

Unfortunately, despite this significant progress around cultural revitalization and increases in Native populations, major problematic health issues remain. A distressing indicator of this suffering is demonstrated by a recent suicide cluster among seven Yurok tribal members over a 15-month period between 2015-2016 that led the Yurok tribe to declare a state of emergency. These victims were all relatively young, ranging in age from 16 to 31.[21] Humboldt County's Health Department statistics show that between 2014-2016, Native Americans in Humboldt County died 12 years earlier than their white counterparts; this data includes higher rates of infant mortality rates and death from unintentional injuries.[22] Furthermore, a recent study by the California Department of Social Services revealed that, in 2016, Native American children represented 7% of the total children in Humboldt County but approximately 37% of the foster care population handled by Humboldt County Child Welfare Services.[23] Close to thirty percent of children in Humboldt County suffer adverse experiences, some of the highest rates in California.[24] Adverse childhood experiences (ACEs) are defined as stressful or traumatic events, including abuse and neglect[25] and are frequently higher in the foster care system. Thus, in considering these troubling figures, it becomes clear that there remains much work in order to ameliorate unnecessary suffering in Northwest California Indian communities.

American Indian Mental Health and its Limitations

Keeping in mind this history, sociopolitical context, and contemporary health status of Indian people, the remainder of the chapter will focus on examining American Indian mental health in more depth, including how to shape the field in order to promote sustainable self-determination among Indian people. For purposes of this chapter, American Indian mental health refers to professional Indian and non-Indian psychologists, researchers, and the institutions (e.g., Indian Health Service, community based non-profits) that serve Indian peoples' mental health needs. To comprehend American Indian mental health, one should first recognize the significance that clinicians and researchers working in the field place on Euro-American colonization to explain elevated levels of psychological and social problems in Indian communities.[26] Over the last four decades, the historical trauma concept has become an integral part of American Indian mental health. Historical trauma has been used to describe the exposure of American Indian communities to over 500 years of large-scale, repeated, cumulative, violent, and dehumanizing events. A critical feature of American Indian historical trauma is that the effects of this colonial violence are believed to be transmitted to subsequent generations through biological, psychological, environmental, and social means, causing a cross-generational cycle of traumatic symptoms such as unresolved grief.[27] More specifically, American Indian mental health clinicians and researchers argue that the current psychosocial suffering (e.g., depression, substance abuse, suicide) of Indians in places such as Humboldt County are best explained by understanding the violent and "traumatic" history described earlier in this essay. This history includes the well-documented Indian Island Massacre as well as lesser-known massacres, such as those during the Indian Wars (Red Cap Wars, Yontocket Massacre), along with the cultural suppression of their traditions throughout the 19th and 20th centuries.

Alongside historical trauma theory, professionals working in American Indian mental health frequently contend that mental health treatment models shaped by European culture conflict with the values and perspectives of American Indian cultures. They stress that the "culture" of the mainstream mental health clinic is misaligned with the "culture" of the Indian community.[28] For these service providers and researchers working with American Indian communities, the leading treatment paradigms taught in psychology training programs are saturated with classifications, ideologies, and practices that are often culturally alien to Indian communities. To this end, by working with western-based experts or American Indian practitioners trained in mainstream institutions that privilege biological and medical knowledge and classify people through a specific diagnostic nosology (i.e., *Diagnostic Statistical Manual-V*), American Indians risk becoming even more assimilated into American society, changing the ways they view themselves and others.

In order to counteract these Euro-American hegemonic practices and help to heal Indian people from the effects of historical trauma and cultural loss, researchers and professional psychologists working in Indian Country advocate for, and implement, interventions that prioritize American Indian cultural traditions. Among these mental health professionals, the therapeutic expression "our culture is prevention" is endorsed, including the use of terms such as "enculturation" to explain how cultural practices may serve as protective factors for American Indian youth.[29] While *acculturation* is the process by which a member of an ethnic minority group adheres to the majority culture, *enculturation* signifies the degree of re-integration within one's own cultural traditions.

Understanding the ways historical trauma theory and cultural-based interventions have promoted healing in Indian communities is critical to understanding contemporary American Indian mental health. Significant advances in tribal communities dealing with mental health and social ills (e.g., addiction, suicide) have resulted from the strong focus on historical trauma and American Indian cultural practices by mental health researchers and community service providers. For example, an enculturation process that helps American Indians to connect to their tribal cultures has been correlated to resilience,[30] improved academic performance,[31] decreased risk of suicide,[32] and lower susceptibility to substance abuse among American Indian youth. Research on the effects of historical suppression of cultures and identities has also increased the awareness of these as causes of suffering in American Indian communities. This research has generated increased funding and expanded culturally-based interventions in many American Indian communities. However, like many treatment models, the key features of American Indian mental health can be enriched.

Scholars have recently investigated the failure of the historical trauma construct to meet the emancipatory goals of Indian communities.[33] These scholars have stated that the historical trauma theory may inadvertently integrate Indians into Eurocentric belief systems, and/or inadequately address the social determinants of health. For example, many current Indian and non-Indian historical trauma proponents have not separated this theory from its clinical and medical origins based on the western biomedical model.[34] Psychological trauma, such as Post Traumatic Stress Disorder, is based in psychopathology and a western-based psychotherapeutic culture that includes particular ways of understanding personhood (e.g., autonomous, rational, individual). These perspectives run counter to many Indigenous views of personhood that have been termed collectivist, socio-centric, or eco-centric.[35]

At this point, it is important to clarify that the critique of historical trauma theory is not intended to undermine former individual accounts of abuse and the after-effects, such as the brutalizing experiences many Indian people faced in boarding schools. Rather, the purpose is to bring attention to how working through the lens of trauma theory limits the parameters of discussions to the effects of settler colonialism, without discussing the destructive ideological foundations of colonialism and their wider consequences.[36] When historical trauma theory is used to locate pathology within the individual, it parallels limited biomedical and psychiatric diagnostic classifications. This continued adherence to the mainstream biomedical model via psychological trauma often leads to "medicalizing" social issues such as poverty, severe underfunding for Indian health services, and institutional racism. Rather than working on the ongoing systemic origins of distress in Indian communities, historical trauma proponents may inadvertently attempt to remake individuals, and consequently fail to transform the social, economic, and political determinants of health. American Indian scholar, Dian Million states, "…the healing [of trauma] would occur while capitalist development might still displace one or require one's land." She asserts that this situation is "…a little like accepting being bandaged by your armed assailant while he is still ransacking your house."[37] In other words, historical trauma theory tends to ignore how *current* colonial institutions, ideas, and practices combine to undermine Indians' access to, and control over, a range of social factors influencing health, including their relationship with the land and the promotion of healthy child development through strengthening Indigenous institutions.

Professional discourses that categorize individuals and their forms of suffering also directly impact their lives, influencing how they understand themselves and others.[38] For example, qualitative research by Hartmann and Gone on historical trauma in a Northern Plains reservation exposed how cultural expectations based on mainstream health discourses can encourage psychological-mindedness, the "individual's ability and interest in reflecting on psychological [internal] processes that structure experiences of self and others."[39] The problem with this sort of discourse is that it again shifts the focus away from factors external to the individual, toward individual psyches. Moreover, psychological thinking is not the way in which many North American Indian communities have viewed the world.[40] Historically, most Northwest California American Indian belief systems about health and illness were based in spiritual teachings. These teachings conflict with the strong emphasis that the mainstream trauma field places on psychological and biological factors to explain the effects of violent acts. Hence, one can see how promoting psychological-mindedness through a historical trauma theory can result in remaking Indian peoples' cultural worldviews (i.e., from spiritual to psychological), further leading to assimilation and disconnecting them from their own cultural ways of being.

Just as historical trauma theory is limited in its ability to promote wellness in Indian communities, the sweeping emphasis on "culture," often used by American Indian mental health professionals, also has its limits. Even when focusing on cultural interventions, the American Indian mental health approach often does so narrowly. Culture is often presented as beliefs and behaviors of an ethnic group or an individual person.[41] When used in this way, "culture" can homogenize and/or essentialize American Indian groups. In effect, by using this single term—"culture"—important socioeconomic differences are frequently diminished, and diverse American Indian communities are treated as one group. This becomes problematic because there are significant socioeconomic differences in access to health-promoting resources. Accordingly, interventions that are not tailored to meet these socio-economic variances may fail to address some of American Indians' most pressing needs.

Similarly, shortcomings of cultural interventions used by mental health practitioners and researchers occur when interventions fail to recognize the importance of the organization, policies, and ideologies of institutions that influence health and inequalities. Many American Indians live in chronic poverty, with limited access to adequate health care, housing, and quality education. For example, from 2010-2014, the Yurok tribe economy was considerably depressed, with 34.5% of residents falling below the federal poverty level.[42] Additionally, the Indian Health Service (IHS), the primary health care provider for most American Indians, has been historically inadequately funded, with recent estimates showing that federal funding only provides 54 percent of needed services.[43] In fact, in 2015, while national per capita health care spending averaged $9,523 annually, IHS spends only about $3,688 per person per year.[44] One could call these *macro-level* cultural factors, and when clinicians and researchers in American Indian mental health do not prioritize these factors, they may obscure the ongoing material dispossession and political domination impacting American Indian communities that have severe health consequences.

Improving Health and Self-determination among Northwest California Indians

Keeping the positive and negative effects of the current American Indian mental health field in mind, the question arises: how can American Indian mental health professionals better serve Indian children? As implied throughout the chapter, individual well-being is profoundly connected to the lives of others. Yet American children, including Indian children, are often told that they will only prosper through extreme individualism. These beliefs largely stem from the meritocratic ethos of contemporary capitalism, which posits that social class is no longer pertinent; therefore, everyone ends up with the socioeconomic lot they earn. This belief system often places self-interest at the center of human motivation, thereby increasing competition, habitual comparison to others, and the pursuit of personal profit at any cost. Accordingly, an improved American Indian mental health system must incorporate more interventions that counter these highly individualistic ideologies.

In *The High Price of Materialism*, psychologist Tim Kasser describes the impact of one of these ideologies, materialism, on mental health. Kasser cites research showing that the greater emphasis one places on materialistic, self-enhancing values (social power, wealth, etc.), the lower one's happiness and life satisfaction.[45] He found that depression, anxiety, and substance abuse trend higher among people with values promoted by a materialistic society.[46] Furthermore, he found that the higher the levels of materialistic thinking, the less individuals are socially minded. In fact, scientists find that materialistic and pro-social values are like a seesaw; as materialistic values increase, pro-social values tend to decrease.[47] Thus, people act in less empathetic, generous, and cooperative ways when money dominates their intentions. Because American Indian youth are immersed daily in mainstream social media, television, advertising, and school curricula that promote individually focused, consumer-based ideologies, it is crucial for their mental health service providers and researchers to acknowledge and prevent the effects of these forces on them.

Fortunately, for American Indians in Northwest California, much of the wisdom about dealing with toxic, antisocial beliefs already resides in their cultural history and traditions. The Wo-neek we ley-goo, or Jump Dance is a spiritual ritual renewing the continuation of humankind. Yurok cultural leader Walt Lara Sr. stated that the ceremony "is all about the health, education and welfare of families…raising children to be in balance with the world." Yurok cultural leader Chris Peters added, "we are here to heal and renew the earth for everyone, not just Yurok people. That is our obligation."[48] These tribal leaders believe that Yuroks have been put on the earth to live with the land in harmony. They are here to renew and heal the world for all beings—a goal markedly different from exploiting the land and encouraging the greed and self-entitlement that modern corporate capitalism often produces. Indeed, revitalizing ceremonies and cultural traditions is critical to the balance and healing of contemporary Indian communities. Indians should practice this healing process in order to become whole again. An improved American Indian mental health system should continue to support these community efforts.

Since the devastating historical events described in this chapter have frequently led to the disconnection of Indian children from their Indigenous ways of being, implementing structural interventions must supplement these cultural interventions. An American Indian mental health system that incorporates structural interventions can advance approaches that clearly articulate a radical transformation of values and interventions countering greed and materialism. For example, mental health providers can give new mothers information about the dangers of screen time for young children, and recommend that American Indian parents block advertisements on phones in order to limit children's exposure to materialism. In addition, American Indian mental health professionals can recommend that tribal leaders ban corporate advertising to children and remove corporate ads from public spaces. Prioritizing cooperation (versus profit at all cost) and other non-competitive behaviors such as empathy and compassion is also imperative. These pro-social values should extend to the environment for American Indian youth. Programs that utilize volunteers to take care of the environment, such as picking up trash on weekends or working in community gardens, are just two examples of mental health interventions that develop pro-environmental values aligned with longstanding Native traditions. For example, Kirmayer found that Cree youth in James Bay, Canada who spent more time outdoors decreased their level of distress.[49]

A recent story on the U.S. opioid crisis featured on CBS "60 Minutes" (October 20, 2017) exemplifies how an expanded, more structurally informed American Indian mental health field may look. CBS' joint investigation[50] with *The Washington Post* described a pharmaceutical industry that approved millions of opiates to be sold to irresponsible pharmacies and doctors' offices for people with no need for those drugs. The report found that the federal government wrote legislation disempowering the U.S. Drug Enforcement Agency's regulatory power, aiding major pharmaceutical companies (e.g., Cardinal Health, Mckesson, AmerisourceBergen) to make billions of dollars, despite dire consequences. These consequences include over 42,000 people dying in the U.S. in 2016 of opiate overdose, up to 400% increase from the previous 10 years.[51] 1,925 Californians died from opioid overdoses in 2016, and 33 of them were in Humboldt County–which revealed the second-highest average overdose rate in the state.[52] Moreover, data from the Center for Disease Control and Prevention shows that American Indians have experienced the largest rise in opioid death rates of any ethnic group.[53]

Political factors related to issues such as drug overdose rates are often omitted from the current mental health model. Instead, the focus tends to be on how to "fix" individuals struggling with addiction. Accordingly, using the opioid epidemic as an example, an expanded American Indian mental health intervention should teach Indian youth and those struggling with addiction about contextual factors (e.g., profit-seeking pharmaceutical companies and the governmental agencies that support them). Encouraging Indian youth to be proactive about finding ways to transform the impact of the pharmaceutical industry on wellness in Indian communities is an important mental health intervention. Specific interventions might include teaching Indian children advocacy skills by engaging in local politics and activism via broad social movements (e.g., Standing Rock), and community organizing skills and critical media literacy in order to diminish the power of the pharmaceutical industry. It is crucial to emphasize that, as much as individual healing is needed in Indian communities, Paulo Freirean style consciousness raising[54] where there is a deep and critical interrogation about the ways in which the American political establishment and corporations negatively impact American Indian mental health is also necessary and a mental health intervention, per se. Rather than separating our understanding of economic and social practices from our understanding of human psychology and development, we need to bring them together and align them for true healing and long-term liberation to occur. We need a new integrated model for mental health, combined with new politics. Such an integrated methodology will create a mental health system that better serves Indian children and, in so doing, support collective struggles for social and political change.

With the relentless erosion of community in the U.S. over the last four decades[55] coupled with elevated rates of mental health issues in Indian Country, attention to structure as an organizing principle in American mental health is vital. If the history of Northwest California described in this chapter tells us anything, it should relate that European-American greed is deeply rooted in the entire structure of U.S. society. Accordingly, to advance thriving Northwest California Indian communities, American Indian mental health must include a deeper interrogation of U.S. society, with structural interventions that promote sustainable self-determination and civic engagement via structural interventions. Indeed, mental health professionals working in Indian Country must more deeply challenge the traditional view of what mental illness is, and what the mental health system and its professionals can do.

Summary

Indian people in Northwest California have withstood over 150 years of persistent assaults aimed at destroying their way of life and overall population. Practicing distinct cultural healing traditions has been central to their survival. However, problems remain that require rearticulating "cultural" presentations in structural terms. Today, American Indian children in Northwest California experience an increasing number of health problems, including elevated rates of suicide and substance abuse. In this chapter, it has been argued that American Indians must address the impact of sociopolitical forces, such as individualism at any cost and corporate greed, on the development and health of Indian children. To this end, American Indian mental health must cast its net wider and investigate the ways in which the current social values of mainstream

America determine and shape the values and beliefs of Indian children. Encouraging and supporting American Indian youth to proactively learn ways to develop structural competence and work to transform the U.S. sociopolitical system is a critical mental health intervention that will ensure a better future for Northwest California Indian communities.

Endnotes

1. Jack Norton, *Genocide in Northwest California: When our worlds cried* (San Francisco, Indian Historian Press, 1979), 1; James Rawls, *Indians of California: The Changing Image* (Norman, University of Oklahoma Press, 1984), 171.

2. Benjamin Madley, *American Genocide: The United States and the California Indian Catastrophe, 1846-1873* (New Haven: Yale University Press, 2016), 12.

3. Benjamin Madley, *American Genocide: The United States and the California Indian Catastrophe, 1846-1873* (New Haven: Yale University Press, 2016), 3.

4. Alfred L. Kroeber, "Principles of Yurok law" in *Handbook of the Indians of California*, ed. Alfred L. Kroeber (Washington, D.C.: Bureau of American Ethnology, Bulletin 78, 1925), 883; The "Yurok Tribe Background Information," The Yurok Tribe, accessed Dec 10, 2017 http://www.yuroktribe.org/culture/history/history.htm.

5. Hubert Howe Bancroft, *History of the Pacific States of North American: North Mexican States. 1531-1800* (San Francisco: History Company, 1883), 474.

6. Llewellyn Loud, *University of California Publications in American Archaeology and Ethnology*, Vol. 14, ed. A. L. Kroeber (Berkeley: University of California Press, 1965), 305.

7. Benjamin Madley, "It's Time to Acknowledge the Genocide of California's Indians," *The Los Angeles Times*, May 22, 2016, accessed December 9, 2017, http://www.latimes.com/opinion/op-ed/la-oe-madley-california-genocide-20160522-snap-story.html.

8. Brendan C. Lindsay *Murder State: California's Native American Genocide, 1846-1873.* (Lincoln: U of Nebraska Press, 2012), 3-5.

9. Tony Platt, *Grave Matters: Excavating California's Buried Past* (Berkeley: Heyday, 2011), 45-50.

10. Nilda Rego, "Days Gone By: 1860 massacre of Native American tribe prompts strong opposition from Brett Harte," *The Mercury*

News, March 26, 2014. Accessed December 3, 2017 https://www.mercurynews.com/2014/03/26/days-gone-by-1860-massacre-of-native-american-tribe-prompts-strong-opposition-from-bret-harte/.

11. Michael Karp, *"Lifting the Redwood Curtain: Work, Violence, and Environment, 1850-1948,"* (PhD diss., Saint Louis University, 2015), 1-18.

12. Thomas Buckley, *Standing Ground: Yurok Indian Spirituality, 1850–1990.* (Berkeley, Univ. of California Press, 2002), 12.

13. Jack Norton, *Genocide in Northwest California: When our Worlds Cried* (San Francisco, Indian Historian Press, 1979), 38-40.

14. Benjamin Madley, "unholy Traffic in Human Blood and Souls": Systems of California Indian Servitude Under US Rule." *Pacific Historical Review* 83, no. 4 (2014): 626-667.

15. Byron Nelson. *Our Home forever: A Hupa tribal history* (Hoopa: Hoopa Valley Tribe, 1978), 65.

16. Kimberly Johnston-Dodds. "Early California Laws and Policies Related to California Indians," *California Research Bureau,* accessed November 7, 2017, http://www.water.ca.gov/pubs/planning/california_water_plan_2005_update__bulletin_160-05_/vol4-tribal-earlycalifornialaws.pdf.

17. Byron Nelson, *Our Home Forever: A Hupa Tribal History* (Hoopa: Hoopa Valley Tribe, 1978), 168.

18. Alice Littlefield, "Indian Education and The World of Work in Michigan, 1893-1933," in *Native Americans and Wage labor: Ethnohistorical Perspectives,* ed. Alice Littlefield and Martha C. Knack (Norman: University of Oklahoma Press, 1996), 120.

19. Byron Nelson. *Our Home Forever: A Hupa tribal history.* (Hoopa: Hoopa Valley Tribe, 1978), 54.

20. Thomas Buckley, *Standing Ground: Yurok Indian Spirituality, 1850–1990* (Berkeley: Univ. of California Press, 2002), 45-46.

21. Joe Mozingo, "How a remote California tribe set out to save its river and stop a suicide epidemic," *The Los Angeles Times,* May 19, 2017, accessed October, 13, 2017, http://www.latimes.com/local/california/la-me-salmon-demise-yurok-suicides-20170519-htmlstory.html.

22. California Department of Public Health, "Humboldt County Maternal Child and Adolescent Health Community Profile, 2017-2018," https://www.cdph.ca.gov/Programs/CFH/DMCAH/LocalMCAH/CDPH%20Document%20Library/Community-Profile-Humboldt.pdf (accessed, December 20, 2017).

23. Humboldt Department of Health and Human Services, *Humboldt County System Improvement Plan Annual Progress Report: California Child and Family Services Review*, by Sheryl Lyons, Jody Green and Cris Plocher, Eureka, CA, August 30, 2016 http://www.childsworld. ca.gov/res/SIPs/2016/HumboldtSIP.pdf.

24. Times Standard, "Grand jury: Humboldt County kids 'ill-served' by system meant to protect them," *The Times Standard* May 30, 2017, http://www.times-standard.com/article/NJ/20170530/ NEWS/170539998.

25. Substance Abuse and Mental Health Services Administration, "*Adverse Childhood Experiences*," accessed November 1, 2018, https:// www.samhsa.gov/capt/practicing-effective-prevention/prevention-behavioral-health/adverse-childhood-experiences.

26. Eduardo Duran and Bonnie Duran, *Native American Postcolonial Psychology* (Albany: SUNY Press, 1995), 1-10.

27. Maria Yellow Horse Brave Heart and Lemyra M. DeBruyn "The American Indian Holocaust: Healing Historical Unresolved Grief," *American Indian and Alaska Native Mental Health*, 8, no. 2 (1998), 56.

28. Joseph P. Gone and Joseph E. Trimble, "American Indian and Alaska Native mental health: Diverse perspectives on enduring disparities" *Annual Review of Clinical Psychology* 8, (2012): 131-160.

29. Teresa D. LaFromboise, Dan R. Hoyt, Lisa Oliver, and Les B. Whitbeck, "Family, Community, and School Influences on Resilience among American Indian Adolescents in the Upper Midwest," *Journal of Community Psychology* 34, no. 2 (2006): 193-209.

30. Mindy Herman-Stahl, Donna L. Spencer, and Jessica E. Duncan, "The Implications of Cultural Orientation for Substance Use Among American Indians," *American Indian and Alaska Native Mental Health Research* 11, no. 1 (2003): 46.

31. Whitbeck, Les B., Dan R. Hoyt, Jerry D. Stubben, and Teresa LaFromboise. "Traditional culture and academic success among American Indian children in the upper Midwest," *Journal of American Indian Education* 40, no. 2 (2001): 48-60.

32. Michael Chandler and Christopher Lalonde "Cultural Continuity as a Hedge Against Suicide in Canada's First Nations," *Transcultural Psychiatry* 35, no. 2 (1998): 191-219.

33. Joseph P. Gone, "Reconsidering American Indian Historical Trauma: Lessons from an early Gros Ventre War Narrative." *Transcultural Psychiatry* 51, no. 3 (2014): 387-406; Maxwell, Krista, "Historicizing

Historical Trauma Theory: Troubling the Trans-generational Transmission Paradigm," *Transcultural Psychiatry* 51, no. 3 (2014): 407-435.

34. Joseph P. Gone "Redressing First Nations Historical Trauma: Theorizing Mechanisms for Indigenous Culture as Mental Health Treatment," *Transcultural Psychiatry* 50, no. 5, (2013): 683-706.

35. Laurence J. Kirmayer, "Psychotherapy and the Cultural Concept of the Person," *Transcultural psychiatry* 44, no. 2 (2007): 232-257.

36. Krista Maxwell, "Historicizing historical trauma theory: Troubling the trans-generational transmission paradigm." *Transcultural Psychiatry* 51, no. 3 (2014): 407-435.

37. Dian Million, *Therapeutic Nations: Healing in the Age of Indigenous Human Rights* (Tuscon:University of Arizona Press, 2013), 106.

38. Ian Hacking, Making up People, in Reconstructing Individualism: Autonomy, Individuality, and the Self in Western Thought, ed. Thomas C. Heller, Morton Sosna, and David Wellbery (Stanford: Stanford University, 1986), 222-36.

39. William E. Hartmann and Joseph P. Gone, "Psychological-Mindedness and American Indian Historical Trauma: Interviews with Service Providers from a Great Plains Reservation," *American Journal of Community Psychology*, 57, no. 1-2 (2016): 230.

40. Regna Darnell, "Reflections on Cree interactional etiquette: Educational implications," *Working Papers in Sociolinguistics* 57, 1979: 1-22.

41. Laurence J. Kirmayer, "Rethinking Cultural Competence," *Transcultural Psychiatry* 49, (2012): 149-164.

42. Yurok Tribe, "American Community Survey, 5-year Estimates, 2010-2014." Accessed January 2, 2018, http://www.yuroktribe.org/documents/DRAFT_CEDS_WEB.pdf.

43. Indian Health Services, "The 2016 Indian Health Service and Tribal Health Care Facilities' Needs Assessment Report to Congress," accessed December 20, 2017 https://www.ihs.gov/newsroom/includes/themes/newihstheme/display_objects/documents/RepCong_2016/IHSRTC_on_FacilitiesNeedsAssessmentReport.pdf.

44. Indian Health Services, "IHS 2016 Profile," accessed December 20, 2017 https://www.ihs.gov/newsroom/factsheets/ihsprofile/.

45. Shalom H. Schwartz, "Universals in the Content and Structure of Values: Theoretical Advances and Empirical Tests in 20 Countries," *Advances in Experimental Social Psychology* 25, (1992): 1-65.

46. Tim Kasser, Katherine L. Rosenblum, Arnold J. Sameroff, Edward L. Deci, Christopher P. Niemiec, Richard M. Ryan, Osp Árnadóttir et al. "Changes in Materialism, Changes in Psychological Well-being: Evidence from Three Longitudinal Studies and an Intervention Experiment," *Motivation and Emotion* 38, no. 1 (2014): 1-22.

47. Tim Kasser, "Materialistic Values and Goals," *Annual Review of Psychology* 67, (2016): 489-514.

48. Yurok Today, "Cha-pekw Descendants Raise it up. Ceremonial Leaders Restore the Stone Lagoon Jump Dance, A Sacred Ceremony to Heal the World," *Yurok Today: The Voice of the People*, October, 2012, accessed November 3, 2017, http://www.yuroktribe.org/documents/2012_october.pdf.

49. Laurence J. Kirmayer, Lucy J. Boothroyd, Adrian Tanner, Naomi Adelson, and Elizabeth Robinson, "Psychological Distress among the Cree of James Bay," *Transcultural Psychiatry* 37, no. 1 (2000): 35-56.

50. Scott Higham and Lenny Bernstein, "The Drug Industry's Triumph over the DEA, *The Washington Post*, October 15, 2017, accessed October 31, 2017 https://www.washingtonpost.com/graphics/2017/investigations/dea-drug-industry-congress/?utm_term=.5d0dcce7060f https://www.washingtonpost.com/graphics/2017/investigations/dea-drug-industry-congress/?utm_term=.aedce61daa46.

51. Center for Disease Control and Prevention, *Prescription Opioid Overdose Data* (Washington D.C., 2015) https://www.cdc.gov/drugoverdose/data/overdose.html (accessed, December 19, 2017).

52. California Department of Public Health, *Report: more opioid prescriptions in Humboldt County than residents* (Eureka, CA, 2017) http://www.times-standard.com/general-news/20171026/report-more-opioid-prescriptions-in-humboldt-county-than-residents (accessed, December 19, 2017).

53. Center for Disease Control and Prevention, *Prescription Opioid Overdose Data* (Washington D.C., 2015) https://www.cdc.gov/drugoverdose/data/overdose.html (accessed, December 20, 2017).

54. Paulo Freire, *Pedagogy of the Oppressed* (New York: Bloomsbury Publishing, 1968), 12-14.

55. Robert D. Putnam "Bowling Alone: The Collapse and Revival of American Community (New York Simon & Schuster, 2000), 30-32.

CHAPTER 5

Sustaining *Hlkelonah ue Meygeytohl* in an Ever-Changing World

Seafha Ramos

THIS CHAPTER WILL UTILIZE FINDINGS FROM INTERDIS-
CIPLINARY, CULTURALLY SENSITIVE WILDLIFE RESEARCH
TO UNDERSTAND HOW TRADITIONAL ECOLOGICAL
KNOWLEDGE (TEK) IS CONCEPTUALIZED THROUGH A
YUROK[1] CULTURAL LENS. In addition, personal and academic expe-
riences in regard to contemporary wildlife research with both Western
Ecological Knowledge and TEK will be discussed. Finally, this chapter
concludes with some of the roles people in the community can take in
the continued effort in survival of Yurok TEK and natural resources
conservation.

Background of Research

Data collection included semi-structured informal interviews with
adult individuals of Yurok ancestry or people who were identified as
being knowledgeable about relationships between wildlife, natural
resources, and Yurok culture. Among the participants were spiritual/

cultural leaders, Yurok Tribe government officials, Yurok Tribe Cultural Resources staff, Yurok Tribe Natural Resources Committee appointees, Yurok Tribe Culture Committee appointees, Yurok Tribe Language Program staff, fishermen, and hunters. Some interview participants explicitly noted their desire for the research to be used for cultural preservation and educational purposes, such as is the intent of this chapter, with the hope that others will gain from it by processing what is shared and using what is right for them.[1] A wildlife survey was designed and conducted with the intention that, where possible, elements would fit within the Yurok TEK framework, integrating Indigenous and Western approaches to research.

The Relationship of 'oohl (Yurok People) and Wildlife in Yurok Traditional Ecological Knowledge

The term "TEK" was derived in academia and came into widespread use in the 1980s. Though there is no universally accepted definition,[2] a commonly cited definition is, "a cumulative body of knowledge, practice, and belief, evolving by adaptive processes and handed down through generations by cultural transmission, about the relationship of living beings (including humans) with one another and with their environment."[3] Many Yurok consider TEK as a way of life. Yurok people, 'oohl, were placed on the Earth to serve as stewards of the land, understanding that if the resources, such as wildlife, are treated with respect, nourished, and taken care of (i.e. "managed"), these resources will continue to be available. Yurok TEK can be thought of as a branch of Indigenous Science and conceptualized as hlkelonah ue meygeytohl ("to take care of the Earth"), a system where Yurok people and wildlife collaboratively strive to create and maintain balance of the Earth via physical and spiritual management in tandem.[4]

In Yurok TEK, people and wildlife depend on each other. Wildlife depend on 'oohl to take care of the land so that the animals can survive. When regalia is made, often with animal parts, it becomes a spiritual life that contributes to the making of spiritual medicine during ceremony. In that sense, wildlife help create the unification of the physical and spiritual, which allows the medicine to fulfill its purpose of contributing to the spiritual and physical health of 'oohl. There are also many species that are traditional foods for the Yurok people. Therefore, 'oohl depend on wildlife for food, teachings, and medicine to survive.

In order to fulfill this relationship, there are times when it is necessary to take an animal's life. The concept of taking life has many layers in the Yurok paradigm. From a Western perspective, one might not consider the existence of a mutual cognitive or spiritual understanding between the hunter and the animal being hunted. However, for Yurok, although the hunter takes the life of the animal, there is an understanding that the animal also willingly gives its life to the hunter. A former hunter shared a story about a time he went hunting for ceremony. None of the dance camps had meat and so he chose to make a rare exception from his teachings to not hunt during ceremony. While on his hunt, he spotted a buck and a doe and he watched them for a little while. He observed the doe walk to the buck; they rubbed heads as if to say goodbye to each other. The doe walked away and the buck turned and looked at the hunter; the hunter then took the buck's life. He recalled his sentiments from that experience:

> "That's the last time that I killed a deer, [the last time] that I hunted, because I understood how sacred that it [the deer] was, and how close that it lived to us, and [I then had] that understanding. I knew he'd come there to give his life to our people… when I sat down there, I cried. I felt really sad and it changed the way that I looked at hunting and taking life and about how we're connected. It knew that we needed it for meat for our camps, and it gave itself willingly, freely. It didn't move, and it just stood there, just a short distance from me, and looked at me and waited."[5]

Equally important in Yurok TEK as the understanding of taking life as something necessary is the taking care of the Earth, and following cultural hunting and gathering protocols, so that populations can persist. A core Yurok value is to only take as much as one needs and can respectfully process without wasting. Yurok TEK also includes knowledge of phenology and resource cycles of knowing when foods and other cultural items, such as basket materials, are in season for gathering. Interview participants named various natural resource gathering seasons, such as pee-'eeh (mussels), kwes-cheen (strawberries), he'-woy (surf fish), woo-mehl (acorns), che-gel' (seaweed), puuek (deer), and ne-puey (salmon).

Changes Over Time

Authors in other chapters of this book have written about several important topics, including the history of the local region, laws, and policies that have been imposed upon Native peoples; Yurok cosmology; and lived experiences in cultural revitalization movements. Underlying or resulting from many of these topics is the fact that the landscape—as well as customary (Indian) laws, beliefs, and values that govern the people—have changed drastically over the last several hundred years. Yurok ancestral territory consists of many land jurisdictions that have been developed since European settlement and subsequent actions by the United States, such as areas of Redwood National and State Parks, Six Rivers National Forest, and the Yurok reservation. Each of these entities manages lands and natural resources with different objectives, and each adheres to federal laws pertaining to their jurisdiction. Forests have been under various models of management, rivers have been dammed, fire ecology has changed, hunting and fishing regulations have been established, and infrastructure has been built. The Yurok Tribe is charged with considering many of these factors simultaneously in decision-making about natural resources management within its jurisdiction.[6]

Some interview participants provided thoughts about how environmental changes and natural resource management have resulted in declines in wildlife and, therefore, limited important resources for food, ceremony, and other community needs. One interview participant mentioned they had contemplated how many animals and various species must have been taken to contribute to the regalia that has been repatriated from museums. Their understanding is that there must have been an abundance of wildlife at one point in time, noting that it has only been in recent times have we detected drastic declines in wildlife.[7] Interview participants attributed these declines to several factors, such as forest clear-cutting. Pesticide and herbicide spraying and other chemicals are also suspected by some interview participants to have contributed to declines in wildlife. Contemporary research has confirmed toxic chemicals in the local area have caused wildlife mortality. Anticoagulant rodenticide—a toxicant used to suppress pest species by use of bait often found in illegal marijuana grows—has been directly linked to mortality of Pacific fishers (le'-goh; *Martes pennanti*), a candidate for listing under the federal Endangered Species Act[8] and a culturally significant species to the Yurok.

Interview participants also noted that the Yurok relationship with wildlife has changed due to factors such as declines in wildlife populations and progressively restricted access to various geographic areas outside of tribal lands. Some species, such as California condor (Pre-go-neesh; *Gymnogyps californianus*), have been completely extirpated from Yurok ancestral lands. Pre-go-neesh is highly significant in Yurok ceremonies. The entire condor population in the United States had plummeted to just twenty-two individuals by 1982 as a result of killing by humans and the bird's susceptibility to lead poisoning from eating carcasses of hunted animals shot with lead ammunition.[9] Such changes in wildlife populations can have direct impacts on the Yurok way of life. For example, with the loss of Pre-go-neesh in Yurok lands and the concurrent ceremonial revitalization, some regalia makers have opted to utilize feather repository services, which provide Native Americans with legal sources of feathers from migratory birds, as they are unable to obtain feathers by traditional means.[10]

Some interview participants acknowledged that the Yurok-wildlife relationship will continue to change as the environment, lifestyles, and laws change. There will be some changes that conflict with what many consider traditional values and protocols. Having the time to live a lifestyle that includes cultural activities that are completely consistent with historical TEK was a concern for many of the participants. One controversial issue that was discussed is spotlight hunting, a method of hunting at night with the use of flashlights or spotlights to more easily detect eyeshine of an animal. Some community members are in opposition to this method of hunting, as they believe it might result in a loss of connection with the environment and an increase the likelihood of over-harvesting. However, one interview participant noted that, "...people just don't have the time to do things the way we used to do... They've got to go to work... So you have to go at night with the spotlight or sometimes wherever the deer are, when you can..."[11]

Efforts to Monitor and Manage Wildlife on
Yurok Ancestral Lands

Research and monitoring of natural resources and the environment are important because the information and knowledge gained can be used in management, as well as in the development of laws and policies that guide such management. The Yurok Tribe has participated in many environmental studies. For example, the inaugural project of the Tribe's Wildlife program was Pre-go-neesh recovery. The Tribe joined with several agencies, such as the U.S. Fish and Wildlife Service and the National Park Service, to conduct Pre-go-neesh reintroduction feasibility studies in Yurok ancestral lands.[12] Another example is the Yurok Tribe's response to large-scale illegal marijuana cultivation within and adjacent to the reservation. As noted, illegal large-scale grows have resulted in wildlife poisoning. They have also led to forest clearing and contamination of the Klamath River and its tributaries, the life-blood of the Yurok people and culture. The Yurok Tribe collaborated with researchers to answer the important question of how much water is diverted from the river and its tributaries for these grows. Knowledge of local surface water demand can be used to inform the Tribe's management decisions and calculate impairments to endangered species' habitats.[13]

The Yurok Tribe also supported a wildlife survey,[14] which was explicitly designed to be culturally sensitive where possible. For example, this survey took into consideration the belief that animals and humans are spiritually no different from each other. Further, animals are perceived to be a people in the Yurok cultural lens.[15] Therefore, the wildlife survey was designed to be non-invasive, where it was not necessary to trap or handle any animals. With the ultimate goal of using genetic analysis of scats to determine species presence, researchers collected scats on Yurok ancestral lands. Many species were detected, including meso-carnivores such as chmuuek (bobcat) and wer-gers (gray fox), as well as large carnivores such as ke-get (mountain lion).[16] This study could be repeated in the future to detect changes in the presence of certain species in certain areas, which could be especially important for culturally significant species.

Sustaining *Hlkelonah ue Meygeytohl*

The cultural community has been in a time of revitalization, and many are aware that it can be a process to continue traditional customs when it is not possible to live as the Yurok lived long ago. Yet, there is a strong desire by many to hold on to a Yurok identity. Despite having many customs taken or lost in dark eras of the past, many 'oohl have fought for cultural survival. Yurok people can continue to learn and live their TEK as a foundation of understanding and perspective, facing continued changes with resilience.

Yurok TEK and Western Ecological Knowledge can be bridged, possibly resulting in culturally sensitive monitoring techniques and solutions to lack of cultural and natural resources. It is important that Yurok people continue asking questions and doing research on the status and health of the environment. When the alignment of Western and Yurok paradigms is not possible, natural resource managers, researchers, and others can consider whether certain research methods can or should be modified.

There are many roles that individuals can take to contribute to the continuation of Yurok TEK and the health of the environment. For example, Yurok people who are trained in both Indigenous and Western science paradigms are needed to serve as academic and professional activists: people who have cultural and academic understandings who can advocate for tribal issues and concerns. Higher education fields such as Natural Resources, Environmental Science, Native American Studies, and American Indian Law and Policy can be especially applicable in such work. Yurok people with interest in natural resources or law and policy are needed to fill future employment positions with the Yurok Tribe. Additionally, there are many aspects of Yurok TEK that one can learn, practice, and teach to ensure that, as a whole, the Yurok way of life is being preserved. Culture bearers of all kinds are needed: language speakers, ceremonial participants, regalia makers, traditional food and material harvesters, etc. Taking part in and facilitating cultural survival at any level is important to build community, and provides opportunities for the transfer of traditional knowledge.

In addition to working within the local community, it is also important to think and work globally. There is a need to learn about the global impacts of humans on the Earth, such as human population growth, the modification of landscapes resulting in the degradation of wildlife habitat, pollution, the impacts of sea level rise, etc. Beyond learning about these issues, it may be important to consider lifestyle changes that are more environmentally friendly to minimize the overall impact on the Earth. For example, some people have made a conscious effort to use less water, drive smaller vehicles, use a bike instead of a vehicle or take public transportation, reduce the use of plastics, or reduce waste by purchasing fewer single-use items. Some have even chosen to have few or no children in an effort to slow the population growth rate. It may be helpful for all people to consider their lifestyle and how it may impact the Earth and, therefore, future generations. This concept aligns with Yurok TEK while also taking into consideration contemporary environmental issues, and can be done regardless of where one lives.

The Yurok culture persists today because many choose to maintain their connection to the people, the land, the spirit world, the language, and the animals. Many choose to stand up as activists against environmental injustices. Many choose to participate in ceremony. Many choose to gather and process traditional plant materials and make baskets. Many choose to consider their impact on the environment and make lifestyle adjustments where possible. Many are employed as environmental managers, researchers, and lawyers, with cultural implications at the heart of their work. Perhaps each individual is not an expert at everything, but each can make efforts to engage and be active in serving a role in the community.

Some Yurok readers of this chapter already have a strong sense of identity, what it means to them to be Yurok, and the role they can take to contribute to the community. However, others are eager to learn and are finding their place. Perhaps they never had the opportunity to learn, or maybe they had every opportunity but chose another lifestyle and, in time, came to realize they missed a crucial piece of themselves. One Yurok belief that was shared by interview participants is that every life—including animals, plants, and humans—has a purpose, and we all depend on each other. Readers of this book are encouraged to consider their purpose. While it is possible to live a lifestyle that is disconnected from the culture, if everyone chose to live completely disconnected, what would that mean for 'oohl, the culture, and the environment upon which they depend?

Endnotes

1. I am deeply thankful to all of my interview participants, Allen C. McCovey, Barbara McQuillen, Christopher Peters, Frank Lara, Marion Frye, Noreen Jones, Richard "Dickie" Myers, Robert McConnell, Rosie Clayburn, Thomas O'Rourke, James Gensaw, Pergish Carlson, Victoria Carlson, aawok Margaret Carlson, Walt Lara, Sr., Callie Lara, Kishan Lara-Cooper, aawok Rebecca "Becky" James, Patti James and Lawrence "Tiger" O'Rourke; the reviewer of this chapter, Gary Markussen, Jr.; the Yurok Tribe Language Program and language community for embracing me as a learner and teacher; my loved ones; and my cultural, professional and academic mentors for guiding me in life.
2. Berkes, 2012, p. 3; Whyte 2013, p. 3-5
3. Berkes, 2012, p. 7
4. Ramos, 2016, p. 50.
5. Interview Participant 14, Personal Communication, October 15, 2013.
6. Yurok Tribe, 1993.
7. Interview Participant 2, Personal Communication, August 14, 2011.
8. Gabriel, et al. 2012, 15 pages.
9. Yurok Today, 2009.
10. Gary Markussen Jr., Personal communication, November, 20, 2017.
11. Interview Participant 6, Personal Communication, December 6, 2012.
12. U.S. Fish and Wildlife Service, 2014, 11 pgs.
13. Thiesen and Plocher, 2016, pgs 3-4.
14. Dr. Ramos conducted as a component of her doctoral research.
15. Ramos, 2016.
16. Ramos, 2016, p. 61-87.

{INTERLUDE}

"Yurok Medicine"

Tene Kremling

Long long ago, everyone one knows there was a Ceremonial Jump Dance to pray for the people at Orek'. There isn't one anymore, so I'm wondering where did the Yurok medicine go, is it lost to us?

You might find the Yurok medicine at the waves of the beach "i u quee Dear Friend," they say.

Or the medicine might be in the cool waves that soothes your aches.

Or in the motions of the waves that calms your heart.

Maybe it is in the gray sand that reminds you of your place in the world and makes your troubles small.

Or it might be in the foam from the waves that sweep away your fears and pain.

Be grateful for the medicine of the beach.

You might find the medicine when you lean your head against the spongy bark of a redwood tree and feel it's strength.

Or you might hear it in stroke of the bird's wing as it flies overhead.

Here you will find the peace that comes in the quiet of the redwood forest.

Be thankful for the medicine of the forest.

You might see the medicine in the sweep of the clear blue sky.

Or maybe it is in the powerful gray storm clouds which
reminds you that change happens every day.
Medicine ripples in the glassy surface of Stone Lagoon.
Looking back, I feel the medicine of this sacred place.
Medicine can be found in the song of the salmon as it surges
up the green river.
And it is in the heart of a young boy as he helps his father and
uncle pull in the fish net.
Be thankful to the medicine of the river.
Surely you find medicine in the laughter and tears of our
people.
As we share our lives, the good and the bad, be assured with
family and friends you are never alone.
And this is powerful medicine.
And always prayer is medicine of the strongest kind.
The wind carries the prayers to the Creator.
Medicine was never lost to us.
We have always had the gift of Yurok medicine.

*—Tene Kremling, Yurok. As a young girl, poem was Inspired
from watching her Auntie Josie Marks, dry surf fish on the
Orick beach, circa 1958.*

PART 2

Lessons to be Learned: Testimonials of Resistance, Renewal, and Advocacy

This section highlights the uniqueness of Indigenous advocacy in California. Each testimonial is deeply rooted in connection to place, relationships, and responsibility.

CHAPTER 6

"Tilted History is too Often Taught": Activism, Advocacy, and Restoring Humanity

Rose Soza War Soldier

ON JANUARY 4, 1968, DURING A CRISP MORNING IN SAN FRANCISCO, DOZENS OF INDIAN COMMUNITY MEMBERS EAGERLY AWAITED THE START OF A SPECIAL SENATE SUBCOMMITTEE HEARING. A little before nine am, they squeezed into the local American Indian Center with standing room only (some sat on the floor), in order to hear testimony at the hearing on Indian Education held by the Committee on Labor and Public Welfare. Some undoubtedly attended for the chance to see popular New York Democratic Senator Robert F. Kennedy, chair of the Subcommittee on Indian Education; the enigmatic young leader's future Presidential bid was palpable in the mind of some early supporters. The other Senator in attendance, Paul Fannin, a Republican from Arizona, pushed to conduct hearings and selected California because of its sizable Indian population. Structured as a quasi-listening tour, the Senators traveled for almost a year to different states to hear about Indian experiences and learn about the various challenges in Indian education. The listening tour encouraged Senator Kennedy to conclude, in his congressional report, that Indian children require, "an education that no longer presumes that cultural difference means cultural inferiority."[1]

At the San Francisco hearing, Rupert Costo, Cahuilla, expressed his concern about California public education, particularly the textbooks used in classrooms. He testified, "There is not one Indian in the whole of this country who does not cringe in anguish and frustration because of these textbooks." He continued, "There is not one Indian child who has not come home in shame and tears after one of those sessions in which he is taught that his people were dirty, animal-like, something less than a human being."[2] Costo could speak with knowledge and passion on the subject because the organization he co-founded and in which he served as president, the American Indian Historical Society (AIHS or "The Society"), had begun evaluating California textbooks in 1965.[3] Costo's assessment was a clarion call. He helped to propel the issue of California Indian educational inequity into the public arena. Curriculum, textbooks, and laws segregating schools all served to keep California Indians in their presumed social place, as a second-class population, generally out of mainstream sight, and certainly out of any historical narrative. Through activism and advocacy, California Indians have spoken out for over fifty years about history education in public schools.

In practical terms, a combination of *de facto* and *de jure* school segregation had been the rule for California Indian children. Until 1916, California Indian children did not attend public schools in significant rates because of prejudicial policies and questions about funding sources and if federal or state monies would pay for educating California Indians. Formal education of California Indians may be loosely divided into three periods that parallel national policies. From 1849 through 1870, a functioning California Indian education policy did not exist. Between 1870 and 1916, California Indian education existed primarily through federal boarding schools, day schools, and some contracts with religious—largely Catholic—schools. Many students were prevented from attending public schools until a successful lawsuit challenged Section 1662 of California's Political Code, which in part, allowed local school districts to exclude children with "filthy or vicious habits" or "suffering from contagious or infectious diseases." The majority of California Indian students were assumed to fall under its parameters.[4]

The third period of formal education of California Indians began in 1924, when the California State Supreme Court issued a pivotal unanimous decision in the case *Piper v. Big Pine School District of Inyo*

County, leading to public school integration. The *Piper* case ended the policy stipulating that Indian children could not attend a public school if a government-run Indian school was located within three miles. This ruling recognized the inherently unequal status of Indian schools. In part, the *Piper* decision held that Indian children could not be prevented from attending public schools solely because they were "of Indian blood."[5] On the same day, the United States Congress issued the 1924 Indian Citizenship Act which unilaterally granted U.S. citizenship to all Native Americans. Combined, the *Piper* ruling and the Indian Citizenship Act ensured access to a public education, though that did not lead immediately to consistently equal treatment or quality education. In California, public school curriculum, textbooks, and the commonly assigned fourth grade unit on California missions have long been flashpoints for many California Indians.

The battle over California Indian history is not a matter of perspective, opinion, or viewpoint; rather, it is a about responsible inclusivity, truth-telling, and accuracy. History is inexorably tied to humanity, since history is the story of humans. Maori Scholar Linda Tuhiwai Smith argues the people who "made" history have a perceived humanity because historians consider members of the dominant society as being naturally "fully rational, self-actualizing human beings capable, therefore, of creating social change."[6] As a result, erasure within history serves to maintain denial for the dominant society and further dehumanizes California Indians. Part of an accurate history includes using the correct word to describe policies, events, and loss.

In 1943, legal scholar Raphael Lemkin coined a new word for an ancient crime. When defining the concept of genocide in 1944, he shared how he combined "the Greek word genos (tribe, race) and the Latin [word] cide," or killing, to describe genocide as any attempt to physically or culturally annihilate an ethnic, national, religious, or political group. In 1948, the United Nations Convention on the Prevention and Punishment of the Crime of Genocide more narrowly defined genocide as, "Acts committed with intent to destroy, in whole or in part, a national, ethnical, racial or religious group, as such: (a) Killing members of the group; (b) Causing serious bodily or mental harm to members of the group; (c) Deliberately inflicting on the group conditions of life calculated to bring about its physical destruction in whole or in part; (d) Imposing measures intended to prevent births within the group; (e) Forcibly transferring children of the group to another group."[7] The United Nations definition created a clear, internationally recognized understanding of the use of the term. Further, it facilitated a growing scholarly consensus in American Indian history, particularly in California, on the application of the term.[8] According to historian Benjamin Madley, "The direct and deliberate killing of Indians in California between 1846 and 1873 was more lethal and sustained than anywhere in the United States or its colonial antecedents."[9]

California Indians received violent, and often deadly, treatment, similar to the treatments of other tribal nations in different geographical areas across the country. However, by the time California entered the Union in September 1850, elected officials, military personnel, and the general population had learned tactics from earlier targeted campaigns on addressing the commonly termed "Indian problem." As a result, California Indians experienced genocide under American rule in a much more compressed time period, with a practiced deadly precision, when compared to other regions. Despite all the available evidence, California's genocidal history is avoided—or aspects are celebrated, since California Indians are often constructed as obstacles to civilization.

Nonetheless, many tribal community members advocate and promote awareness on the subject of California Indian history. For some, their advocacy is coordinated and strengthened through organizations; for others, it is a direct and personal challenge to their children's curriculum at their local school. For example, an assignment given to students in the Union Hill School District of Grass Valley circulated on social media in November 2017. The assignment included a hand-out titled, "Native American Helper Name," asking parents of kindergartners to select an "Indian name" for their child during Native American Heritage Month. The assignment mentioned that Indians received names based on actions and mannerisms, and listed examples such as "Climbing Girl" and "Snoring Bird." The assignment text included the quote that "braves wore feathers in their headdresses to signify exceptional deeds," and asked parents to list three good deeds the child has done for the family. Finally, the assignment included listing a child's "real name," the child's "Native American Helper Name," and having the child write, "why I like it."[10] The assignment is problematic for a myriad of reasons, but perhaps most glaringly for its dismissive tone, deafness to the cultural significance of names, inappropriate use of "braves" and "headdresses" in California, and the nearly omnipresent lumping together of diverse tribal communities.

In another example, ten-year old Alex Fierro, Wukchumni, from Visalia Unified School District, brought home lyrics to the song "Twenty-one Missions." In part, the lyrics read, "To save the soul, soothe the savage breast" and described the "noble goal" of "praying, teaching, searching, reaching out to the red man's soul." Fierro's mother, Debra, described her reaction to reading the lyrics: "I just got this pit in my stomach. I felt horrible."[11] She wrote letters to the teacher, principal, and school administrators. In addition, she contacted Wukchumni tribal chairperson Darlene Franco, who also sent a letter to the school district. Within a week the school district responded to Fierro's letter, pulled the song from curriculum, and apologized to Fierro. By the time the District removed the song—which had been approved for use since 2000—from its curriculum, the song had been utilized for over a decade. Assistant Superintendent of Visalia Unified School District, Doug Bartsch, commented, "I like to think of myself as culturally sensitive, but we all miss stuff. We want to continue working with local tribes, to get together and listen more, to think about what we can do better in the future."[12] Bartsch recognizes the importance of listening and working with tribal communities, yet his comment leaves unspoken the painful legacy of stereotyping and its impact on Indian children and their self-worth. Experiences like these are nothing new. Countless students have had similar experiences over the past century which have gone unrecorded.

California Indians have been organizing and working to address educational and societal inequalities for decades. Indigenous social and political movements emphasize the centrality of land, sovereignty, and treaty rights. In the period from the early to the mid-20th century, many California Indian-based organizations were formed including: Mission Indian Federation, California Indian Rights Association, California Indian Brotherhood, Federated Indians of California, American Indian Historical Society, and California Indian Education Association, among others. On a daily basis, tribal community members are advocates and activists for issues in larger society, in school, and at home. An "activist" refers to a person actively working towards bringing cultural, social, or political change, generally associated with some form of direct action. An "advocate" refers to a person who defends a person or cause; their approach may include direct action. Activism is not inherently physical or violent. It can be powerfully quiet and promote what Taiaiake Alfred, Mohawk, calls "creative contention," the strategies and tactics on the middle path between armed rebellion and conventional protest.[13] Alfred also discusses a significant aspect of cultural restoration and decolonization as, "a dedicated commitment to loving our mother, the earth, and teaching our children their responsibilities." He continues, "If my kids can be more Indigenous than I am, then to me that's decolonization."[14]

When examining the activism of Rupert Costo or Debra Fierro, their speaking out derived from concern for young students, Indian and non-Indian, in California public schools. They emerged as activists and advocates and approached issues in a non-violent manner. Most importantly, their activism and advocacy led to constructive dialogue involving non-Indians on how to change and revise the educational institutions and structures. Through speaking out, they challenged the notion—largely the result of formal education—that Native people exist only in the past. They re-centered Native voices as present makers of history.

A common misguided perception of activism has at times led to the view and categorization of all forms of activism and advocacy as negative due to the construction and perception of activism as is reported broadly across popular culture news outlets. For example, activism may be evaluated as connected to individualism and ego. However, it is important to recognize the importance of family, community, and concern for future generations that informs many California Indian activists and advocates. For Indigenous communities specifically, a foundational basis for activism and advocacy is sovereignty, land and water rights, and culture. The centrality of these issues establishes the inherent differences of the struggles of Indigenous communities from those of other underrepresented populations in the United States. In addition, for California Indians, contemporary activists and advocates follow in the steps of earlier organizations and community members committed to maintaining Indian rights, thus contemporary advocates represent a historical cultural practice of speaking up and speaking out.

The cultural maintenance by Indian people, and the continued identity as a member of a tribal Nation, is in itself a political act. California's formation occurred under three national flags—Spain, Mexico, and United States of America—and had a violent history, yet California Indians maintained their diverse cultures. Therefore, the continued cultural existence of California Indian people into the 21st century is a political declaration, since formal federal, state, and local governmental policies sought to eliminate and destroy California Indian cultures and lives through genocide.[15] In part, activism and advocacy has been central in protecting and preserving the Indigenous way of life. One approach to restoring the humanity of California Indian people is through advocating for historical accuracy and truth-telling. Thus, what is taught in public schools about Indians is important. It is more than political correctness; it is a step in restoring humanity.

In the fall of 2015, nineteen-year old California State University, Sacramento (CSUS) student Chiitaanibah Johnson, Maidu and Navajo, attended her U.S. History 17A class. A general U.S. survey course, it examines 1607-1877 and fulfills the "Race and Ethnicity in American Society" graduation requirement. At one of the first class meetings of the semester, her history professor Maury Wiseman stated, "I don't like to use the term 'genocide' because 'genocide' is something that is done on purpose, but needless to say European diseases primarily will wipe out Native American populations..."[16] His broad statement supports the commonly held belief that disease was the primary cause of devastating population loss, which was thus unintended. Wiseman avoided consideration of specific California policies, such as the 1850 "Act for the Government and Protection of Indians," which legalized slavery for over a decade. Or voluntary state militias, which killed California Indians explicitly and purposefully for paid bounties on Indian scalps, heads, or other body parts as proof of death. State newspaper editorials regularly called for the "extermination" of California Indians and detailed actions of voluntary militia companies and their deadly actions. In 1863, the *Marysville Daily Appeal* reported that the Honey Lake residents of Lassen County raised funds to pay "twenty-five cents for Indian scalps taken by the company."[17] Newspapers also celebrated the movements of notorious Indian killers, as illustrated in the 1870 *Marin Journal*, "Buckskin Joe with 47 Indian scalps passed through Elmira [Solano County] recently. The 47 Indians who formally owned the scalps did not accompany him."[18] The preponderance of evidence invalidates the idea perpetuated by Wiseman of inevitable conquest, or unintentional spread of diseases as the primary cause of deaths. Indeed, his statement about genocide is historically inaccurate, particularly in the city where CSUS is located. A search on California Digital Newspaper Collection reveals a well-documented pattern of state-sponsored systematic policies of murder, slavery, kidnapping, and, as July 1860 *Sacramento Union* termed the sexual abuses of California Indian women, "concubinage" with details "unfit to commit to paper."

Too upset to question his assertion at the time, Johnson did some research and came to the next class meeting on Friday, September 4, 2015, with supporting material she had printed, including the United Nations definition of genocide. However, during the exchange, Wiseman reportedly stated she had "hijacked" his class, and he dismissed class early, and asked to speak with her after class.[19] When interviewed by *News from Native California*, Johnson asserted, "It's like it's easier to pull the trigger and say, 'Alright, I'm going to stand up and do it,' when you think about all the sacrifices and miracles it took just to be an Indigenous person alive. Period."[20] Her comment illustrates her connection to her family, and the ease with which she found herself speaking up. Further, she recognizes the role she holds as a descendant of survivors, and is compelled to speak up. Thus, she follows in the footsteps of advocates like Costo, Fierro, and many additional California Indians.

On September 6, 2015, *Indian Country Today* published an online story entitled, "History Professor Denies Native Genocide: Native Student Disagreed, Then Says Professor Expelled Her From Course." This story about the CSUS exchange received wide-spread attention throughout Indian country. It quickly spread through social media and gained attention from numerous media outlets, including the *Sacramento Bee*. Some articles and public comments highlighted the perception of Johnson interrupting the classroom environment and disturbing her classmates' learning experience. However, other publications used the opportunity to reveal a more nuanced critical analysis of the meaning of history, social memory, and cultural maintenance.

Frequently overlooked in the discussions about Wiseman's lecture is the nature of the history class itself, which serves as a graduation requirement for CSUS. The U.S. Survey classes are generally the last history class a college student will ever take, and, as such, therefore likely include the last history books they will ever read. If professors want to generate curiosity in their students and facilitate the growth of well-informed citizens, students need to engage in critical thinking and debate. Further, any professor in the historical field, not to mention their students, would be better served if they tried to become familiar with the local history where they teach. When speaking up, Johnson repeatedly positioned herself as an Indian woman who received an education at home from her relatives. Thus her activism and advocacy is not about her, specifically; rather it centers around her communities. Her act of speaking out is not new or about her as an individual; rather, it represents a continuation of California Indian activism focused on history that has been occurring in California for over fifty years.

The California History-Social Science Project is one of several institutions involved in a broader effort to revise and reform the fourth-grade curriculum and its mission unit, which is generally the first exposure California public students receive about Indians. One of the common activities completed for the mission unit is to have students build a mission model or diorama usually out of sugar cubes. The twenty-one missions along coastal California on *El Camino Real* (the Royal Road, or the King's Highway), which eventually became tourist sites were built with forced Indian labor. However, this aspect is overwhelmingly ignored by the assignment as is the historical reality of mass burial sites paved over for public parking.

In Fall 2017, the State Department of Education announced its new educational history-social science framework, adopted July 14, 2016, because it had determined the mission unit was offensive and taught little historically accurate information.[21] Nancy McTygue, Executive Director of the California History-Social Science Project, commented, "This activity is just wrong on so many levels—it's offensive to the Native peoples whose lives were largely shattered by the mission system, it's a waste of time and money, it doesn't build reading or writing skills, and it doesn't teach anything of substance about our past."[22] Leading up to the framework revisions, some California Indian students indigenized the mission model. Vincent Medina, Ohlone, shared how he helped his younger brother, Gabe, with his fourth-grade mission project. Rather than the typical sugar-cube or popsicle stick model, they built Mission San Jose under siege to demonstrate the rebellion led by Estanislao in 1829.[23]

The mission model has been a California pedagogical mainstay for decades. While nearly ubiquitous, the mission model was never a part of the official state curriculum or guidelines; rather, many teachers included it as a hands-on activity. The history-social science framework revisions attracted the attention of educators, parents, and students across the state, as well as several newspapers which ran headlines describing the historical ending of mission models—for example, the *San Diego Union-Tribune*: "Fourth Grade Mission Model Project Could be History," and the *Sacramento Bee*, "No more Sugar Cubes and Popsicle Sticks? State Urges Teachers to scrap 4th-grade Mission Project." The public comments illustrate the position that, for some, the framework revision represented political correctness run amok. In the public comments to the *Sacramento Bee* story, one comment asserted, "History is being used as a weapon here, and the only casualties will be Latino and Hispanic Californians, especially those who are Catholic." And another: "Socialists love to rewrite history." It is telling that some readers perceived the framework revisions as not being connected to historical accuracy, which reveals their lack of historical knowledge. Others commented: "It's about time," "Teach the kids the truth," and "History was rewritten when they made it seem the missionaries were loved."[24] Further, it is a false equivalency to perceive any curriculum revision as an affront to Catholic Latinos of the state. The correcting of the mission unit is less about Spaniards or Mexicans and more about centering California Indians.

Another group, the California Indian History Curriculum Coalition, emerged from the 2014 California Indian Conference held at CSU San Bernardino "to promote the creation, adoption and implementation of California Indian-vetted curricula."[25] The Curriculum Coalition held a California Indian History Curriculum Summit at CSUS on October 9, 2017, where California educators had the opportunity to learn about different sources to include in their classrooms.[26] It stands as an example of an emerging collaborative effort between educators and California Indian community members. Many California Indians talk about history, textbooks, and curriculum within families and tribal communities, but unless there is curiosity and engagement from non-Indian people, it is a one-sided conversation. California will not produce well-informed citizens as long as public school systems, both K-12 as well as colleges and universities, permit unquestioned assertions and continue the promotion of inaccurate historical narratives.

The California State University system represents a primary training ground for many K-12 teachers for the state, and is therefore best situated to expose the next generation of teachers to inclusive and accurate material. Yet there is no state requirement to learn Native histories as part of the teacher training program. One notable exception is the Child Development major at CSU Humboldt, which prepares college students for careers as social workers, counselors, teachers, curriculum specialists, and child advocates, among others. It requires students to take two American Indian Education classes as part of its core curriculum. This is particularly important because in *The State of American Indian & Alaskan Native Education in California*, Dr. Joely Proudfit,

Luiseño, reveals that, according to the latest data, there are 34,704 Indian and Alaskan Native K-12 students in public schools, and only 1,530 Indian and Alaskan Native K-12 educators, representing .52% of 276,824 K-12 teachers.[27]

In a recent example of a tribal nation taking the lead, the Agua Caliente Band of Cahuilla Indians signed a memorandum of understanding with Foundation for Palm Springs School District to collaborate on developing an elementary and middle school Native American Studies curriculum. The tribe agreed to underwrite the costs involved in development and in the implementation into existing units. According to Foundation Director Ellen Goodman, "This new curriculum will help establish a real groundwork of familiarity on students' parts with the importance and impact of the Agua Caliente Band of Cahuilla Indians."[28]

For some educators in K-12 and in college, the term "genocide" to describe the history of California is seen as too extreme and not appropriate for elementary students. As a result, by the time students arrive to college, it is a shocking realization when their professors use that term. In a review of history textbooks used in California public schools, historians Clifford Trafzer and Michelle Lorimer note, "It is easier for the authors of the text to reconcile Spanish (Catholic) violence against Native populations than to tarnish the image of pioneers (primarily Protestants), Manifest Destiny, and the Gold Rush era."[29] While their study reveals the lack of historically accurate information in textbooks, educators also have a role. Educators could utilize scaffolding wherein, perhaps, they do not overtly describe the violence and death to elementary school students, but introduce the concept that not every person who arrived in California was a decent person who treated California Indians with compassion. As students grow older, educators could then introduce concepts of competition for resources and land, state policies, unratified treaties, and, eventually, introduce students to genocide in California. A great resource available is the special edition of *News from Native California*, "Saying our Share: Surviving the Missions," which offers a plethora of articles written by California Indians.[30]

One of the greatest dangers for California Indians is the persuasive silence surrounding history. For a lengthy period of time, silence was violently imposed by colonizing powers. As Deborah Miranda, Esselen and Chumash, commented, "Fourth graders, their parents, their teachers, tourists to the missions, even historians, often learn and perpetuate only one story about California Indians: conquest, subjugation, defeat, disappearance."[31] Costo went a step further and asserted, "…tilted history is too often taught in our universities and general education;" it filters into public education and is cause "for alarm."[32] The cause for alarm is apparent when school assignments make the news like February 2018 news story which shared the 20-exercise grammar worksheet at Stonegate Elementary in West Sacramento.[33] The worksheet included the statements: "Indians belong to the red race," "The women were called squaws, an Indian word for women," and "Their skin is of a copper color," among additional stereotypical tropes. There remains work to be done to ensure students are not taught historically inaccurate information based on caricatures, stereotypes, and assumptions.

For most of the 20th century, California Indians practiced everyday activism and advocacy throughout the state. Community members identified their personal skill set and applied them. For some, it is through the art form of letter writing, campaign, or personal phone calls. For some, it is the physical occupation of space. For some, it is raising children to be proud of their ancestors and know their tribal histories, languages, and cultural practices. For some, it is practicing an art form, from basket weaving to abalone jewelry to making gourd rattles. For some, it is earning the academic degrees necessary to be in the room and at the table with decision-makers in order to influence policy and represent the community. Of course, these are not the only forms of activism and advocacy, and many engage in several forms. For many, activism and advocacy is deeply rooted to family, community, and concern for future generations. The relatively small California Indian population requires an effective combined effort of activism and advocacy. There is not one correct way to approach activism or advocacy, but we all need to take part in action.

Endnotes

1. U.S. Congress, Senate Special Subcommittee on Indian Education of the Committee on Labor and Public Welfare, *Hearings on Indian Education: The Study of the Education of Indian Children Part 1*, 90 Cong., 1 and 2 sess. (1968), 5.

2. Ibid, 243.

3. Rose Delia Soza War Soldier,*"To Take Positive and Effective Action": Rupert Costo and the California Based American Indian Historical Society.* (Dissertation, Arizona State University, 2013).

4. Nicole Blalock-Moore, "Piper v. Big Pine School District of Inyo County: Indigenous Schooling and Resistance in Early Twentieth Century," *Southern California Quarterly* 94 (Fall 2012): 361.

5. *Piper v. Big Pine School District of Inyo County*, 226 Pac. 926 (Cal., 1924).

6. Linda Tuhiwai Smith. *Decolonizing Methodologies : Research and Indigenous Peoples.* London ; New York : Dunedin : New York: Zed Books ; University of Otago Press; Distributed in the USA Exclusively by St Martin's Press, 1999, 32.

7. United Nations Office on Genocide Prevention and the Responsibility to Protect, http://www.un.org/en/genocideprevention/genocide.html (accessed December 1, 2017).

8. Rupert Costo and Jeannette Henry-Costo, eds. *The Missions of California: A Legacy of Genocide.* San Francisco, Indian Historian Press, 1987; Brendan C. Lindsay, *Murder State: California's Native American Genocide, 1846-1873.* Lincoln: University of Nebraska Press, 2012.; Benjamin Madley, *An American Genocide the United States and the California Indian Catastrophe, 1846-1873.* Lamar Series in Western History. 2016; Jack Norton, *Genocide in Northwestern California.* San Francisco: Indian Historian Press, 1979.; Clifford E. Trafzer, and Joel R. Hyer. *Exterminate Them! Written Accounts of the Murder, Rape, and Enslavement of Native Americans during the California Gold Rush.* East Lansing: Michigan State University Press, 1999.

9. Benjamin Madley,. *An American Genocide : The United States and the California Indian Catastrophe, 1846-1873.* Lamar Series in Western History. New Haven: Yale University Press, 2016, 358.

10. Union Hill School District Facebook page, https://www.facebook.com/pages/Union-Hill-School-District/122309757825893, (accessed November 30, 2017)

11. Alysa Landry, "10-Year-Old Gets Mission Song Stricken from

California School District Curriculum," *Indian Country Today*, https://indiancountrymedianetwork.com/history/events/10-year-old-gets-mission-song-stricken-from-california-school-district-curriculum/ (accessed November 10, 2017).

12. Ibid.

13. Taiaiake Alfred, *Wasáse: Indigenous Pathways of Action and Freedom.* Peterborough, Ont.: Broadview Press, 2005, 228.

14. Taiaiake Alfred, Practical [sic] Decolonialization, https://www.youtube.com/watch?v=pq87xqSMrDw, (accessed November 11, 2017).

15. Rupert Costo and Jeannette Henry-Costo, eds. *The Missions of California: A Legacy of Genocide.* San Francisco, Indian Historian Press, 1987; Brendan C. Lindsay, *Murder State: California's Native American Genocide, 1846-1873.* Lincoln: University of Nebraska Press, 2012.; Benjamin Madley, *An American Genocide the United States and the California Indian Catastrophe, 1846-1873.* Lamar Series in Western History. 2016; Jack Norton, *Genocide in Northwestern California.* San Francisco: Indian Historian Press, 1979.; Clifford E. Trafzer, and Joel R. Hyer. *Exterminate Them! Written Accounts of the Murder, Rape, and Enslavement of Native Americans during the California Gold Rush.* East Lansing: Michigan State University Press, 1999.

16. Maury Wiseman, "Sac State Professor Explains his use of Genocide," *The State Hornet*, https://statehornet.com/2015/10/sac-state-professor-explains-his-use-of-word-genocide/ (accessed November 11, 2017).

17. *Marysville Daily Appeal*, February 20, 1863, 2.

18. *Marin Journal*, September 17, 1870, 2.

19. Chiitaanibah Johnson, "Native American Student at Sac State Shares her Story," *The State Hornet*, https://statehornet.com/2015/10/native-american-student-at-sac-state-shares-her-story/(accessed November 11, 2017).

20. Vincent Medina, "A Word with Chiitaanibah Johnson," *News from Native California* 29, no. 2 (2015):7.

21. California Department of Education, 2016 History-Social Science Framework, https://www.cde.ca.gov/ci/hs/cf/sbedrafthssfw.asp (accessed 11/12/17).

22. Nancy McTygue, "Enough with Mission Projects Already," *The Source* (Summer 2012):3.

23. Vincent Medina, "Plastic Siege: A New Twist on the Fourth Grade Mission Project," *News From Native California* 27, no. 1 (Fall 2013):4-5.

24. Diana Lambert, "No More Sugar Cubes and Popsicle Sticks?' *Sacramento Bee*, http://www.sacbee.com/news/local/education/article170884897.html, (accessed 11/12/17).

25. California Indian History Curriculum Coalition, http://www.csus.edu/coe/cic/, (accessed 11/12/17).

26. California Indian History Curriculum Coalition Summit at Sacramento State, https://www.youtube.com/watch?v=5hW_S6bFKmA, (accessed 11/12/17).

27. Joely Proudfit with Theresa Gregor, *The State of American Indian & Alaskan Native Education in California 2016*, https://www.csusm.edu/cicsc/projects/projects_docs_images/2016SAIANEC_FINAL.pdf, (accessed 11/25/17).

28. Agua Caliente Band of Cahuilla Indians, News and Events, http://www.aguacaliente.org/content/News%20&%20Events/?showStoryID=116 (accessed 11/12/17).

29. Clifford E. Trafzer and Michelle Lorimer. "Silencing California Indian Genocide in Social Studies Texts." *American Behavioral Scientist* 58, no. 1 (2014): 75.

30. *News from Native California* 28, no. 2 (Winter 2014/2015).

31. Deborah Miranda, *Bad Indians: A Tribal Memoir*. Berkeley: Heyday, 2013, 193.

32. Rupert Costo and Jeannette Henry-Costo, *Natives of the Golden State: The California Indians*. San Francisco, Indian Historian Press, 1995, xviii.

33. Racist homework? West Sacramento School Assigns Controversial Worksheet, KCRA3, https://www.kcra.com/article/racist-homework-west-sacramento-school-assigns-controversial-worksheet/17004436, (accessed February 25, 2018).

CHAPTER 7

The Past is Our Future: Thoughts on Identity, Tradition and Change

Jack Norton

IN SPRING OF 1997, MY WIFE INVITED FRIENDS AND COLLEAGUES TO MY RETIREMENT LUNCHEON. Attending were Humanistic psychologists, historians, and office administrators, which included my second cousin, former students, and a group of merry Anthropologists. In mock solemnity, the Anthropologists presented me an honorary degree in their discipline. The certificate was signed by A. L. Kroeber, considered the putative Dean of California Indian Anthropology, who died in 1960. This satirical moment was based upon my years of criticism and—as some have said—diatribe against Kroeber's studies on California Indians.

In my twenty-five years as Professor of Native American Studies at Humboldt State University in northwestern California, I was fortunate to be part of a dynamic shift in academe and the Indian community. Beginning in the 1970s, curriculum in American Indian Studies developed in the universities of California. At Humboldt State University, a strong Native American Studies Department was supported by collateral programs such as the Indian Teacher Education Program, Center for Community Development, and Native American Careers in Science and Engineering and Administrative Leadership. As a state university that admits students throughout California and abroad, Humboldt resides within the heart of Indian country and has a large Indian student body. The nearby Yurok Nation is the largest tribe in California, with nearly 4,000 members. In addition, the Hoopa Reservation is the largest in the state, all of which provides a strong Indigenous presence and influence. This was particularly demonstrated in 1985, when Alistair McCrone, the President of the University, along with members of his staff and the Affirmative Action Officer, attended the Hupa White Deerskin Dance at Tsemeta.

My tenure at Humboldt State was unique. First, I was recruited from the public schools where I had taught for fourteen years. Second, a search for the position in Native American Studies was conducted by not only the typical hiring practices of the university, but by a committee of Indian people from the community and the student body. Thus, I never lost ties and commitment to a unique place, and integral human societies, which had resided upon the land for thousands of years.

My father, Jack Norton, Sr., was only twelve years old when he left Hoopa Valley to attend Phoenix Indian School in 1915. His father, Sherman Norton, was an outspoken critic of the Bureau of Indian Affairs' (BIA) assimilation policies. My grandfather often challenged the economic and educational inequities on the Hoopa Reservation and was threatened with removal by the Superintendent. In 1918, my father left Phoenix to attend Haskell Indian School in Lawrence, Kansas. My mother, Emma Norton, arrived at Haskell when she was about fifteen years old. Both my parents had lost their mothers when they were young, and their fathers had hoped that they would become educated in a rapidly changing world.

My father was the first college graduate of the Hupa Nation. Following his graduation from Northeastern University in 1929, he was employed by several school districts in Oklahoma but later moved to the Navajo Reservation. He became Superintendent of Schools for Kinlichee, Klagetah, Tohatchi, and several day schools. These were the tumultuous years of the New Deal and the Indian Reorganization Act, which was often at odds with Indian traditional values. For example, many Navajo families were compromised when their valuable sheep were declared surplus and killed by the thousands. Their social and economic status took years to recover.

Years later, I learned that the Hupa and Navajo are Athabascan speaking peoples. I remember my mother telling others that she never worried where I was as a small child growing up on the Navajo Reservation. I could always be found, she said, in a circle of old Navajo men singing. Sometimes, a resonance of similar sounds and songs reverberate deep within me still.

In 1942, our family returned to northwestern California. We farmed the Sugar Bowl Ranch, which included the traditional Hupa village of Xaime, but the ranch was now several miles south of the Hoopa Reservation boundaries. I attended fifth and sixth grades in the old Indian boarding school buildings. I met my cousins, aunts, and uncles as classmates or employees in the Indian service. After years of farming, my parents were employed by the Hoopa School District. My mother taught first grade while my father was a civics teacher and coach. The school was located at old Fort Gaston and the BIA agency grounds. Some of the original buildings were used as classrooms, and the school cafeteria was in Fort Gaston's mess hall. These buildings lined the square parameter of the parade grounds, which now had two tennis courts in the center of the square. We lived in a BIA duplex near the old adobe where Captain Ulysses S. Grant supposedly stayed during a short visit to Fort Gaston.

Our house was not far from the old commissary building and, as young kids, my friends and I knew where the World War I uniforms were stored. On rainy days we would go down to the commissary basement and pull out shirts and pants from the crates, looking for our sizes. We tromped across at least three feet of discarded uniforms, which filled the entire room. After a successful search, we put on the shirts and pants, went outside, found the biggest mud hole, and splashed through it.

Following the successful years as football and basketball coach at Hoopa High School, my father was hired as Assistant Football Coach and Physical Education Teacher at Humboldt State University, and our family moved from Hoopa to Arcata. During the next several years, while attending Arcata High School from 1949 to 1951, I often competed against my friends and relatives in football, basketball, and track, as Arcata and Hoopa met in interscholastic sports. Although Hoopa High School was one of the smallest schools in the league, they did well against the larger schools of Eureka and Arcata, beating them several times in football and basketball.

While still in high school, I received a check for $150 from the Federal Government. However, I was too immersed in typical teenage bravado to question why. Years later I learned the truth.

When, in 1851, news of the murder and mayhem committed by miners, individual citizens, and vigilante groups against California native people reached Washington, Congress finally acted by sending three Treaty Commissioners to California. By July 1852, eighteen treaties, setting aside 8.5 million acres, were sent to the Senate. However, a coalition led by the two senators from California called for non-ratification. The senators declared that, "too much good land was being given to Indian savages." The hearings were held in confidence (secret) and the treaties were not ratified, but merely filed without notification to the Indian nations. In fact, some of the Indian people had already left their ancestral homelands and moved to the designated treaty areas. This obvious injustice was litigated by the Court of Claims in 1942. California Indian people were awarded a $17 million settlement. However, before any compensation was distributed, a $12 million offset for services was subtracted. Despite evidence that many goods and services—such as needles, shovels, World War I uniforms, and paved roads—were inadequate, the U.S. Court of Claims upheld the offset. This left approximately five million dollars to be distributed among 36,000 "Indians of California."

The phrase "Indians of California" has had pernicious consequences upon federal policies toward California Indian people. "Indians of California" nullifies constitutional responsibility of making treaties with nations, which, in America, is the supreme law of the land. For example, California is made up of many sovereign California Indian nations within the definition of universal law. This law recognizes separate and distinct nations with agreed-upon boundaries, social structure, history, and a common language. These Indian nations were signatories to the eighteen non-ratified treaties. Thus, the term "Indians of California" is as unacceptable as referring collectively to the "white men of Europe" if the sovereign nations of France, Spain, and Germany litigated a suit against the United States.

In 1954, I was the apparent master of my fate. I was majoring in Biological Sciences at Humboldt State University and doing rather well. The Latin terms for the purple sea urchin, Dungeness crab, and the twenty-rayed starfish rolled easily across my lips and I had some vague idea of becoming a doctor, laboratory assistance, or technician. I certainly was not going to be a teacher like my parents. Fate, however, as the philosopher Schopenhauer wrote in a paper entitled, "On an

Apparent Intention in the Fate of the Individual," seems to have its own script. "Often," Schopenhauer wrote, "the lines and events of our lives are written in seemingly small letters, but when viewed from a perspective of years, they can be seen as the twist and turns that have led to the present condition." Finally, Schopenhauer adds, we all probably at one time or another ask, "who wrote this book anyway?" (Schopenhauer as cited in Campbell, 1988, pp. 229-230).

After graduating from Humboldt State in 1955, I tested the boundaries of parental forbearance and common sense. I bought a Harley Davidson motorcycle with the grandiose idea of touring Mexico. However, riding through the Mohave Desert in mid-summer and breaking down several times quickly demonstrated the reality that this was no easy ride. I turned around in Kingman, Arizona, and sought out the kinder temperatures of the California north coast and the graciousness of my friends and family. I spent the next several years in Hoopa. My friends and I would often travel to Eureka for entertainment, to see a movie or for a bite to eat. I was surprised to find that many of my companions refused to go to the Eureka Inn for refreshments. "Oh, no, we're not allowed up there," they would comment, afraid of being ridiculed or feeling out of place. In the movie theatres we sat upstairs with the rest of the "colored people." It was not until later that I realized how individuals seeking societal approval and acceptance internalize the narrowness of others.

Later, I spent six months in San Francisco where I was completely out of place and thoroughly miserable. When I recall my exile in San Francisco, I am increasingly aware of the potential suffering of thousands of Indians that were relocated from reservations to large urban centers. The consequences of assimilation for these Indian people have been monumental, ranging from a loss or confusion of identity, high suicide rates, alcoholism, poor health, isolation, and uncritical acceptance of values that were often at odds with previously held worldviews. For many California Indians, this latest manifestation of victimizing the victim weighs heavily upon the collective Indian soul. However, if we see how and why these assimilation policies were enforced, we have a means to address them.

Beginning in the mid-1950s, under the guise of employment assistance, the BIA "helped" Indian adults receive training and employment in San Francisco, Oakland, Los Angeles, and other populated areas. As a result, many Indian people became welders, beauticians, mechanics, or labored hundreds of feet under the San Francisco Bay, working on the Bay Area Rapid Transit tunnels. Surrounded and often ridiculed by ignorant people for being Indian, or told "not to drink too much firewater, Chief," by their foreman, Indians often sank deeper and deeper into depression and poverty. Fortunately, some survived and raised families hundreds of miles away from their original communities. However, the real intent of the Employment Assistance Act, passed by the Republican Congress in 1953, was to assimilate Indians into American society.

The Federal Government assumed that if American Indians were fully acculturated, they would be more likely to terminate their treaty rights. Indian reservations contained vast resources of minerals, coal, and gas, and held paramount and prior rights to all water that arises on, traverses, or flows beneath the reservations. Relocation was a deceitful and hypocritical governmental policy because employment training could have been developed on the reservations or in Indian communities without the fragmentation of family, relatives, and culture. Finally, the influx of large numbers of non-California nations such as the Sioux, Cherokee, Navajos, and others introduced differing cultural expressions that splintered indigenous values and left many, particularly the young, disoriented and alienated.

In the later part of 1957, the local draft board enforced my two-year obligation under the Selective Service Act. I had been deferred from military service during my graduate studies. However, before reporting to Fort Ord, California, for basic training, the Hoopa Tribal Council and my father, who was chairman, were confronted with the possibility that the Hoopa Valley Reservation with its large timber resources and water rights on the Trinity River, might be terminated, and the original homelands of the Hupa people be lost. The Bureau of Indian Affairs, had marked the reservation for termination through the Sacramento office, and was using all means of persuasion and coercion for compliance. But the Tribal Council held fast. However, nearly forty reservations and rancherias in California were terminated under the Rancheria Act of 1958.

After basic training, I was assigned as a clerk typist at Fort Bragg, North Carolina. I learned that if I got a job as a public-school teacher, an early release could be obtained. I saved up my leave and, in the spring of 1958, I interviewed at Fortuna High School, Fortuna, California. There were "no openings in Biology or the Sciences," the Superintendent informed me, but there was one in History! "Would I be interested in that?" the Superintendent inquired. "Absolutely," I quickly responded, and yet another twist of fate was recorded.

I was in Fort Bragg in July when Congressman Clem Miller called and said procedures were in motion and I should be released by August. Thus, in the fall of 1958, I started my 40-plus years of teaching. I taught World and U.S. History, and in those early years, if I worked hard, I could be at least one chapter ahead of the class. On some days I was not prepared, but I learned to listen to the concerns and interests of my students. I discovered early on that teaching was a two-way communication of mutual trust and respect. Years later, upon chance meetings, some of these first students recalled with fondness those shared experiences. In 1963, I took a year's leave of absence from Fortuna High School and majored in History at Humboldt State University.

As I look back to see the patterns and intents of my life's unfolding, perhaps 1963 was a critical year. In that year, I moved from a general background in the Sciences to the Humanities. It is not that I neglected knowledge from biology and chemistry, but rather I found there were theories and information from the Sciences that enhanced and enriched insights in the Humanities. For example, from biology it is proposed that ontogeny recapitulates phylogeny. That is, the history of the species passes through the history of the phylum. As humans, we are assigned to the phylum vertebrata or vertebrates. Those species or animals that have a backbone or vertebral column such as horses, buffalo, eagles, fish, mice, and humans are related. We share the same basic structure. Were Indians throughout North America merely being poetic when they declared that the horse is their brother, or did they have a fundamental understanding into related species? We may not be able to discern an answer, but a multitude of knowledge and the mystery of dreams may enrich us all.

In addition to my epistemological broadening, 1963 was the nascent year of Indian awareness following the Civil Rights Movement. New programs and governmental policies under the democratic aegis supported a growing concept of self-determination for Indian reservations. The National Congress of American Indians and tribal representatives took action against the termination policies of the Bureau of Indian Affairs. Meanwhile, President Johnson's Great Society began to fund projects through the Office of Economic Opportunity (OEO). Federal funding for housing, health, community action, and education became available. For example, in 1966 the Navajo Rough

Rock Demonstration School was established to reverse the 50% or more dropout rate of Indian youth. The Navajos hoped that an all-Indian school board and teaching facility would provide a meaningful and culturally significant education.

In 1969, Humboldt State University received a federal grant to train Indian teachers for employment in the California Public School System. The major intent was to mitigate the high dropout rate of Indian students. In general, this program was a success with Indian graduates returning to their communities. Few, however, taught classes in the public schools because there was such a critical need for leadership. Indian graduates, in those early years, often became directors of community action groups such as the Johnson O'Malley Program, the Inter-Tribal Council of California, and the California Indian Legal Services. Years later, many returned to the classroom and made significant contributions in California Indian education.

Intellectual expressions and grass roots activism joined in 1969 in a surge of energy and pride in one's ancestry that ignited Indian and American interest and confrontations. N. Scott Momaday became the first American Indian to win the Pulitzer Prize in Literature. His novel, *House Made of Dawn*, evoked symbolic and sensory modes with syntactical precision when, for instance, Momaday described the dilemma of many Indian people living in two worlds and perhaps not comfortable in either. Vine Deloria, Jr., another native writer at this time, wrote books such as *Custer Died for your Sins*, which satirically broke new ground by shattering old images of stoic, monosyllabic Indians, the all-knowing white Anthropologist, and the paternalistic governing agencies. In the following years, Deloria wrote numerous books, articles, and monographs on American Indian religions, philosophy, treaty-rights, and politics.

As a result of these works and many others, The Citizens Advocate Center published an indictment of the failure of government-Indian relations in *Our Brother's Keeper: The Indian in White America*, edited by Edgar Cahn and David Hearne. In essence, these editors wrote that, "despite three centuries of systematic effort to destroy or absorb the American Indian, he shows no sign of disappearing. His culture has been deeply and purposely eroded yet it persists" (1969, "Foreword," p. vii). The book reads as an exposé of lies, deceit, and bureaucratic bumbling by the U.S. Government. However, Cahn and Hearne make no recommendations. Rather, they make a strong observation that, "Indians do not need one more white-man's plan for their betterment;" it must come from the Indian people themselves (pp. 187-193).

These sentiments and realizations had numerous consequences, particularly in Indian protests and actions, which began to define self-determination. Perhaps the most symbolic of these activities was the occupation of Alcatraz Island in November 1969. Most people are familiar with the sequence of events, but relatively few know that it was based on law—albeit with some interpretive features. U.S. Code Title 25 compiles congressional laws relating to Indians. Various statutes declare that abandoned federal properties of ten or more years shall return to its original owners. Alcatraz, a federal prison, had closed six years earlier in 1963, therefore a strict application of U.S. Code Title 25 did not apply. However, the intent of the law would be cited in future occupations.

Meanwhile, a small group of Sioux activists filed claim to Alcatraz Island under the 1868 Fort Laramie Treaty that recognized ownership of unused federal lands would return to the Indian people. Armed with these declarations and a need for a new community center in San Francisco, Indian students from universities and colleges, and members from the urban relocation programs, began the occupation of Alcatraz. By March of 1970, seventy-eight Indians were arrested at Fort Lawton, Washington, as they claimed the facility as an Indian cultural center.

In July of the same year, members of the Oglala Sioux demanded the return of a deserted gunnery range taken by the military during World War II. In November, Indian and Chicano students occupied an abandoned army communications center near Davis, California, in order to demand the establishment of a unique university that served and was administered by Native Americans. In May 1971, members of the American Indian Movement (AIM) took over the unused naval air station in Milwaukee, Wisconsin, under the terms of the 1868 treaty. This action tested Article VI of the U.S. Constitution that declares treaties are the supreme laws of the land.

Simultaneously, Indian nations throughout the United States refused to be categorized as one more complaining minority. Various Indian communities declared that, as signatories to contracts or treaties between sovereign powers, obligations and immunities are to be upheld by both parties. However, the 375 treaties between Indian nations and the U.S. Government have been unilaterally broken or disregarded by the United States. Therefore, in the summer of 1972, Indian leaders organized a caravan from San Francisco to Washington, D. C. This caravan, known as the Trail of Broken Treaties, focused attention on a list of twenty points to be addressed by President Nixon on the eve of his re-election. Over one third of the twenty points dealt with treaty relations, while the remainder covered issues concerning land reform, termination, protection of Indian religious freedom, and housing and employment. National attention on these issues, however, was soon diverted by the more sensational Indian "take-over and occupation" of the Bureau of Indian Affairs office in the nation's capital.

Not since the War of 1812 had Washington, D. C. been occupied by threatening external forces. However, within a week, the occupation ended. The Indians were paid $60,000, all charges were dropped, and they returned home. The White House finally answered the twenty points of the Trail of Broken Treaties the following year. Their response would be convincing to most, yet Indian leaders replied point-by-point and created an important document of Indian-U.S. Government relations.

The following February of 1973, U.S. military maneuvers against the Indian occupation of Wounded Knee caused more distractions. The FBI and the U.S. military, in an attempt to starve the protesters, set up barricades on all roads leading into the small compound located on the Pine River Reservation. Many of my students traveled to Wounded Knee. They sneaked passed the military outposts with food and supplies for the besieged Indians. One young man, who later became a well-known AIM leader, never graduated because protracted and spurious trials conducted by the FBI sidetracked his academic career.

In the meantime, California Indians were experiencing their own ordeals from unjust governmental activities. Earlier, in 1964, California Indian nations were again lumped together as "Indians of California" in a Land's Claim case for the return of approximately 60 million acres. In a series of BIA machinations, the "Indians of California" received only forty-seven cents an acre as "just compensation" for lands fraudulently taken. Payment of $1.25 an acre for any land in America had been established in 1820. However, the California Indian people were coerced to accept the judgment of forty-seven cents an acre and received a federal check for $668.51 on December 22, 1972, three days before Christmas. Along with others, I never cashed my own check. For several years the BIA asked me if I had deposited the check. To this day, I have never responded to those inquiries.

In 1976, I became increasingly critical of U.S. federal policies as patriotic slogans and historical platitudes asked for "true Americans" to celebrate 200 years of "America's greatness." The purposed Bicentennial celebrations galvanized my efforts to document obvious genocidal acts in northern California. "Indians have nothing to celebrate in 1976," I stated, and, "If they do, their ancestors should come back and haunt them." Given my strong statements, I had to accurately record accounts of inhuman activity in my book entitled *Genocide in Northwestern California* and to place them within international condemnation as crimes against humanity. I believe the book was generally well-received and, recently, the respected Anthropologist Thomas Buckley confirmed my perceptions in his book on Yurok culture and epistemology, *Standing Ground* (2002).

The following years were a jumble of positive gains and negative setbacks in Indian and U.S. governmental relations. Several judicial decisions affirmed Indian tribal sovereignty and inherent rights. For example, the Boldt Decision (U.S. v. Washington, 1974) recognized that tribes in the northwest were entitled to one half the "harvestable" off-reservation catch of salmon. In New Mexico, the Mescalero Apache exercised their right to regulate non-Indian hunting and fishing on ancestral lands. Further gains were made in Indian education, and by 1991 there were twenty-two tribally controlled community colleges and at least 70,000 Indians attending college nationwide. By 1990, Congress passed certain acts pertaining to Indian religious freedoms, Indian child welfare, and protection of Native American graves and return of remains and cultural items. There was also a feigned attempt to acknowledge governmental complicity in genocide when Congress issued an expression of "Deep Regret" for the 7th Calvary's 1890 massacre of 300 men, women, and children at Wounded Knee.

Conversely, however, the rudimentary policy to assimilate Indian people and resources into the fabric of the American society has never changed. In 1981, Reagan-economics drastically reduced—by at least 26%—federal funds for Indian housing, education, employment, and vocational acceptance. The Supreme Court ruled in Montana v. U.S. that the state had authority to regulate hunting and fishing on the Bighorn River that flowed through the Crow Reservation. This ruling, along with similar decisions and legislation, confused issues of tribal sovereignty and the Indian's right to enforce their own laws.

Additionally, Congress passed the Nuclear Waste Policy Act in 1983, which allowed the Environmental Protection Agency (EPA) to dump nuclear and radioactive waste on reservation lands. Although this required tribal council approval, many reservations became torn between tribal membership and leadership due to conflict and distrust.

An example of the inherent misunderstandings between the Reagan administration and Indian nations was demonstrated when Interior Secretary James Watt stated on national television that, "if you want an example of the failures of Socialism, don't go to Russia, come to America and see the American Indian reservations." A few years later, President Reagan told students at Moscow University that, "maybe we made a mistake. Maybe we should not have humored them [Indians] in wanting to stay in that kind of primitive lifestyle." As disconcerting as these ignorant remarks were, the greater liability to Indian integrity and self-government was the passage of the Indian Gaming Regulatory Act in 1988. In response to complaints by non-Indian businesses and state officials, Congress was determined to regulate Indian gaming on reservation lands. The claim of congressional authority over Indian nations had been fraudulently and unconstitutionally assumed in Lone Wolf v. Hitchcock, 1903. Thus, not only should the Indian Gaming Regulatory Act be challenged, but all Indian governmental relations should be reviewed. Indian-government relations must be based upon treaty agreement and not arbitrary and deceptive congressional acts.

In 1992, the Quincentennial, the 500th anniversary of Columbus' voyage, offered an opportunity for review of the moral consequences of his historical journey. The Quincentennial allowed for a debate as to whether Columbus was a harbinger of democracy and liberty or was the agent of death and suffering for millions of indigenous people. Special curriculum was developed for the public schools, and *Time* and *Newsweek* magazines published articles emphasizing a review of the meeting of the two worlds. However, little changed, and in the following years, textbooks still seemed to imply that the discovery of a New World was an introduction of civilization to a backward people. A Walk for Justice in 1994 was organized by the AIM leadership to bring attention to continuing incidence of mistreatment of Native Americans in urban areas and on the reservations. In particular, AIM demanded clemency for Leonard Peltier. Peltier, who had been arrested at the protest at Wounded Knee in 1973, and given a life sentence for the murder of two federal agents, was considered to be a political prisoner by many since there was no solid evidence linking him to the murders. As a result his case received world publicity by Amnesty International, yet the

U.S. Justice Department refused to review his incarceration. Also, the Walk for Justice ordered the return of the Black Hills to the Sioux and resolution to the Navajo-Hopi land dispute. The protest march began in the winter from San Francisco and ended in Washington, D. C. that summer. Although the protest served as a catalyst for young Indian people, it failed to resolve these issues.

After my retirement from Humboldt State University in 1997, I became the first California Indian appointed to the Rupert Costo Chair in American Indian History at the University of California, Riverside. The Rupert Costo Chair was established in 1986 and was the first endowed academic position in American Indian History for the University of California system. The chair's primary mission is to enhance and continue scholarly studies and research in Native American affairs, particularly in California Indian history. It is also expected that the chair holders continue leadership in local, national, and international developments of American Indian rights and sovereignty.

During my tenure as the Costo Chair, I met outstanding members of the southern California Indian community, and in 1998 we planned a conference on California Indian cultures. The San Manuel Tribe of Serrano (Yuhaviatam) people, working closely with California State University, San Bernardino, sponsored a conference to commemorate the legislative bill AB 1953 that declared the fourth Friday of September as an official holiday to be observed as Native American Day. This week-long conference has been held every year since 1999. Over 25,000 students throughout southern California have attended and have learned about the history and the diversity of Indian cultures in California.

I officially retired from teaching in 1999, after 41 years in a career that, if you recall, I was not going to be a part of. Yet, I was fortunate because my academic career and interests were immersed in the multitudes of Indian protests, activities, and responses that were circumscribed by legislative laws and arbitrary enforcement. From these conditions, I realized that Indian-governmental relations were the consequences of American laws based in the attitude, desires, and reactions of its citizenry. In a democracy, laws do not need to be morally just; they just have to be passed by a majority. The will of the majority may be crafted by truisms that permeate the society. For example, Western democracy assumes a superior stance in the unfolding of history, which is upheld by technology and religious dogma. From the early doctrines of discovery, such as Manifest Destiny all the way through to the resolution of the Cold War in Europe, America has claimed the right to spread its ideals throughout the world. Only recently have some of these inculcated virtues been questioned or challenged.

In the 1960s and 1970s, many—particularly the youth—became disenchanted with the war in Vietnam, nuclear disasters, and the despoliation of the environment. The 1980s witnessed an intellectual revisionism of American history, where some of the old values were re-evaluated. Richard Drinnon's *Facing West: The Metaphysics of Indian Hating and Empire Building*, for instance, documented the psychological costs to the American psyche as crucial historical events were re-examined. As Drinnon exposed these events of America's past, he more clearly associated genocide with western expansionism and Indian-white relations.

In the meantime, Indian people responded to these ever-changing events. Some joined militant movements and confronted century-old injustices. Others believed in change through educating themselves and society. They expected that a fundamental union could be potentially forged between those who supported Western individual rights and Native American communal and treaty rights. Finally, there were those Indian people who rejected any communication with American society and retreated into isolationism and exclusivity. Of course, there were many gradations between these arbitrary categories, and individuals moved through them depending upon times and conditions.

Today, an understanding and acceptance of differing worldviews is difficult to obtain because there is an inherent contradiction within the American psyche and society. On the one hand, a virtue of rugged individualism is fostered and admired where a freedom from declaration is sustained by a corollary of a "right to create one's own reality." On the other hand, the requirement of American democracy is the consensus of commonly held values.

Thus, this tension between the individual and the majority consensus can create real or imaginary enemies that call for a united action and perhaps a suspension of individual rights. A facile politician or government can mold the citizenry into action, and nullify, for the moment, previously held convictions, as we have seen in the most recent presidential administration. This situation conflicts with the commitment to communal values that support and validate individual expressions that are evaluated within common experiences of the group. Most Indian communities share an idea of place, a homeland that carries the racial memories and energy of a people and where cultural and social mores along with spiritual beliefs are demonstrated. Religious activity then confirms viable communal expressions that are not considered universal truths for all humankind. An opportunity to develop consensual value of a meaningful life can be achieved. When, for example, an individual decides upon a course of action, the results can be anticipated by asking, "Does this affirm life, or does it deny life?" Life, in this regard, refers to all things: animals, trees, physical landscapes, biosystems, and other human beings. Perhaps differences in our respective cultural values, as well as the native world view that embraces the natural world as a sacred relation, and not as a resource for exploitation, have only served to separate and exacerbate the relationship between Indians and non-Indians today.

An inherent misunderstanding of Indian beliefs has developed over thousands of years and reflected communal expressions to place. For many Americans, religious experiences occur between an individual and a transcendent being. The concept of a sacred area in nature or a wilderness is difficult to grasp because nature is perceived as often dangerous and needs to be overcome. God can be communed with anywhere, but preferably in a man-made structure like a church, where written doctrines and instructions are given.

There are, however, examples where Western ideas have reflected the concept and value of place. An aspect of this can be found in the establishment of national parks such as Yosemite, Yellowstone and the Grand Canyon. These areas, and others like them, are seen as places for reflection upon the beauty and solace of nature for all individual Americans. Also, the concerns of many environmentalists and conservationists such as the Sierra Club, the Audubon Society, and specific interests as Save the Mount Shasta Coalition, have all sought the setting aside of valuable lands.

In 1975, however, when the Six Rivers National Forest Service constructed a logging road that bisected the sacred High Country of the Yurok, Tolowa, and Karuk peoples, the attempt to protect sacred areas for communal spiritual purposes was vehemently resisted. As a result, a coalition of representatives of the tribes and environmentalists filed suit in the federal district courts in San Francisco. The suit charged that the logging road would impair or destroy the required solitude and privacy necessary to exercise and practice the traditional religion of the native groups. Thus, the United States Government was violating the

First Amendment rights of Indian people.

Both federal district and appellate courts ruled in favor of the Indians. When the case, entitled Ling v. Northwest Indian Cemetery Protective Association, reached the Supreme Court in 1988, it was dismissed. Justice Sandra Day O'Connor, writing for the majority, implied a threat to government property would ensue if an individual standing before the Lincoln Memorial had a religious revelation and therefore claimed the right to protect their religion. Justice O'Connor did not elaborate upon the diversity of beliefs in America nor the rights of the First Amendment Protection Clause. The First Amendment Protection Clause does not distinguish between public or privately held lands in the protection of religious freedom. The court also decided that the American Indian Religious Freedom Act, 1978, had no jurisdiction in this case because the road was federal property within the Six Rivers National Forest. The American Indian Religious Freedom Act prescribed that Native Americans came under the "Free Exercise Clause" of the First Amendment of the United States Constitution, which stipulates that "Congress shall make no law respecting an establishment of religion, or prohibiting the free exercise thereof." However, it was decided that the American Religious Freedom Act lacked the power of enforcement because it was passed in the form of a joint resolution of Congress. Therefore, the forest service logging road known as the Gasquet-Orleans or Go-Road could be completed.

In the summer of 1988, after the Supreme Court decision, a unique event occurred. Quietly, several Karuk spiritual leaders prepared a ceremony to balance and heal the energy within the sacred area. They sent word to the dance leaders of the five High Dance tribes, and that summer, in Elk Valley just below Chimney Rock, a special Jump Dance or Mountain Dance was held. Two years later, Congress added the disputed lands in the sacred area to the California Wilderness Act that had been passed earlier. The paved two-lane road from Gasquet on the north side of the Siskiyou Mountains, and a similar road from Orleans on the south side, abruptly stopped at the edge of the sacred High Country. The entire area was, at least for the moment, free from disruption and harm.

However, this is my greatest concern. If a people and their representatives in government support the laws and decisions within a democracy, including Supreme Court decisions, then resultant laws are reflections of an inculcated compulsory educational system. In the future, the tenets of rampant individualism, of man over nature, of technological resolution to problems and immediate gratification are generally accepted by the majority of Americans, an understanding and recognition of Native American worldviews may be nullified. However, as an educator and a singer and dancer in the ceremonies of the Five High Dance tribes, I believe that someday there will be a gracious acceptance of views whereby all life will be enhanced, not lessened. Hopefully, from this paradigm, integrity of beingness will be nurtured for all.

Before this can occur, we must meet each other honestly and openly. We must address our similarities and differences. All Euro-Americans are not dupes of societal dogma and governmental policies. There have always been individuals who have believed and acted for the common good and have sought an authentic and genuine relationship to place. However, non-Indians must accept responsibility for the actions of their ancestors and must be willing to discover legitimate spiritual means by which they may come to know all things.

Nor are all Indians spiritually guided beings. There are those who have become materialistic and isolated from their communities as any other modern person. Recent attempts within Indian country to exclude certain members of the community, by removing them from tribal membership based on blood quantum, may reflect an internalization of trauma and not traditional practices. However, this does not, I believe, doom us all to live, as Thomas Hobbes wrote in his 1651 treatise *Leviathan,* to a life that is "poor, nasty, brutish and short" (*Of Man, Being the First Part,* vol. 34, Part 5). We can decide to seek out and make alliances with those who hold comparable values, no matter from what culture one would assign them. Obviously, if enough associations were made, then political actions in a democracy would be successful.

In the meantime, we as Indian people have responsibility to strengthen our own integrity by affirming the traditions of living graciously within the lands and ideals that sustained our people for generations. Today, one hears throughout Indian country that the past is our future. For me, this affirms responsibility to the earth, the community, and each other by seeking a balanced existence within an ever-changing world. The traditional Yurok, for example, recognized as a Pegerk as a real or honored person one who acknowledged the forces of good and evil, and their many attendant forms. These individuals sought a means to keep discord in check by becoming doctors, dance leaders, or spiritually aware participants in the community. The high ceremonies such as the Jump or Mountain Dance, or White Deerskin Dance are said to "fix or renew the world." When societies become riddled with mischief, misfortune, calamity, multigenerational suffering and trauma, depravity, corruption, prejudice, mean-spirited gossip, and the multitudes of maladies that befall humans because they are of their own making, then a great ceremony can be held to return the world to balance. Those who earnestly participate in this undertaking including cooks, wood gatherers, regalia makers, members of the audience, and many others. All have the opportunity to stand within the radiance of healing energy. The ceremonial leaders, dancers, and closely related individuals have journeyed into the High Country for periods of fasting and isolation. There they may address energies from within and without and may be given insights or lessons about their own lives, and how to become better human beings.

In my own experience, the ebb and flow of teaching and serving both the native and non-Native communities for over 40 years in an attempt to articulate meaningful ideas, thoughts, and concerns, has become the mainstay of my life. These thoughts, reflections, and subjective interpretations coalesced with scholarly information and personal knowledge. As my perceptions matured over time, what I once saw in an abrupt or judgmental way—for I was quick to categorize and assume—became, as the years passed and experiences broadened, more inclusive, and I sought out a commonality of human strengths and weaknesses.

Hence, I learned that all individuals must take responsibility for their own actions. They must ask themselves if their actions enhance life or if their actions demean or lessen life. And by life, all things must be included: animals, plants, rocks, rivers—the entities of our natural world—as well as other cultures and races of human kind. Every society has a code of ethics that defines and emphasizes their responsibility to others. It is only when individuals distort, narrow, or set aside these moral obligations do inhuman acts such as genocide find their way into human history (Norton, 2014, "If the Truth Be Told," p. 53).

Thus, it is imperative that young people in Indian country today understand and come to know, each in their own way, the vitality and meaning of the ceremonial systems. It is imperative that they feel the transcendent forces for spiritual wholeness and move upon this earth with purpose, to keep their hearts open by showing kindness to all things. They must pass to each succeeding generation the knowledge and responsibility of keeping the world in health and harmony.

It is also imperative that non-Indian people also feel the rhythms and energies of this earth, for they too may walk gently and share their kindness with all. They too must seek out their own original instructions and come to know how to feel connected to their centers. Because in each of us there is this central focus, this center-of-being in which we all share the energy and mystery of the cosmos. In this manner, we all may become a person who sees all things as beautiful within the integrity of being and belonging. (Norton, 2007, "Songs of Continuance," p. 174). The decisions made while living upon this earth will enhance all things and will not lessen the integrity of others, so that justice and reconciliation can offer us new insights into human behavior to live more graciously upon this land.

Our ancestors knew this. This we may also know. In this way, the past is our future.

CHAPTER 8

Resilience and Resistance Through Grassroots Organization

William J. Pink

MY JOURNEY INTO THE DECADE OF 1970 BEGAN IN VIETNAM. After completing a tour in Panama with the 8th Special Forces Group, I was assigned to the 5th Special Forces Group in Vietnam. To most people of my generation, these simple facts were so normal that they almost become meaningless. Why I don't consider this to be true for me goes back to the age of three when I learned to read my first word. That word was "WAR." It was posted on every newspaper those days and was in reference to the Korean War.

I was plagued with nightmares as a child. I can remember my mother leaving me with my grandparents and, at the time, I did not understand why. I do remember my grandmother talking to me about my nightmares. The dreams were very graphic, active, and frightening. My grandmother would tell me that the dreams occurred. She knew because I slept with my right hand over my heart.

What was significant about those events wasn't the dreams but the way my grandmother talked to me. Her voice was without doubt, and even at the age of four, I recognized that. It was at that moment that my full faith in Indian beliefs was established. The next nightmare I had, I was calmed by the fact that I awoke with my right hand over my heart. I moved my arm and went back to sleep. The nightmares didn't frighten me anymore and would just remain as expressions in my lifelong learning.

In 1980, I was appointed by Governor Brown to serve as the Executive Secretary of the Native American Heritage Commission. The job revolved around the protection of various Indian sacred sites, burial grounds, and traditional activities. The most significant case of the time was the "GO Road," which was short for the Gasquet-Orleans Road. It was a proposed United States Forest Service Road that was designed to provide greater access for loggers in Northwestern California. There are several sacred areas along the proposed road that were threatened by the project.

During a meeting with my predecessor, I mentioned that I was going to the GO Road area to get a first-hand look at the proposed road route and some of the areas considered to be sacred. He looked at me and said, "Do you really believe in that stuff?"

I cannot remember another time in my life where my mind went utterly blank. It was like a six-second-long pause while my brain was searching for an answer. I had to look at him to see if there wasn't some other point to his question, but he was dead serious. I answered him, "Yes." I have to say even more today, "Yes I do."

I had joined the military service at the age of seventeen, and Indian politics were just as foreign to me as was Vietnam. I know we went to tribal meetings. We visited Warner Springs or Agua Caliente, the place where my grandfather was born and forcibly removed in 1903 to a Reservation located in the Pala Valley. What were not foreign to me were the various religious activities that we attended as children, either with my grandparents or my mother. These included wakes and funerals, fiestas, candle lighting, clothes burning, and year-after ceremonies. These were all separate from the government policies that were affecting the everyday life of Indians throughout America.

The other part of believing is the realization that it is just there. Things happen and they just are. Yes, *Tahquitz*, the spirit eater, does appear in the sky as a fireball. Yes, the raven sings the war song. Yes, if the owl calls your name, you have three days to get your house in order. Yes, if the coyote crosses your path, you are to end your journey and return home. Yes, if you do not sing your ancestors out, they will bother you until you do what is right.

I returned home from Vietnam in 1971. My tour was not without incident and I have many stories related to the Indian perspective. I often flew in the CH-47 helicopters, which were capable of carrying 45 passengers plus crew. It was during one of these flights that we were shot down over Cambodia. We were at an elevation of 8,000 feet when I noticed that we were red-lighting. The crew chief informed me that we were crashing. He began to panic. I looked at him and motioned for him to sit down. He sat next to me and became very calm. Our descent was taking a toll on our Vietnamese passengers. Some began to vomit while others held their ears, trying to stop the pain from the pressure building up on their eardrums. We were prepared to crash.

We were 500 feet from the ground when the secondary controls kicked in and the pilot regained control of the aircraft. Even so, the helicopter began to shudder like it was going to fly apart. The helicopter was slowing its descent, but we could feel the force trying to press us through the floor. Without any hover time, we set down firmly on the ground—or, as some like to call it, a hard landing. We were in Cambodia in a helicopter that could explode at any time. We forced the passengers to disembark while the pilot and co-pilot remained with the helicopter.

Almost immediately there were four Huey helicopters circling over-head, offering us cover if needed. It would not be long before the Viet Cong would be on our position. I asked the crew chief who the circling helicopters were, and he responded, "They are 7th Air Cav." He then looked at me and said, "You really do have a guardian angel, don't you."

My brother had been killed while serving with the 7th Air Cav. I didn't say that to the crew chief, but it was immediately on my mind. In the meanwhile, the aircraft was repaired and we were airborne again. The crew chief then explained his remark, stating that I got them in and out of places and situations all the time, and it was talk amongst the flight crews that I had a guardian angel.

In another situation, I was woken one night by a Huey crew chief. He was leaning over my bed with his flight helmet on, appearing almost alien. He asked me if my name was Pink. I told him yes. He then said, "Trang Sup is under attack and they are not just asking for help, they are crying for help. They are out of ammunition."

I led the crew chief to our ammo bunker and asked him what he could carry. He said they would take 1,500 pounds of ammo at a time and we could fly three sorties. He said, "We will stack the ammo around you, and when we enter the camp you will push it out so we do not have to land." So we did it. We carried out three successful sorties and Trang Sup was able to repel the final wave attack of Viet Cong.

That morning, there were several pictures from the body count floating around the mess hall while soldiers celebrated the victory and began the flurry of war stories. One of the team members from Trang Sup sat at my table with a handful of photos saying, "Do you want to see what you did last night?" I really didn't. In the background was one of the older soldiers moving around repeating the same question at every table he visited, "Does anyone know where that helicopter came from. Did anyone get a tail number?" Satisfied that he had visited every table he finally said out loud, "It must have been one of those ghost ships."

So where did the helicopter come from? No one knew the answer but it was real and solid enough to carry me and three sorties of ammunition to the battle front. It was indeed a ghost ship. It did have me thinking that these men, most of them twice my junior, believed in something. They had seen something in their experiences that caused them to believe without question. No one questioned it. It was a ghost ship. It was no different to me than my great uncle transforming himself into a bear. It is about more than believing; it's truly more about knowing.

Even with all this knowing, maneuvering through the 1970s was no easy task. The Bureau of Indian Affairs (BIA) and various study groups were releasing report after report stating that Indians performed poorly because of low self-esteem. It seemed to be the hallmark of the time, and every grant of money, every Reservation project, and every change in Indian education focused on improving Indian self-esteem.

After more than 80 years of forced assimilation and acculturation, Indian belief systems were near collapse. It must be remembered that there were only 16,000 California Indians left at the beginning of the 20th Century. When you divide that population of 16,000 up amongst 150 tribes that is only 105 Indian persons per tribe. The reality is that several of the tribes were nearing extinction or extinct. Remarkably, there were tribes that were still thriving in parts of Northern California, and many of the tribes in Central California were reclaiming their heritage with actions like the burning of the "Digger Indian."

California Indians were confused by the influx of Plains Indians that were being relocated to California under the BIA re-location program. The 1970s saw the population of non-California Indians surpass the number of California Indians as most of the Indians from the Plains sector were re-located to Los Angeles, San Jose, and San Francisco

Bay Area. Most California Indians were very welcoming and received the other Indians as family. The treatment was not reciprocal. Soon the landscape was being dominated by Pow Wows, Sioux sweats, Sundance, and the American Indian Movement. This domination included the occupation of Alcatraz and the Longest Walk.

During this time, California Indians were still reeling from the California Indian Land Claims Settlement. We were forced to accept a settlement of $0.47 cents per acre. Some tribes refused to accept their settlement payments while others were outmaneuvered by the BIA, whose planned distribution of settlement checks began arriving just one week before Christmas. 70,000 California Indians received $668.51 each as part of the Claims Settlement.

The 1970s also saw the effecting of various legislative acts that would directly impact the everyday lives of many California Indians. These laws included Public Law 93-638, the Indian Self-Determination Act, the California Environmental Quality Act (CEQA) and Public Law 91-190, and the National Environmental Policy Act (NEPA). A major provision of the National Environmental Quality Act states:

> It declares that it is the policy of the Federal Government to use all practicable means to create and maintain conditions under which man and nature can exist in productive harmony and fulfill the social, economic, and other requirements of present and future generations of Americans.

As is typical with post-war activities, bomb-building dollars had to be diverted to other projects, and the post-war eras of World War II, the Korean War, and Vietnam War kept California's growth surging. The housing boom in California was being driven by VA loans and lax banking rules. It wasn't long before suburban sprawl was knocking on the door of culturally sensitive areas of many California Indian Tribes.

During this time, Indian people were still being treated as second class citizens with no particular rights or a minimum of rights. They did not share the same Constitutional rights as did other citizens of the United States. The BIA was the voice of Indian People and the transition from Indian Ward to tribal self-governance and tribal sovereignty was clouded by the BIA's corruption in implementing Public Law 93-638.

There is no clear line of demarcation as to when tribes became self-governing. Even with the Supreme Court decision SANTA CLARA PUEBLO v. MARTINEZ, 436 U.S. 49 (1978) 436 U.S. 49, there was no great heralding of "Free At Last." The BIA—and, more so, the United States—took no direct action to correct the way the BIA was treating tribes.

There was no concern on the part of the BIA to reach out and protect the rights of their Indian Wards with respects to religion, property, and civil rights. Instead, archaeology and archaeologists became the interface between federal, state, and local governments when it came to cultural matters. Indians, regardless of tribal affiliation, were recruited to monitor project development while the archaeologists did what they thought was satisfactory compliance with environmental laws. This did not include ultimate protection of Native American grave sites and sacred sites. The basic requirement for getting CEQA or NEPA approval of a project was that 1% of 1% of a Native American Cultural Site (Archaeological Site) had to be recovered to consider the site to be fully mitigated. In the case of a one-acre site, this meant that only a 0.4 square meter of the site was required to be excavated and the cultural materials removed for study.

So what would happen if the one-acre site was an Indian burial site? Under the environmental laws of the 1970s, there was nothing an Indian person could do to change the outcome of satisfying CEQA and NEPA. So the archaeologist would enter a Native American burial site, dig up a few graves, take possession of the human remains (including the associated grave goods), and leave the rest for the bulldozers. This was happening at an accelerated rate, since California was undergoing its business and housing boom.

There was massive confusion in the world of California Indian Culture. Traditional Indians were demanding full protection of all Indian burial grounds. Tribal governments did not share the same interest because of the rapidly growing needs of implementing Indian Self-Determination. Archaeologists were declaring their scientific needs as paramount to Native American beliefs. Local governments saw traditional Indians as obstructionists. Every California public utility had a pet "Indian chief." The biggest question of the time was, "Who can speak for all of the Indians?"

The competition to become that one Indian person was vicious and unproductive. Several Indian organizations made attempts to answer the call by federal, state, and local governments to have a single voice amongst

Indian people. There was the California Tribal Chairman's Association, the Intertribal Council of California, the Southern California Tribal Chairman's Association, the California Indian Education Association, and several Indian tribal centers with growing political power. Even the Indian Cattleman's Associations saw themselves as leaders within the Indian community. The American Indian Movement was often stealing the spotlight away from California Indians.

If all this was not enough, there were the "Indian Fakers." These impostors were known for cultural consumption, exploitation, and "playing Indian." The most famous of all Indian Fakers was Iron Eyes Cody, whose real name was Espera Oscar DeCorti. He was an Italian actor who played the role of an Indian in several movies. As gentlemanly and kind Iron Eyes was as a man, he was not an Indian. "Indian Fakers" were detrimental to the movement of California Indians by hording the spotlight, misrepresenting themselves and tribes, and utilizing Indian identity for their own personal gain. In my lifetime, I have had to work with a number of these types of people.

My very first project after being appointed to serve as Executive Secretary was to intervene in a housing project located in Stockton. The developer, with the blessing of the Stockton City Council, had hired a non-California Indian and an "Indian faker" to monitor the removal of human remains and associated grave goods. The burial site was large, and I estimated that at least 2,000 graves were being impacted. I contacted William (Bill) Franklin, since the site was located in Miwok territory, and Bill put me in touch with Karl Mathieson of Chicken Ranch Rancheria.

Karl and I did everything that we thought was right. To us, the site was obviously an Indian cemetery and should be afforded appropriate protection under the State's cemetery laws. After all, the State Health and Safety Code states:

7003 "Cemetery" means either of the following:
(a) Any of the following that is used or intended to be used and dedicated for cemetery purposes:
    (1) A burial park, for earth interments.
    (2) A mausoleum, for crypt or vault interments.
    (3) A crematory and columbarium, for cinerary interments.
(b) A place where six or more human bodies are buried.

This includes recent amendments, but the section we saw as applicable to our case was the simple language, "A place where six or more human bodies are buried." English can't get any simpler than that, right!? Wrong. We quickly learned that there were several requirements for a cemetery to qualify as a cemetery. Each burial plot has to be surveyed and recorded, with the name of the interred person known and recorded. Just this fact alone was enough to disqualify every Indian burial site from protection by state law.

Treatment of the burial site in Stockton was wide open. We had to be innovative and creative. Most of all, Karl and I had to identify the issues affecting the developer and the City of Stockton. Karl was expedient at getting the "Indian Faker" removed from the site. We learned that he was selling the remains and artifacts to various collectors on the East Coast. He later succumbed to an unknown lung infection thought to be associated with his activities at the burial site. Meanwhile, Karl and I negotiated with the developer to have the excavated remains buried on site and portions of the burial ground preserved.

With Stockton behind us and lessons learned, Bill and I were called out to investigate a project in Morgan Hill in Santa Clara County. Again, it was a massive Indian burial site being destroyed by another housing developer. The site was guarded by several archaeologists and we were refused admittance on to the property. We watched through the fence as earth movers made repeated passes across the land and, at each pass, exposing human remains. As the remains were exposed, archaeologists would run across the path of the heavy equipment and pick up as many human remains as was possible before the next earth mover began its pass. It was like watching ball boys at a tennis match, only these were the bones of Indians instead of tennis balls.

Bill and I then went to the County Coroner Office for Santa Clara County. We met directly with the Coroner, who stood behind a counter while we talked to him. I told him about his duties as the Coroner and responsibility to investigate the discovery of human remains. After describing the situation to him, he stepped back from the counter and said, "I don't have to do anything." I asked him why not and he responded, "Because Indians are not human." With that he walked away, but not before Bill Franklin became visibly enraged. There was nothing we could do.

After two major setbacks with respect to protecting Indian burial sites, it was obvious that the laws needed to be changed in order to protect Indian burial sites. So what were the issues? First, Indians were being treated as a resource and funneled into the protections offered by CEQA; second, Indians were not being treated or recognized as human; third, archaeologists served as the voice and, in many cases, the final determiner as to the disposition of Indian human remains; and fourth, associated grave goods were not to be separated from the remains. Of these four major issues, it was the "Associated Grave Goods" that became the biggest obstacle in obtaining comprehensive burial protection for Indians. Reaction from the archaeological community was swift. The ink was barely dry on the bill proposed by then-Senator John Garamendi when we were overwhelmed with opposition because of legislative language which simply stated, "A place where six or more Indians are interred is a cemetery."

A major player in maneuvering the legislation through the various committees was Senator Garamendi's top aid, Gladys Ikeda. She was brilliant, and listened with the same fervor as if she had experienced a ghost ship or an uncle changing in to a bear. She never questioned or doubted any expressions we had to make regarding our Indian ancestry. She and Senator Garamendi recommended that we carry the bill as a two year bill. This gave us time to develop the legislative language that we needed to achieve real protection for Indian burial sites. Critical language included terms such as *associated grave goods*, *most likely descendent*, *knowingly disturbing*, and *accidental disturbance*. Also critical was the right of final determination and disposition of the human remains.

The opposition had time to organize as well. The American Committee for the Protection of Archaeological Collections (ACPAC) was formed, and they spearheaded opposition for the archaeological community. The University of California, Board of Regents and the Academic Senate sent their lobbyist to oppose the legislation. We had to appear before several committees and were often outnumbered by the opposition during these sessions. We did have very strong support from several anthropologists and archaeologists, as well.

What was not obvious was that this was not a fight between science and "the Indians," but a fight between the developer and "the Indian." Behind the scenes, the Californian Building Industry Association sat relaxed and poised with confidence that they could have the bill defeated at any time. In their favor, we amended the bill to include an exemption from CEQA in resolving burial issues affecting developers.

The legislative process was foreign to me, so it was fortunate when

Wanda Lee Graves was appointed to serve on the Heritage Commission. Wanda Lee knew her way around the halls of the Capitol, and every time I hit a closed door or road block, Wanda Lee found a way around it. I can remember her saying to me more than once, "Just shut up and listen." Listen I did, and the clearing of so many obstacles was becoming magical.

The most memorable moment for me came when Assemblyman Robert Frazee, a Republican, changed his vote. Assemblyman Frazee has to be described as the gentleman of the Assembly, whose politeness and candor was matched by no one. Still, after meeting with him, he advised me that he would be voting against the bill. During the committee hearing he offered his own testimony. He said, "The other day I went to visit the graves of my grandparents. When I got there the cemetery was gone. It had been moved for construction of the I-5 Freeway. Now I know what it feels like to be an Indian. I vote in favor of the bill." And so it happened. The bill became law with the signing of the legislation by Governor Brown.

It was not the first time a State had passed legislation to protect Indian burial grounds. That honor goes to the State of Wisconsin. However, as goes California, so goes the nation. After that came the passage of the Native American Graves Protection and Repatriation Act, PUBLIC LAW 101-601—NOV.16, 1990.

Parallel to these events were the developing and growing economies of tribes. It is not enough to have your culture preserved. Every culture needs an economic base from which to operate. Tribal Sovereignty has always been meaningless without economic sovereignty. The preservation of tribal independence while maintaining cultural belief systems was a matter very internal for tribes, and was also a very singular matter. No tribe is going to resolve the core religious issues of another tribe. However, there are the practitioners of tribal beliefs that do not share the same problems, as does a tribal council. I will let the State of California describe in its own words this conflict:

The basic facts are not disputed. On April 5 and 19, 1964, respectively, a department game warden seized defendant gill [246 Cal. App. 2d 32] nets, as the meshes of each exceeded the mesh size permitted by sections 8664 and 8686 of the code. fn. 3 The first net, subsequently claimed by Grover Reed, was approximately 53 feet long and 12 feet deep and was strung across the Klamath

River about one-quarter mile downstream from the mouth of Pecwan Creek; the second net, subsequently claimed by Dewey George, was about 91 feet long and was in a boat partially lodged on the bank of and partially in the Klamath River near Superstition Rock. Both nets were found within that portion of the Hoopa Indian Reservation known as the Hoopa Extension.

Grover Reed and Dewey George are both full-blooded Yurok (or Lower Klamath River Indians), fn. 4 descendants of Lower Klamath River Indians who were allotted specific tracts of land in the Hoopa Extension. Both were born and had lived and fished most of their lives in the area where the nets were found. Both were enrolled as Klamath River or Yurok Indians and as "wards" of the federal government on the 1931, 1937, and 1940 rolls of the Bureau of Indian Affairs (hereafter Bureau), as well as the Bureau's roll of living allottees and direct descendants of allottees on the Hoopa Extension.

Grover Reed and Dewey George were individual Indians exercising their traditional rights central to their cultural beliefs and a centerpiece in the heart of all Indian matters as to the issue of being a practicing Indian.

It is not enough to just boast of being Indian. It is so much more than that. In another State of California case:

(Cite as: 61 Cal.2d 716, 394 P.2d 813, 40 Cal.Rptr. 69) The PEOPLE, Plaintiff and Respondent, v. Jack WOODY et al., Defendants and Appellants. Cr. 7788. Supreme Court of California, In Bank. Aug. 24, 1964. The Attorney General argues that since "peyote could be regarded as a symbol, one that obstructs enlightenment and shackles the Indian to primitive conditions, the responsibility rests with the state to eliminate its use. We know of no doctrine that the state, in its asserted omniscience, should undertake to deny to defendants the observance of their religion in order to **free them from the suppositious "shackles" of their "unenlightened" and "primitive condition."**

Understand that there is no separation for Indian people when it comes to cultural practices. Gill net fishing is considered no less a spiritual event than the use of peyote. And so it is that the Indians right to practice their culture is often challenged. The Court found in the case of Dewey George and Grover Reed:

> As it is undisputed that since [246 Cal. App. 2d 41] 1855 the Lower Klamath Indians, whose main subsistence was fishing, have fished in the area in question and that even in the absence of any treaties or formal agreement, their right to do so was apparently informally recognized by the federal government prior to the enactment of Public Law 280, we think the trial court's conclusion was correct.

Fishing or taking peyote possess real substances that can be held, utilized, and even confiscated as a matter of dispute, and therefore these are tangible cultural practices. On the other hand, intangible resources and practices, such as the right to sit in a tranquil environment and achieve the necessary learning to become a full practitioner in one's faith, seems to paralyze the United States Constitution with respects to religious freedom. In Lyng v. Northwest Indian Cemetery 485 U.S. 439 (1988), also known as the GO-Road case, Justice Sandra Day O'Conner delivered the opinion of the Court:

> This case requires us to consider whether the First Amendment's Free Exercise Clause prohibits the Government from permitting timber harvesting in, or constructing a road through, a portion of a National Forest that has traditionally been used for religious purposes by members of three American Indian tribes in northwestern California. **<u>We conclude that it does not.</u>**

Can it get any more blunt than that? It does not! Native American rights to religious freedom, when practiced in a similar manner as Christian religion, is not afforded equal protection.

I was recently reminded by the ethnographer Robert Laidlaw of a conversation with Ruby Modesto regarding electrical transmission lines that would cross Desert Cahuilla sacred areas. The utility company was confident that it would not be an issue since there was already an existing line in the project area. Ruby offered the analysis that, if someone entered the Sistine Chapel with a can of spray paint and proceeded to paint over half of the works of Michelangelo, would you not consider that to be sacrilege? Yes, you would. So the question is, would you invite him back to finish the job?

After defending this country's belief systems in Vietnam, I took time to tour America. One stop on the tour was Lincoln's tomb in Springfield, Illinois. The first thing I noticed was that the copper statues that were located throughout the tomb area did not have any noses. I asked one of the care keepers why this was, and it was explained to me that visiting black people would rub the noses on the statues of Lincoln as an act of thanks and reverence. It was done so often that the noses wore off. The care keeper explained that the noses have been replaced several times.

When I entered the tomb, I proceeded to take a photograph of Lincoln's resting place and I was immediately stopped by one of the guards. His words to me, "It is too sacred for you to photograph. No photographs allowed." It wasn't so much that he stopped me that got my attention. It was the fact that he truly believed it to be sacred simply on the promise that, indeed, Abraham Lincoln was buried there under ten feet of concrete. It was sacred because of the works of a man—not a god or spirit entity, but a man. No Indian community holds in reverence any man. No man represents a spiritual connection between God and the Indian belief systems.

Yet here we are challenged and denied the right of true religious freedom. Congress has made attempts to correct this, but these actions have no effect. The American Indian Religious Freedom Act, Public Law No. 95-341, 92 Stat. 469 (Aug. 11, 1978) (commonly abbreviated to AIRFA), was as worthless as any treaty promising, "*As long as water flows, or grass grows upon the earth, or the sun rises to show your pathway, or you kindle your camp fires, so long shall you be protected from your present habitations.*[1]" AIRFA stated in SEC. 2: The President shall direct that various Federal departments, agencies, and other instrumentalities responsible for administering relevant laws evaluate their policies and procedures in consultation with Native traditional religious leaders in order to determine appropriate changes necessary to protect and preserve Native American religious cultural rights and practices. Twelve months after approval of this resolution, the President shall report back to Congress the results of his evaluation, including any changes which were made in administrative policies and procedures, and any recommendations he may have for legislative action.

The President of the time was Jimmy Carter, and he would not issue the necessary Memorandum allowing implementation of AIRFA. Was it because it conflicted with his Christian religious beliefs? I believe that to be the case, but I also remember that Jimmy Carter signed legislation terminating the Vietnam Veteran's education benefits.

I do not know of any tribe in California that does not respect their ancestors. Central to that fact is the belief that we will all be living together again. We do everything we can to protect the graves of our ancestors. The problem is with the "Everything we *can*," because there are still restrictions and challenges that limit what we can do. Private land ownership is probably the number one issue serving to prohibit Native American religious free expression. Private land ownership precludes gathering rights, ancestral territorial rights, burial rights, and ceremonial rights. Still, some private owners allow and even welcome events on their property.

Property is the one tangible defining asset when it comes to describing Native American religious beliefs. But even that has been violated—whether knowingly or unknowingly, the impact is the same. There are certain sacred values associated with one's life that transcend this world unless we direct it to be otherwise. "Associated grave goods" are items that are placed in the grave of a person because there is an unbreakable bond between that person and the material culture which that person chose to define one's self. At any time during my life, I can choose to part with, give away, or even sell any part of the material culture associated with me. If I do not, then it is forever mine and not to be disturbed even in my grave.

Dwight Dutschke once offered me this explanation: robbing a grave is the same as walking in to a person's home and removing the furniture, the television, and other personal possessions while the only thing that person can do is sit there and watch it happen. In the instance of Indian burials, the associated grave goods are their possessions in the next world and the property of no one else.

So, is Indian religion material-based, spiritual in nature, monotheistic, god-fearing, ancestor worship, or simply a conglomeration of fairy tales and myths as is the common representation taught in schools? The simple answer is that Indian religion just *is*. It is because it happens, just like the ghost ship in Vietnam or my great uncle changing into a bear. It is built upon beliefs that we have been blessed with resources that define our culture and religious practices. Why do the fish come back? Why does the deer stand and offer itself up as food? Why does the Blue Jay gossip? Why does the coyote really howl at the moon? Whether we know the answer or not, the simple fact is that these things just *are*.

Know your enemies' ways. It is through this knowledge that we may achieve peace. I learned this at a young age, and it seems to be universal among many Indian communities. But what has the American citizen learned about the American Indian, for years known as their enemy?

I had an opportunity to meet and speak with the State Superintendent of Public Instruction a year before the writing of this. I asked him, "When will California schools start teaching the truth about Captain Jack, the Modoc leader?" His response, "Who is Captain Jack?" I told him that is exactly the point. Everyone studying California Indian history should know the story of Captain Jack. I can guarantee you that the schools have moved nothing forward in teaching an accurate history of the California Indian. Did you know that more than $4 billion has been spent on mitigating Native American Archaeological sites? And what has the State gained from this expenditure of billions of dollars, and the average citizens' understanding of California Indians? The answer is an unequivocal, "Nothing."

The inability of the average citizen to believe in things that are evidenced to them because governments represents those things as not possible, is in itself blasphemous. If I see an Unidentified Flying Object or UFO, why do I need a government to validate what I saw? This is how it is for Indian people. The United States government operates in such a way that our religion is only valid when we are validated by Congress or the courts. We are because we are, and our religion is because it is. It is not surrounded with doubt and a need for miracles and prophets. It is God and us, and us and God.

Endnotes

1.   President Monroe, 1817.

CHAPTER 9

Across the Lagoon: The Inspiration behind the Northwest Indian Cemetery Protection Association (NICPA)

Walt Lara Sr. & Kishan Lara-Cooper

I AM CALLED "BLACKSNAKE" BY CLOSE FRIENDS AND BY PEOPLE WHO SIMPLY LIKE THE NAME. Once, somewhere around 1945 when all the Yurok kids from Requa, California were playing, they chose names from comic books of famous gun slingers like Black Bart, Lone Ranger, and Hop-Along Cassidy. After I finished my chores, I joined them, but all the good names were taken. The group told me that I had to be Blacksnake, the bad guy hero! Reluctantly, I took the name. Bill Tripp, who was getting out of the crummy,[1] heard the teasing and continued to call me "Blacksnake," and the name stuck. Bill worked for Coast Redwood Logging Company, located on AhPah Road five miles south of Klamath, California, as a timber faller. He liked that I was a hard worker, so three years later he hired me, at age fourteen. My job was to pack his gear and equipment; thus began my

Figure 2: Auth Weyatch traveling to the village of Chapekw.© 2019 Gary Colegrove. Courtesy of Ka'm-t'em Photography Project.

training in the woods as a timber faller. In 1952, I enlisted in the Army Airborne, unassigned. I served as squad leader platoon sergeant, acting field first sergeant, and jump master paratrooper trainer. I spent most of my time training the troops on how to survive in infantry combat. I believe that my experience in the woods, my leadership in the service, and my love for our people and guidance from my elders have led me to a life of advocacy for our people.

In this chapter, I would like to briefly share with you my memories and experiences that influenced the creation of the Northwest Indian Cemetery Protective Association (NICPA); the goals of the NICPA organization, including the struggle for cultural survival and autonomy, the preservation of our ceremonial sites and burial sites, and the repatriation of the bones and artifacts of our ancestors; and how the NICPA seriously impacted archaeological diggings, public attitudes about the desecration of native graves, and environmental and logging practices. At the end of the chapter, I would like to share a little about the revitalization of the Chapekw Jump Dance.

My grandmother, Josie, has been the biggest influence in my life. She came from the village of Espeu, known today as Gold Bluffs, located in the California State Park along the Pacific Coast. Miners had pretty much infiltrated the Pacific North Coast in their quest for gold during the turn of the century. Espeu became a target for their greed.

At eight years old, my Grandmother and her immediate family were given one day to vacate the village. Grandma Josie and her family traveled south to Chapekw, where the other side of her family lived. Once, my brother and I were playing on the beach, and I found a piece a gold. I immediately brought the gold to show my grandma. It brought back haunting memories for her, and she told me to "get rid of it, it will only cause trouble." From those types of occurrences, I learned at a young age that my grandma was a survivor.

Chapekw village crested Stone Lagoon, and during high tides the ocean water flowed over into the lagoon. This is where my grandmother grew up. Later, she and my grandfather raised five children at Oosamich, which was across the lagoon and up the hill from Chapekw. Oosamich overlooked Freshwater and Stone Lagoons. It was a traditional hunting area that my grandma's people would travel to when she was young. It had a hole, six feet deep by eight feet in diameter, that they dug. The perimeter of the hole was covered with brush. When they hunted, they would run elk down a v-shaped brush shoot into this pit, and then use their bows and arrow to kill the elk. Although not nearly as deep, the pit is still there today.

My Grandparents planted gardens, grew oats for the animals, raised livestock, fished daily, and had deer meat, since the deer would raid the oat fields on occasion. By the time I came along, my Grandparents were quite good at survival during a time of such tribulations for Indigenous people.

Grandma Josie was known for her sun-dried surf fish, as well as other sea foods that she could preserve or prepare. There were always friends and family that would travel from the Klamath River or Hoopa to trade for a suitcase or gunny sack full of her specialties. There was so much knowledge and history of the Yurok people that my grandmother shared. Stories that would make a person laugh and cry at the same time. I think about how hard she worked and it always brings a smile to my face.

At six years old, I learned to paddle my grandmother across the lagoon in a redwood dugout canoe, *Auth Weyotch*, to the village of

Chapekw to visit our uncle, Johnny Skirk. He was the last living resident of our village. I paddled my grandmother across the lagoon to visit every weekend. On our journey, Grandma told me about a hiding ground that was located across the lagoon just east of Chapekw. The first time that settlers came to Chapekw to invade the village, her family took shelter at the hiding ground. From there, they watched the destruction of their village, homes, baskets, and regalia. In the coming years, they would find themselves at the hiding ground on a number of occasions to escape genocidal acts. A few years ago, I was told that this hiding ground was "discovered" by archaeologists and identified as a village. However, this was a place of hiding for the people of Chapekw village. It's a shame that they had to use it so often that it had the same indicators of a village site. Grandma also talked to me about the Wonik-we le ga, Jump Dance Ceremony, that was held at Chapekw for the balance and healing of the world and the human beings within it. When the raids of Chapekw became rampant, they stopped having the ceremony and would pray in secret. They feared that they would all be killed if they were caught in prayer together. She described to me the last dance that she saw at Chapekw. I don't remember if she specifically told me, or if it was just understood, but it seemed clear that she invested this knowledge in me because she knew that I was going to be a part of making a change.

When I became an adult, Johnny Skirk passed away and we buried him at Chapekw in our ceremonial manner. I am hesitant to discuss the matter of burial, but I have come to the realization that these things need to be discussed so that our Indigenous knowledge will never be forgotten. I have learned that our people don't go to a "heaven" or a "hell" after their death. Rather, there are different dimensions of this earth where they reside. Although we may not see them, their energy is present, particularly in ceremony. When a person passes on to that next realm, we have a specific protocol that we follow. My elders have instructed me that we need to take care of business within three days, if possible; not to sleep or eat among non-living; to take the body out the window or side wall of the home; to spread ash along the exit; and to feed the spirit for ten days, just to name a few parts of the process. The most pertinent matter to this discussion is the inclusion of burial items or associated goods with the deceased. Not every person has associated grave goods buried with them. However, most of our people are "sent off" with three shells of dentalia to compensate the boatman for taking them over three different crossings. In addition, some of our people are buried with items that identify them with their contribution to the human realm. For example, a contributor to the Jump Dance might be buried with a Jump Dance feather. These items ensure their placement with our ancestors and our creators. To make certain that these items are in different form than they are in the human realm, we will break the items in specific places. These are a few of the guidelines that we followed in the burial of Awok[2] Johnny Skirk.

During the winter months, I was raised at Oosamich. On a daily basis, I could look across the lagoon to the old village of Chapekw. Throughout my life, I have been deeply connected to this place. In my late thirties, one morning, I awoke to witness several archaeology students digging up his (and others') graves. They were carrying buckets and shovels along the Chapekw village site. It took me about thirty minutes to get down the hill, cross the road, and drive up the beach to the village location. The County Sheriff met me at the beach and, upon closer investigation, we found a group of twenty or more people from Sonoma State University digging up bones and artifacts. This was not the first incident there. I had covered large holes around my Awok Aunt Maggie Skirk's grave with mesh screens from previous diggings. Looting of Indigenous graves had been a serious problem. It was a common practice for the State Park to allow universities to dig in village sites throughout California in the name of science. I think it must be said that it was not that long ago that genocidal practices to Native people were done in the name of God. In his book *Genocide in Northwestern California*, Jack Norton states:

> These aggressive invaders of the 1850s saw the valleys and forests as obstructions to their goal of Manifest Destiny. They were instructed by scripture, they said, reinforced by success, and driven by individualistic will, to believe they were destined to be the civilizers of the earth (p.3).

Whether it's in the name of God, science, or individual will, genocide is genocide, no matter what name it is done in.

Anyhow, the Yurok Tribe was not yet organized[3] at the time, and we hadn't received any help from the Bureau of Indian Affairs (BIA) to stop this injustice. So, Awok Milton Marks, Awok Glenn Moore I, Awok Luwana Brantner, Awok Dewey George, Awok Ella Norris, Awok Josephine Peters, Awok Annabelle Downs Doyal, and I immediately formed the Northwest Indian Cemetery Protection Association (NICPA) in the late 1960s. NICPA's mission was to protect Indian cemeteries, preserve ceremonial sites, and repatriate bones and artifacts. My uncle Milton had a vision that this organization would protect our burial sites from grave robbers, as well as protect our ceremonial sites. He and I brought together representation from all the local tribes in Northwestern California (175 members). He became the first chairperson for NICPA and dedicated his time to developing the NICPA constitution and bylaws, as well as grant writing. We were able to set up an office in Humboldt County and hired Jim Benson, an archaeologist. He also brought in funding for investigating and surveying roads that were being built over Indigenous sacred sites. Although we received some resistance from the non-Indian community, particularly those who had made a living on the artifacts of our ancestors, we obtained full support from the Board of Supervisors in Humboldt and Del Norte counties. We soon joined the Inter-Tribal Council of California, where we received state and national political support. Our advocacy was influential in making positive change in federal policy. NICPA met with John Echohawk, a lawyer and director of the Native American Rights Fund, to discuss issues in repatriation and protections of sacred sites. Soon after, in 1978, President Reagan signed the American Indian Religious Freedom Act, passed by Congress.

Governor Brown put together the California Native American Heritage Commission and appointed Uncle Milton as a commissioner. After Uncle's death, I served out his term, as well as an additional three terms, on the Commission, under four different Governors. I also served as the chairperson of NICPA. During that time, laws were developed addressing looting and desecration of "Indian"[4] graves and ceremonial sites. Through the Heritage Commission, we obtained access to the human remains stored in the warehouse of the State Park in Sacramento, California. Another member of NICPA and I made the trip to Sacramento to collect the human remains and associated grave goods that had been taken from the local villages of our area. As we walked through the warehouse, we were overtaken by the magnitude of devastation concealed in hundreds of labeled boxes. It was one of the most difficult tasks I have ever had. Although we brought home what we could on that trip from Sacramento, there was still another load that we were scheduled to pick up at a later date.

Within hours of our departure from Sacramento, the California

Archaeology Society filed an injunction, claiming that they wanted to keep the bones for the study of venereal disease. They had already had these bones for 45 years, yet they wanted to keep them to study a disease that made its way to America on boats! We took boxes of human remains back to Sumeg, Chapekw, Oreq, and Hoppel villages for reburial. *Awok* Ella Norris, the eldest member of our tribe at the time, struggled with the appropriate prayer (words) for reburial since there had never been such an atrocity of humankind known in our way of life.

During the 1980s, the United States Forest Service was considering building a paved road that would cut through the Chimney Rock area of the Six Rivers National Forest. They were also considering timber harvesting in the area. A study commissioned by the Forest Service reported that harvesting Chimney Rock area would irreparably damage grounds that had historically been used by Native Americans to conduct religious rituals. After the Forest Service decided to construct a road, the NICPA filed action against the Secretary of Agriculture, Richard Lyng. Chris Peters and Awok Sam Jones were key plaintiffs in the case. The Chimney Rock, aka Doctor Rock area, has been used for many generations by my people and the local tribes of Northern California and is still used today as spiritual training grounds. The question before the Supreme Court was, "Did the First Amendment Free Exercise clause prohibit the government from harvesting or developing the Chimney Rock area?" The Supreme Court concluded, "…even where the Government uses federal land in a manner that threatens the very existence of a Native American religion, the Government is simply not 'doing' anything to the practitioners of the faith"[5] and although "…the court accepted that the GO Road could have 'devastating effects on traditional Indian religious practices,'" it nonetheless held that "…the government was not *coercing* the Indians to act contrary to their religious beliefs."[6] Justice Sandra Day O'Connor held that, "The Constitution simply does not provide a principle that could justify upholding [the Indians'] claims…However much we wish that it were otherwise, government simply could not operate if it were required to satisfy every citizen's religious needs and desires."[7]

I often ponder on this statement. If not the first peoples of this land, whose religious needs and desires is the government "required" to satisfy? The answer to this question should serve as motivation to all young people to continuously advocate, educate, and engage in the protection of our religious freedom.

Following the five to three Court decision that the Forest Service was free to harvest the lands, we met with Congressmen Doug Bosco, who attached the preservation of Chimney Rock area to the Siskiyou Wilderness Bill. I am happy that to this day, our sacred area is protected. However, I can't help but be frustrated and hurt at the epistemicide, the threat to our way of knowing and understanding the world. I find injustice in the implication that a Wilderness Bill can protect animals, but the U.S. Constitution is not "required" to protect human beings. Furthermore, the decision on the Gasquet-Orleans Road set precedent and became the "Supreme Law of the Land." The Hawaiians, for example, have been affected by this court decision in their fight to protect their ceremonial areas around the volcanoes and parks. Our intent wasn't to set precedent for other Indigenous peoples; rather, we wanted to assert our Freedom of Religion.

As tribal governments became established throughout the state, they developed their own tribal preservation programs. NICPA trained those first cultural observers. Now this responsibility is done by the Tribal Historical Preservation Officers (THPO). I am pleased that my daughter has become a THPO Officer for the Hoopa Valley Tribe.

Thanks to many contributors, NICPA remained active and provided political advocacy to Indigenous peoples of Northwest California for nearly twenty years. Through these years of service, we developed cooperative working relationships with socially responsible archaeologists (such as Jim Benson, Rich Stradford, Janet Eidness, etc.) and helped to develop the field of compliance archaeology. Once tribes developed their own preservation programs, identified THPO officers, and asserted the Native American Graves Protection and Repatriation Act (NAGPRA)[8] and the American Indian Freedom of Religion Act, there was no longer a need for NICPA. We served our purpose in ensuring that our ancestors were protected.

Several years later, with the help of descendants from Chapekw and Chotchkwee, we were able to revitalize the jump dance ceremony at Chapekw. There is an intricate interaction between the human, natural, and spiritual realms during this ceremony. It is a time when we feed our ancestors; our dancers dance along the line of the physical and spiritual worlds; we pray to oolekwisha (the energies of the world); and our ancestors prepare to dance when we are finished. As such, the revitalization of this ceremony required extensive preparation. First, we had to ensure that the physical remnants of our ancestors were not disrupted.

Second, we had to make certain that their associated grave goods were protected. Then, we had to rebuild prayers items. Countless pieces of regalia had been burned in raids, stolen and sold to large collectors, or destroyed during natural disasters such as the 1955 and 1964 Klamath River Basin Floods. Numerous community members have contributed to cultural revitalization by learning to weave baskets, peel maple bark, construct feathers, tan hides, build canoes…and the list goes on.

Next, we had to bring back our other ceremonies to put us in compliance. We brought back the healing ceremonies at Requa, Wehlk-wew, Weitchpec, Sregon, and Sumeg; the prayer for humankind at Pecwan; the prayer for world renewal at Weitchpec; and the celebration of the transitioning of a young girl to a woman at Sumeg. I feel like these steps all had to take place before bringing it back home to the Jump Dance at Chapekw.

As daylight barely hit the island of Chapekw and the fog began to lift off of the lagoon water, I watched the soonay[9] and their helper paddle across the lagoon to build the fire that would begin the ceremony after an absence of 130 years. I was compelled by the emotion of the Auth Weyotch that glided with such purpose, the mist that surrounded it, and the memory of ancient knowledge that was shared by my grandmother. For ten days, we prayed for the balance and harmony of the world. We were presented with many life lessons that continue to inform us. My greatest reward through several Jump Dances at Chapekw now, has been seeing the young children learn and understand their significance in this world. They have never known a time when there was not a Jump Dance at Chapekw.

When I was 17 years old, I entered the service. I sent my hazardous duty monthly checks home to Grandma so that she could buy food. When I returned home from the service at twenty-one years old, my Grandma brought out a coffee can full of money and set it on the table in front of me. "What is that?" I asked her. "It is all of the money that you sent me," she replied. I told her that I sent her the money for her to spend, it was a thank you for all that she had done for me. "If you want to thank me for all that I have done," she responded "then you can do for your children as I have done for you."

Throughout my life, I have been influenced by my promise to my Grandmother. I have spoken out, fought, loved, collaborated, and strategized to protect sacred knowledge. I hope that I have been a good grandson and I wonder if I have done right by her. Now that

I'm wondering about things, I wonder where she buried that damn coffee can! Now that you have had a laugh, I need to say something to those that follow. You come from extraordinary people. You are resilient. You are powerful. You are humble. You are gifted. As such, you have a responsibility to "protect the treasure," the sacred knowledge of our ancestors.

Endnotes

1. An old converted truck used to transport loggers to and from work.
2. A Yurok term used to reference the deceased.
3. The Yurok Tribe was federally recognized but did not have a constitution, bylaws, or financial credibility at the time.
4. Quotes are used around "Indian" to indicate that this was a term utilized by the federal government at the time to refer to Indigenous peoples with their only tribal identities.
5. Caroline Kennedy and Ellen Alderman. *In Our Defense: Bill of Rights in Action.* (New York: HarperCollins Publishers, 1991), 67.
6. Ibid, 66.
7. Ibid, 66.
8. Native American Graves Protection and Repatriation Act, November 16, 1990. Public Law 101-601; 25 U.S.C et seq.
9. The man and woman who pray to the fire.

CHAPTER 10

Protecting Our Sacred Sites: Lyng V. Northwest Indian Cemetery Protective Association

Chris Peters & Chisa Oros

TO FULLY UNDERSTAND THE UNITED STATES SUPREME COURT CASE LYNG V. NORTHWEST INDIAN CEMETERY PROTECTION ASSOCIATION, OR THE GO (GASQUET – ORLEANS) ROAD CASE, ONE MUST UNDERSTAND THAT FOR INDIGENOUS PEOPLES OF NORTHWESTERN CALIFORNIA, RELIGIOUS BELIEFS AND EVERYDAY LIFEWAYS ARE ONE IN THE SAME. For those of us involved in this precedent-setting case, our young lives were greatly influenced by our elders who had been victims of violence and immense persecution from the California Gold Rush, the boarding school era, and the continuous racism and prejudice in our region. Our elders, and ourselves, were greatly impacted by the destruction and exploitation that occurred against our homelands and our ancestors by way of settler colonialism, the logging industry, degrading gold mining practices, and the numerous power and money-hungry manifestations of such industries that we were forced to partake in for our own survival. However, we always knew where we came from.

Whether we learned the place names later in life, or we were instilled with knowledge from our grandparents throughout our life, we knew that we belonged here.

First trip to Elk Valley

At an early age, we understood there was something very special about the area in the Siskiyou mountain region of what is known as the Puhlik-lah High Country. Our grandfather, Charles Stevens, and later uncle James Stevens (Uncle Jimmy), constructed or cleared trails from the coastal areas over the mountains into the interior Klamath River region. Generally, such trails would follow already established routes that were used for many years by local Native Peoples for passage or hunting. Often these trails would lead into the High Country and bypass many significant sacred places. Many stories passed through family members of the numerous adventures in remote places such as Flint Valley, Peak Eight, Doctor Rock, and Elk Valley. Uncle Jimmy would talk quite extensively about the beauty and the sacredness of these places and of their unique power and draw or special calling that would occupy his mind and his return on several occasions. Little did I know that these places would later become very significant in my personal life as well. My name is Chris Peters and I was a plaintiff in this long and protracted litigation to safeguard these and other sacred places throughout Native America.

My grandmother, Rose Donnelley, was taken from the Klamath River against her will and placed in the Indian boarding school at Carlisle, Pennsylvania in the early 1900s. As a result, she was heavily influenced by Christian theology. Uncle Jimmy also attended church and was not what one might define as a "traditional Native person." He did not participate in cultural activities or involve himself in ceremonial recovery. However, as a young man he would often hear stories from Native elders that knew of his adventures in the Doctor Rock area, and they would speak to him about the spiritual powers of the area that were sought and held by Puhlik people for many generations. These special powers were and are used for healing, "making medicine" for ceremonies, and often for individual strength or personal self-actualization. He also heard stories of the "Bad Place," a large rock located in the High Country used to secure negative energy or power for making bad medicine on other people, families, or sometimes an entire village community.

All the traditional knowledge contained within the stories was still very current and ever-present on the minds of many of the elders that recalled individuals or family members who had dedicated their lives in search of spiritual power. Uncle Jimmy thought that perhaps it was his fascination with such stories that was responsible for his persistent desire to return to the High Country—or, possibly, it was the spiritual nature of these places that beckoned his return on repeated occasions.

In the early 1960s, I was perhaps twelve or thirteen years old when I accompanied Uncle Jimmy and a close cousin, Don Young, on a trip to Elk Valley. Both of them worked together at the old Morick Lumber Mill and had been planning this trip to Elk Valley for many weeks. This would be my first camping trip into the High Country, and I was somewhat excited to see the spectacular nature of the area and the many sacred places used by our people for generations of time. My uncle had an old 1952 Chevy truck and it was loaded to the max with camping gear, but still I could secure my location in the back of the truck among the many boxes of food and sleeping bags. As we began our journey, I recall having countless and conflicting emotions that ranged from excitement at one end to a haunting fear at the other extreme. Our destination was Elk Valley a very remote place located in the Siskiyou Mountains, far from any town or other human beings; we would be isolated and very much alone. The route taken was up through the forks of Bluff Creek and over the mountains, connecting with small "roads" that might best be described as goat trails. I quickly learned that my foremost responsibility, and perhaps the primary reason for my invitation to accompany them on the trip, was to run ahead of the truck to roll large rocks off the road to enable the truck's passage. My location in the back of the truck bed made it easy to access the road for removing rocks.

The 1952 Chevy truck was old at the time; however my uncle had all the confidence in the world that this vehicle could make it to places where others could not. On this one-way road, we came upon many rockslides that sometime required more road repair or re-construction before we could continue. Often these rockslides would be in areas where there were steep embankments on the driver's side of the vehicle, with vertical cliffs reaching hundreds of feet below. At such locations, I was always impressed with how the old truck could continue to move across these narrow passages, and even more impressed with the desire of my uncle and our friend to continue the journey.

At the top of Serpentine Ridge, we stopped to look at the mountains; across the deep valley stood Chimney Rock in all of its majestic prominence, and just below was Turtle Rock. On both of these large rocks, one could find many naturally formed seats where our ancestors would sit for many days in deep meditation in search of spiritual intervention. Off in the distance, my uncle pointed out small outcroppings on the ridge that led from the gradually sloping mountain of Peak Eight to the infamous Doctor Rock, where Puhlik medicine women would find their special powers to heal Puhlik-lah members suffering from human illness. I would hear my uncle and Don Young discuss these locations and future dates when journeys would take them that way.

As we started to descend into Elk Valley, the road became even more narrow and treacherous, requiring a greater amount of repair to allow access for the truck. It was a late summer evening as we reached the valley floor. I could sense a presence in the air that I had not ever experienced before, a palatable manifestation of past events and a lingering mist that was somewhat scary and had restricted my radius of exploration to only a short distance away from camp. The campsite was situated in a small valley that was very green and dissected by the headwaters of Blue Creek. The valley was sheltered with brush that covered the water, in such a way that only small areas of the creek were open to dip into for drinking water. The base of the valley was shaded by towering Cedar and Douglas fir trees and various smaller brush that masked the valley floor.

As we set up camp, we discussed short hikes that were planned for the coming day. Throughout the night, the sensations that I described earlier continued to plague me, as I awakened many times to sounds of animals and an occasional falling branch. During those awaking times, I recalled the story that Elk Valley was a place where elders and spiritual leaders would historically meet to arbitrate significant concerns and plan strategies that could be jointly implemented to overcome issues that confronted our village communities. I was confident that at such meetings our leaders would call in the ancestors and the Wo-gay (the spiritual beings) to help in their deliberations.

In the morning, we quickly gathered our camping gear and a supply of fresh drinking water from the creek and made our way back up the rugged road for a few miles to Flint Valley for the remaining days of our camping. Perhaps Uncle Jimmy and Don also sensed the presences of an unexplainable sensation that filled the air. No one discussed this feeling, however all of us were confident that something profound was present, possibly the spirit of our ancestors or just a knowing that we shouldn't be in the valley now and we needed to find a different camping spot.

Throughout my teenage years, I was fortunate to make several other trips in to the High Country and even returned to Elk Valley, but I never have felt the same sensations or experienced the same level of mystery that I had during my first visit to this wondrous valley.

Pre-GO Road

In the late 1960s, I had returned home from college during the summers and had secured employment with a logging company. At that time, the logging and deforestation was taking place in the mountains near Orleans, where they learned that the U.S. Forest Service had begun to construct a high-quality highway from the small community of Orleans leading in to the mountains. They did not know for what purpose, or the destination the highway would take, but all of the Native American loggers were very much aware that it was heading directly into the Puhlik-lah High Country. Little did they know that the U.S. Forest Service, who is responsible for managing the National Forests, was assisting the timber industry to increase their financial profits by building a logging road directly into our sacred High County and through our sacred places. In fact, the U.S. Forest Service had initiated planning for the GO Road and logging the abundant forest of Blue Creek watershed as early as 1963.

In 1972, the U.S. Forest Service became more public about what would soon become known as the *Blue Creek Unit Management Plan.* This presented a plan in which, among other horrendous things, the timber industry could increase access to the large forests within the Blue Creek drainage. The plan was "sold" to the public as necessary to provide recreation access to the area and to control wild fires. Later, in 1974, the U.S. Forest Service circulated a Draft Environmental Impact Statement of the proposed Blue Creek area, and within this document they described their intent to desecrate our sacred areas at the instigation of the logging industry. The U.S. Forest Service Regional Archaeologist, who completed his investigation, "concluded that there will be no adverse effects on the Native Sacred Places."

In 1975, I had completed his university career and returned home with the intent of reengaging in the cultural and spiritual lifeways of the Puhlik-lah. This was an exciting time for the local Native communities; a renaissance of Tribal cultures and ceremonial practices were beginning to flourish. Indian card games, brush dance ceremonies, and regalia making were blossoming, and it seemed that almost everybody was involved with rebuilding Native lifeways in some respect or the other. Over the course of the next few years, I joined with a small cadre of local Native peoples who were also interested in cultural revitalization.

At that time, they would often gather collectively and organize song and dance classes and traditional regalia making activities, and would come together for many ceremonies. Among them were Puhlik-lah and Karuk people such as Walter Lara Sr., Brian Tripp, Julian Lang, and many others who proved to be notable individuals in the quest to reestablish the spiritual understanding and cultural lifeways among Native Peoples. They, too, were mentored and received ongoing direction from many significant elders of our tribes and families.

After several trips to Chimney Rock and conversations with Tribal Mentors where they deepened their understanding of esoteric knowledge associated with Earth Based Spiritual Theology, a greater urgency for the reestablishment of the Pecwan Jump Dance was forced upon them. The U.S. Forest Service indicated they were moving forward with plans to construct the GO Road, and they began to execute their persistent threat to destroy many sacred places. The Chimney Rock area was needed to secure the spiritual energy that would bring purpose and meaning to the Pecwan ceremony, and now this important area lay directly in harm's way.

A small coalition of Native leaders was emerging who knew quite well that the GO Road had the potential for inflicting a significant blow on the cultural renaissance that was currently blossoming in Northern California. They also realized that this pernicious plan of the U.S. Forest Service had to be stopped for the future of the Puhlik-lah. After extensive administrative review, including consideration of other routes and appeals by the environmental and Native American groups during 1976, the Secretary of Agriculture authorized the construction of the Chimney Rock Corridor.

Figure 3: Walt Lara Sr. standing at the end of the GO Road in the High Country. © 2019 Gary Colegrove. Courtesy of Ka'm-t'em Photography Project.

Community Organizing

Here in Northern California, the mid 1970s presented many critical and ongoing urgent issues that demanded immediate time and attention. Our community organizing throughout rural and reservation-based Native communities was beginning to gain success, and we could now rally Native peoples to assert their basic human and cultural rights as well as to articulate the cultural and socio-political responsibilities associated with such rights. Other issues that figured prominently were the need to stop both clear-cut timber harvesting and the desecration of species habitat that had both been unchecked for many years in local forests. The widespread and indiscriminate use and abuse of herbicide and pesticide spraying, which proved to be very carcinogenic and presented a significant health risk for local Native basket weavers, was another major organizing challenge. Additionally, the mercury or quicksilver runoff of Gold Rush era mining practices continued to poison and plague our people. Even 125 years after the mines actively stopped using mercury to separate gold particles, this historic practice continued to inflict major health problems and birth defects within Native communities.

At this critical time of change and transformation in Northern California, many of us were also involved in front line battles to protect cultural resources (such as grave protection and repatriation of human remains and burial items) as well as the assertion of our rights and responsibilities to continue fishing on the Klamath River. This was a time when Native communities began to assert our own self-determined futures and build movements that shocked the long-standing foundation of Euro-American society and white imperialist hierarchy which was so prevalent in Indian Country.

In addition to all the above, much of my personal community organizing focused on the establishment of a regional, Native-directed, community-based organization called Tri County Indian Development Council, Inc. The organization was comprised of local leaders who would assume responsibility for bringing about change and cultural restoration throughout our homelands. Our organizing efforts sought to engage Native community organizations in a three-county region including Humboldt, Del Norte, and Siskiyou county. It would also involve Tribal Nations including Puhlik-lah, Tolowa, and Karuk peoples. The Tri-County Indian Development Council was critically necessary to secure programs and services to address the many social and economic conditions within local Native communities. It also proved to be a valuable funding vehicle needed to support and maintain the expanding cultural renaissance that was flourishing in many of our communities. Lastly and perhaps more importantly, Tri-County Indian Development Council supported the local movements to rebuild stronger Native communities, and funded much of the opposition to the white settler colonial imperialism that had oppressed Native identity and cultural paradigms for generations.

Although much time and valuable resources were committed to such a monumental organizing task and front-line battles, many Native community organizers continued efforts to restore sacred dance houses, organized ceremonies, and continued the valuable work with our many cultural mentors. During this organizing and community engagement, we would hear a growing opposition from Native Peoples regarding the U.S. Forest Service plans to construct the GO Road, including the threat that it would impose upon the Earth Based Spiritual Theology and lifeways of Native Peoples. I recall several meetings in the homes of the late Sam Jones and Calvin Rube, as well as other Puhlik-lah cultural leaders, where strategies were discussed to launch administrative appeals and ultimately to file suit in opposition to the government's intrusion into our sacred places and the proposed logging activities that would destroy the High Country. At one such meeting, I recall Mr. Rube, a man of significant standing within the Yurok cultural community, voice his vehement opposition to filing any litigation to stop the GO Road in federal court. On repeated occasions, he would caution us not to litigate spiritual issues in the American court system because it would result in a significant loss of spiritual and ceremonial rights throughout the nation; such adjudicating would also set a dangerous precedent that would cause irreparable damage to the natural world. In retrospect, we should have better considered the wisdom of this cultural icon.

As these discussions among cultural leaders continued, it became more apparent that proposed route of the GO Road would dissect the Chimney Rock complex and destroy a sacred area that is central and indispensable to the spiritual life of our peoples. The elders were very clear that this place held sacred knowledge that is central to the efficacy of Earth healing and Earth renewal Ceremonies. The concept of a "place" holding esoteric knowledge may only be germane to the Indigenous paradigm, but nonetheless, this place and the knowledge it holds has guided Native spiritual life since time immemorial. Perhaps more importantly, through stories and oral history, the elders described a deep cultural knowledge, passed through generations of ancestors, that these sacred places were not only sacred for human/spiritual benefit but for all of life.

To destroy the sacred High Country would have an everlasting negative impact on the entire ecosystem of the Blue Creek drainage and beyond. We also came to realize that the loss of these sacred places would destroy our spiritual and human consciousness and, sometime, in the not-so-distant future, would destroy our cultural and sovereign identity as well. We would cease to be a Tribal Nation. These conversations were happening at a time when we were beginning to uncover our own personal and spiritual identities and revitalizing traditional ceremonies and Earth Based Spiritual practices throughout the Yurok Tribal homelands.

Concurrent to our organizing efforts was an ongoing battle along the Klamath River for fishing rights. These battles often included violent struggles with the state and federal government and local and regional law enforcement agencies. The fishing rights battle will be the subject of another chapter of this writing, so we will refrain from detailed discussion of this historic conflict; suffice to say that Native Peoples stood strong and asserted our rights on the Klamath River. Other front-line battles with unemployed timber and lumber mill workers were just as fierce, as they blamed Indians for the sharp decline in the forest industry. Many aggressive conflicts grew from our effort to stop the U.S. Forest Service's diabolic plan of timber cutting in the Blue Creek Drainage.

The final and perhaps deepest dagger in the backs of our community organizing came from own Tribal folks who were involved in the Jessie Short case, where individual Native Peoples of the Klamath River region sought to clarify issues of land rights. The plaintiffs in the Short litigation often criticized us for community organizing in our Puhlik-lah homelands and for reasserting Tribal consciousness. It had been the long-standing legal position of the Short litigants that we Puhlik-lah (Yuroks) did not exist as a Tribal Nation, and were now only members of an extended Hoopa Valley Reservation. This denial of our birth right as a distinct nation of peoples, for personal economic gain, was contrary to our assertion of Puhlik-lah religious freedom in the GO Road case.

As many Puhlik-lah elders proceeded to increase their involvement with the Yurok High Country and made more strategic efforts to stop the GO Road, I was approached in my office by Abby Abananti, who was at that time the Directing Attorney for the California Indian Legal Services (CILS). CILS had assumed the role as lead attorney for a growing number of Tribal elders who were opposing the GO Road construction, and as such were involved in filing several administrative appeals on behalf of the elders. During her visit, Abby requested that I join in the litigation as a plaintiff and formally oppose the construction of the GO Road. Little did I know that her visit would change the direction of my life and formalize my involvement in what would soon become a national legal case in Native America. As she approached me, she brought a small wall hanger, a sign that read, "*If you're being run out of town, get in front of the crowd and make it look like a parade.*" This wall hanger summarizes the opposition that we were facing in all aspects of community organizing, and served as a constant reminder of the opposition that we would face in the near future as the GO Road Case proceeded.

Native Use of the High Country

The historic relationship that Native Peoples of Northern California have experienced with the U.S. Federal Government, as well as with non-Native settlers, was particularly destructive and genocidal in nature. Most non-Native Americans revere the United States as a nation that is enshrined in a philosophy that protects religious freedom and adheres to the dictates of acceptance of all nationalities. However, the reality of daily life for Native Peoples of Northern California was replete with public and legalized brutality, slave auctions, rape of women and young girls, government-funded murder, and some of the bloodiest massacres that have ever been perpetrated upon human beings. Our ancestors struggled to preserve a cultural/spiritual identity that defines who we are today. They have fought and died for a spiritual belief-system that intricately linked the well-being of humanity to the natural world and the health of our place on Earth. During this bleak history of our peoples, the fundamental right to freely exercise traditional, Earth-based spiritual belief systems has been consistently undermined, ever since this nation's settlement by non-Native people. In fact, despite the highly-celebrated list of "freedoms" bestowed within the United States Constitution, Federal Law and Policy has imposed a "conquerors" mentality and disposition on the lives of Native Peoples, and, to this day, has seriously threatened the physical and spiritual survival of our peoples.

In 1977, the U.S. Forest Service issued a draft Environmental Impact Statement (EIS) that described their proposal for upgrading the existing unpaved road that ran through the Chimney Rock Area. This is the same non-maintained goat trail that I had traveled on with my Uncle Jimmy and cousin Don during a trip into Elk Valley. Despite the cultural and spiritual significance expressed by many local community members on this draft EIS, the U.S. Forest Service commissioned a study of American Indian cultural and religious sites in the area. The study was implemented by Theodoratus and Associates, a cultural anthropological research firm, and was to inform the U.S. Forest Service on the effects of the EIS and resulting actions it would have on Native religious and culture practices in the Chimney Rock area. This would, of course, include the planned timber cutting in this section of the Six Rivers National Forest.

Theodoratus and Associates completed a comprehensive ethno-graphic, archaeological, and historical assessment of the High Country, and in doing so reached out to a significant number of *Puhlik-lah*, Karuk, and Tolowa cultural leaders. I recall sitting on top of Doctor Rock with Dr. Dorothea J. Theodoratus and Karuk cultural leader Brian Tripp as we explained the purpose and use of this sacred location. We each told stories that were shared with us by knowledgeable mentors, stories that described women or sometimes men who were recognized in our communities as having special powers for healing other Tribal members. After periods of time in the sweathouse and completing other purification rituals, those with special powers would make their long journey to Doctor Rock to acquire spiritual power to enhance their personal healing abilities. We explained that this ritual might include many days of fasting, deep and prolong periods of meditation, dancing, singing, and jumping until the person achieved a heightened level of spiritual consciousness—or, as some might suggest, a connection with I'lah-lik-washaa (the creative energy that is all around us)—and in this manner, the person would acquire a special energy and perfect their innate healing ability. As we sat with Dr. Theodoratus, we also pointed to Chimney Rock and described the proposed route of the GO Road and the significant intrusion that it would have on this sacred area and on the pristine nature of the ecology.

A part of Theodoratus and Associates was Dr. Joseph L. Chartkoff, who led the archaeological investigation. Shortly after his arrival he retained the services of James Stevens, my Uncle Jimmy, to serve as a Cultural Resource Person—more aptly described as a "Cultural Guide"—to help locate the many sacred places in the High Country. The archaeological team described these places as "Prayer Seats." My uncle had already known the location of many of such places, but after becoming familiar with the area, the investigative team was able to locate several hundred more prayer seats throughout the High Country. Many were located in areas that would be destroyed with any intrusion road building would bring.

As the Theodoratus Study was still in progress and the administrative appeal process was proving to fall upon deaf ears with the U. S Forest Service, Congress passed the American Indian Religious Freedom Act, (Public Law No. 95-341, 92 Stat. 469 (Aug. 11, 1978) (commonly abbreviated to AIRFA), codified at 42 U.S. C. § 1996, a United States federal law, enacted by joint resolution of the Congress in 1978.). Prior to the AIRFA, many Native American religious practices had been prohibited by law and criminalized. To rectify this deplorable situation,

AIRFA was enacted to return "…basic civil liberties, and to protect and preserve for American Indians their inherent right of freedom to believe, express, and exercise the traditional religious rights and cultural rights." These rights include, but are not limited to, access to sacred sites and freedom to worship through ceremonial and traditional ritual. The Act also required policies of all governmental agencies to eliminate their interference with the "…free exercise of Native American religion, based on the First Amendment, and to accommodate access to and use of religious sites."

Finally, we believed that Congress had taken the action needed to stop the GO Road. We anticipated that the U.S. Department of Agriculture would soon establish the necessary policies that would cause the Six Rivers National Forest Service to cease and desist all intrusion into our sacred places and allow us to freely exercise our First Amendment Rights.

Still energized from the passage of the American Indian Religious Freedom Act and the potential victory that it presented, we were equally excited when the Theodoratus Report was finally completed. The report, titled *Cultural Resources of the Chimney Rock Section, Gasquet-Orleans Road,* was submitted to the Six Rivers National Forest Service in April of 1979. In its final recommendations, the report criticized the U.S. Forest Service for not considering the physical and historical significance and religious importance of the Chimney Rock section. From the many interviews with Puhlik-lah, Tolowa, and Karuk cultural leaders, the Theodoratus Report further stated that, because of the long and continuous use of the area—as well as the documented connections of Native use—from a long time prior to the arrival of settler colonialism in our region, the only appropriate management of such land should be its preservation in a natural state.

Please keep in mind that the Theodoratus Report was commissioned by the U.S. Forest Service in order to "…evaluate policies and procedures to protect Native American religious cultural rights and practices." In effect, the Report was to establish a "guideline" by which the U.S. Forest Service would be able to understand the importance of land to Native American culture and spiritual beliefs.

The commissioned study found that the entire area, "…is significant as an integral and indispensable part of Indian religious conceptualization and practice." It also found that the continuations of such practices are dependent upon maintaining privacy, silence, and an undisturbed natural setting. The study concluded that constructing a road along any of the available routes "…would cause serious and irreparable damage to the sacred areas, which are an integral and necessary part of the belief systems and lifeway of Northwest California Indian peoples," and recommended against completing the GO Road.

In May of 1981, shortly after the findings and recommendations of the Theodoratus Report were submitted to the U.S. Forest Service, the Keeper of the National Register of Historic Places declared 13,500 acres of the Puhlik-lah High Country eligible for listing as a Historic Place. The area would be referred to as the "Helkau District," or a place of spiritual significance used for "prayer" by Puhlik Peoples. Shortly thereafter, the Advisory Council Chairman wrote to Secretary of Agriculture John R. Block stating: "…it is fundamentally wrong to so seriously impact an area held sacred by a group of American citizens, if any feasible alternatives exist."

The GO Road Litigation

In 1982, despite the findings in Theodoratus Report and the opposition of their internal staff in the Department of Agricultural and several other federal agencies, the U.S. Forest Service issued the Final Environmental Impact Statement that included the construction of the Gasquet-Orleans Road. The Forest Service claimed it could mitigate the adverse impact on the free exercise of the Puhlik-lah, Tolowa, and Karuk Tribal Nation's religions by avoiding any archaeological areas and protecting specific religious sites from road constructing and logging activity. Again, the position taken by the Forest Service was in stark contrast to the recommendations from their own commissioned report, the Keeper of the National Register of Historic Places, and the provisions of the American Indian Religious Freedom Act.

Immediately thereafter, distinguished tribal elders such as Jimmie James, Sam Jones, and Lowana Branter, who were purposefully selected by Abby Abinanti as plaintiffs for this legal battle, petitioned the U.S. District Court for an injunction against the U.S. Forest Service-planned road construction and timber cutting in the sacred High Country. Although the California Indian Legal Services filed the petition, Abby had left the organization to establish a private practice. The lead Attorney for CILS was now Marilyn Miles. I was selected as a plaintiff to serve as a liaison with the "younger Native Community" and to provide an important link for the continued use of this sacred area for future generations.

Later, our case was consolidated with other actions that included the plaintiffs of several nonprofit corporations, including many environmental organizations as well as the Northwest Indian Cemetery Protective Association (NICPA), who would assume the role as the lead plaintiff in this protracted legal battle. We were also joined by the State of California, acting through and on behalf of the Native American Heritage Commission. At that time, we firmly believed that because of the passage of AIRFA, the designation of a historic place, and the growing levels of support from all sections of society, that we were prepared and well poised for this court case.

After the U.S. District Court heard the case, including testimony from several Puhlik-lah elders who shared personal and esoteric knowledge of the area, the District Court Judge agreed with the plaintiffs and issued a permanent injunction stopping the Forest Service from constructing the Chimney Rock section of the Gasquet-Orleans Road and from implementing their plan to clear-cut much of the Blue Creek Forest. (Northwest Indian Cemetery Protective Assn. v. Peterson, 565 F.Supp. 586 (1983)). The court found that both the plans for road building and tree cutting would violate our First Amendment rights to freely exercise our religion. In this case the court held that the proposed Forest Service Action "…would seriously damage the salient visual, aural, and environmental qualities of the high country." The local Native communities were elated!

This represented a major victory for the High Country and for American Indian Religious Freedom for all Tribal Nations. Perhaps even more importantly, this decision legally recognized that religious and sacred places existed here in North America and that sacred places were not associated only with Abrahamic Religions, which contend that sacred places exist only outside of the Americas. Thus, this was truly a victory for all U.S. Earth Based Theologies. And, because of the unique paradigms that such spiritual theologies hold, this was a victory for all humanity.

In retrospect, many of the people that were closely associated with the court proceedings believe that it was the persuasive and compelling testimonies provided by the elderly Puhlik-lah women that were solely responsible for this favorable and critical court decision. However, as suggested earlier, when litigating spiritual issues in the American judicial system, victories are sometimes short-lived. The U.S. Forest Service appealed the District Court injunction to the U.S. Court of Appeals for the Ninth Circuit.

The Pecwan Wela-Welagah

In early September of 1984, following the significant victory of the Northwest Indian Cemetery Protective Assn. v. Peterson at the U.S. District Court, a small group of burgeoning cultural leaders launched the Earth Healing Ceremony at the village of Pecwan. It had been over 45 years that this sacred ceremony, the Wela-Welagah, lived only in the memories of Tribal Elders. In preparation for ceremony, they had completed several trips to Chimney Rock and were already very spiritually active within the High Country. The cultural interviews and the re-discovering of the "Prayer Seats" described in the Theodoratus Report, as well as the culturally rich and esoteric knowledge provided in the testimony of Puhlik-lah and Karuk elders during the District Court Hearing, confirmed their resolve to move forward with the Pecwan Wela'welagah Ceremony. The knowledge and directions of re-establishing a profound relationship with the spirits that they found in the Puhlik-lah High Country was confirmed with this Jump Dance Ceremony, and their participation in a growing campaign to stop the Gasquet-Orleans Road was significantly enhanced.

From the knowledge and inspiration gathered, they came to understand that their elders and ancestors are/were very intelligent human beings. Either from their astute observations of the natural world or from "Original Instructions" provided at some very important time in our cosmology by the spirit people or the Wogay, they understood that certain places in our homelands contained special powers and are considered sacred. Doctor Rock, Chimney Rock, Little Medicine Mountain, and other places in the High Country contain such sacredness and are central and indispensable to the Puhlik-lah spiritual values and lifeways. The connections with such places are critical to the ongoing efficacy of the many ceremonies of the Puhlik people. Specific protocols, passed through generations of ancestors, provide instructions on how humans can access spiritual power or knowledge used for health, healing, and self-actualization. The elders and ancestors knew from legends how Ceremonies came to be and the important connection and spiritual protocols that each ceremony has with the sacredness of the High Country.

In the effort to re-establish the Earth Healing Ceremony, or Wela'welagah, at Pecwan, Elders spoke extensively about the need to complete "Training in The High Country," an important first step that we had come to believe was the conditioning of our physical body for the demanding ordeal of fasting, grueling hikes in mountainous regions, and scaling large rocks. So, they began to exercise and build physical endurance. Although this enhanced endurance proved to be very much needed, the Elders reference to "training" was quite different from the building of physical strength; rather, they were encouraging an enhanced mental and psychological stamina that would accommodate prolonged periods of concentration and focused meditation. They came to the understanding that to receive a spiritual connection, they first had to clear their minds and open themselves to achieve such transcendence. For the Wela'welagah to successfully happen, they knew that building mental fortitude was needed, and "Training in the High Country"—or more specifically, at Chimney Rock—was an important aspect of this practice known as "Medicine Making." With the support and direction of elders, and for the efficacy of the Pecwan Jump Dance, they found themselves engaged in the process of Medicine Making.

In the evening hours, as directed, we "spoke to the fire" and burned woth pey or medicine root. Later we would jump, sing, and call for the Wo-gay to help establish a connection with the creative force of I'lah-lik-washaa (that which is all around us). The Wo-gay are spirit beings; some suggested that they also include the ancestors, provide a vital link to the spirit, and fulfill the process of Medicine Making.

The process of jumping, singing, and calling for the Wo-gay would last for many hours, and often times well into the night. The daylight hours were dedicated to a much more difficult process that included deep meditation and prolonged and continuously driven thought. As directed by our mentors, the focus of this concentrated thought was to open their minds and souls to receive the spiritual power needed to achieve the profound purpose of the Wela'welagah: to heal the Earth. They would return to Chimney Rock and engage this process of Medicine Making several times before the Pecwan Wela'welagah Ceremony.

Victories for Sacred Places

On September 24, 1984, just a few short days after the completion of the Finish-up Dance of the revitalized Wela'welagah at Pecwan, the U.S. Congress passed the California Wilderness Act (PL 98-425, 98 Stat. 1619). In addition to mitigating California's concern for the RARE (Roadless Area Review and Evaluation) by designating and expanding several of the States Wilderness Areas and National Parks (Lassen, Angeles, John Muir act.), the legislation also created the Siskiyou Wilderness area that encompassed a significant portion of the Chimney Rock section of the Gasquet-Orleans Road. With this action, Congress removed the main purpose for constructing the GO Road by officially stopping the Forest Service's plan for timber cutting and associated logging road building in the Puhlik-lah High Country. However, despite all of the favorable provisions of the California Wilderness Act, the construction of the GO Road was still under review by the U.S. Court of Appeals for the Ninth Circuit, so the Wilderness Act left a strip of land needed to build the controversial road out of the wilderness designation. Little did we know that this set-aside of a small, six-mile strip of land would require the intervention by the Supreme Court of the United States.

In 1986, subsequent to the passage of the California Wilderness Act, a three-judge panel of the Court of Appeals, Ninth Circuit, affirmed the lower court's ruling and held that "…building a road through, and harvesting timber in, the High Country would burden the Indians' freedom of religion." Historically, all First Amendment cases brought before the U.S. judicial system were required to pass a public interest test, whereby the State (Government) is responsible for demonstrating an "overriding public benefit" for any action where legal opposition is raised. In the case of the GO Road, the provisions of the California Wilderness Act eliminated all timber cutting within the High Country and rendering any argument for overriding public benefits moot. Therefore, the government held that the Forest Service had failed to show a compelling public interest in Gasquet-Orleans Road Project.

The decision of the Appellate Court's to uphold the religious freedoms of Native Peoples here in Northern California was considered a major victory. However, because of the precedent-setting nature of the Gasquet-Orleans Road case, the decision was also very critical for the protection of the sacred lands used by Native Peoples throughout Indian

Country. For many American Indians, sacred sites are vital storehouses of traditional power and spiritual knowledge, and to have the American judicial system recognize the vital importance of such places was considered a major victory for all Native Nations. The grievous danger posed by mining operations, deforestation, recreation development, and other corporate and governmental interests to sacred lands mandated one of the most urgent calls to action throughout Indian Country. Many Tribal Nations whose Sacred Lands stood in harm's way of such pernicious land management practice were closely following the progress and setbacks experienced in the battle to save the Puhlik-lah High Country. Historically, the greed of land developers and their desire for profit had been more quickly considered and incorporated into land management policies than were the religious traditions of Native Peoples and the fact that our sacred lands were being desecrated. Before the lower courts rendered their favorable decision in the GO Road case, we could only anticipate the continued ravaging of our sacred lands, much the same as our ancestors had experienced in the late 1800s by the U.S. Cavalry.

The Supreme Court Hearing

This glorious taste of victory again proved to be only short-lived. The Forest Service, under the leadership of Richard Lyng, Secretary of the U.S. Department of Agriculture, appealed the decisions of the two lower courts to the U.S. Supreme Court in *Richard E. Lyng, Secretary of Agriculture v. Northwest Indian Cemetery Protection Association*. It should be noted that much of the clear cutting of ancient forest and road building in the Chimney Rock area was legislatively stopped with the California Wilderness Act. The only issue that was brought before the Supreme Court was the First Amendment Rights of Native Peoples. The First Americans rights to freely exercise our religious beliefs were being questioned by the highest court in the nation.

During the few years leading up to the 1987 Supreme Court Hearing, the meaning and understanding of this Court action moved slowly within the local Native Community. The adverse impacts that a negative Court decision would have on the spiritual beliefs and lifeways of Native Peoples here in Northern California was very difficult to imagine, but the larger impacts that such a negative decision could potentially bring to the spiritual paradigms of Native Peoples and the natural systems throughout the Nations was even more difficult to comprehend. But we were winning! So, much of the negative consequences of the Supreme Court was eliminated from our thinking. In fact, the very nature of the spiritual understanding that we sought to protect forbid such negative thinking and mandated positive directed thoughts. As discussed earlier, Medicine Making requires a formal process of positive and continuously driven thought directed at achieving a desired result or goal. For the situation that we now faced, the magnitude of focused, positive energy would need to be monumental and would require the involvement of many Native communities of peoples. I recall conversations with Cultural Leader Calvin Rube where he suggested that the GO Road case needed to reach beyond the local Tribal communities and seek the support and involvement of Tribal Nations that still practiced the High Mountain Medicine. The spiritual energy of Native Peoples that understood the magnitude of this situation needed to be sequestered if we were to forage a victory.

Native Peoples began to realize that, after the overwhelming victory at the District Court, our direct involvement in the litigation to protect our religious rights seem to be trivialized. Through the Appellate Court, and as we prepared for the Supreme Court, consultation with Native Cultural Leaders became less frequent due to the litigation process where only established court proceedings were reviewed. Therefore, only the legal issues were contemplated by attorneys and judges. Our involvement in the case ceased to be significant, and the outcome of the case quickly fell from the positive directed thinking of Native Peoples where it resided for the past several years.

As the Supreme Court Hearing date drew closer, our grassroots organizing and public awareness campaigns were mobilized and more attention from the local Native communities was captured. Teach-ins and fundraising events were organized throughout the Humboldt and Del Norte County region, and Native Peoples became increasingly involved and supportive. We felt confident that our posters, informational brochures, and public media (radio and television) effectively blanketed the region and stimulated awareness and involvement, at least within the Native Communities.

In 1987, we had raised enough money to pay for a large delegation of Cultural Leaders to travel to Washington D.C. and attend the U.S. Supreme Court Hearing. We were joined at the hearing by several other Cultural Leaders, the Northwestern Indian Cemetery Protection

Association, and the State of California's Native American Heritage Commission. Again, the participation and opinions of Native Peoples were not permitted in the court. Later, many renowned Native Cultural Leaders would complain bitterly that their involvement was rendered to the status of a spectator while the decision being made about our spiritual existence would be everlasting. The late Elizabeth Case, Karuk Medicine Woman, complained that her seating at the Court was so far removed from the Justices and action of the Court that her personal spiritual energy was rendered ineffective in influencing any positive outcomes of their decisions. The hearing was quick. Our attorney, Marilyn Miles, did her utmost best in representing our assertion for First Amendment Protection and to freely practice our Earth Based Spiritual Theologies.

In 1988, the U.S. Supreme Court rendered its historic decision that ruled against applying any U.S. Constitutional protections of the Free Exercise Clause of our religious beliefs and the Earth Based Spiritual Paradigm(s) of Indigenous Peoples. In the GO Road case, the court effectively divested Native peoples of our right to religious freedom, and in doing so threatened the destruction of our entire Earth Based Spiritual Theology. By permitting the U.S. Forest Service to construct the Chimney Rock section of the GO Road, a mere timber access road, the Court willingly and with foresight and premeditation, rendered a decision that was nothing short of a sentence to forever-lasting DEATH for Native Earth Based Spiritual beliefs. With the long and brutal history of extermination, forced assimilation, and entangled Federal law and policy, this decision by the Court was the final phase of cultural genocide to be perpetrated on Native Peoples and Nations.

This sinister 5 to 3 majority Court decision was written by the first woman, Justice Sandra Day O'Connor, to be seated on the Supreme Court, and in fact was the very first legal Opinion that she authored as a Supreme Court Justice. In her historic denial of First Amendment Protection to Native Peoples' worship at sacred sites, she and the Court held that, "Even if we assume that we should accept the Ninth Circuit's prediction according to which the GO Road will 'virtually destroy the Indians' ability to practice their religion…The Constitution simply does not provide a principle that could justify upholding respondent's claim."

In making this decision, the Court set aside its long-standing balancing test that required the Government to substantiate an overriding public benefit to any and all actions taken by the Court. In the GO

Road Case, the Court declared all federal land management agencies exempt from the most basic balancing of government interest with constitutional rights. This means that the primary responsibility of any federal land management agency—managing public lands—is virtually immune from Free Exercise scrutiny. In fact, the Court referred to the government's "right to use its land," and, thereby, implicitly equated the U.S. Forest Service to a private landowner who need not include other parties, even the beneficial owners, the American public, in their management decisions.

In this decision, and under a very constricted interpretation of U.S. Constitution law, the Supreme Court also stipulated that the only way in which a First Amendment claim can be raised within the American Judiciary is when the Government punishes Native Peoples or coerces us to violate our religious beliefs. Since, in contemporary times, it is very difficult to imagine a rare instance in which that might occur, the decision in the GO Road Case renders the Free Exercise Clause a virtual nullity for the protection of our spiritual beliefs and Earth Based Spiritual Theologies.

In his dissent, Court Justice Brennan noted that the U.S. Supreme Court's decision in the GO Road Case would amount to nothing more than the right to believe that our religions will be destroyed by government action. "Today, the Court holds that a federal land-use decision that promises to destroy an entire religion does not burden the practice of that faith in a manner recognized by the Free Exercise Clause. Having thus stripped respondents and all other Native Americans of any constitutional protection against perhaps the most serious threat to their age-old religious practices, the Court assures us that nothing in its decision 'should be read to encourage governmental insensitivity to the religious needs of any citizen...'"

As indicated earlier, the GO Road Case has established legal precedent in adjudicating First Amendment, religious Freedom cases for Native Peoples. To be perfectly clear about what was decided in the GO Road Case, the U.S. Supreme Court affirmed that Native Peoples of the United States never did have religious freedom. The Court asserted that the U.S. constitution does not have a provision that could uphold our legal claim to freely practice our age-old Earth Based Spiritual Theology. Sacred places that are central and indispensable to our spiritual understandings, throughout the United States, now can be destroyed with impunity. With this action, Native spiritual leaders are left without legal recourse within the America justice system. The GO Road Case has effectively closed the courthouse doors on all Native Americans who seek relief from governmental infringements upon our free exercise of Religion(s) as long as the Government does not violate their very constricted interpretation of the U.S. Constitution.

Due to the precedence of the Supreme Court, the ruling in the GO Road case will be applied to Native spiritual practices throughout the United States and beyond. The adverse impacts of the GO Road Decision were felt immediately throughout Native America. San Francisco Peaks, Medicine Lake, Mount Taylor, Red Butte, Bagger Two Medicine, and at least thirty other sacred places are now in harm's way and can/will be destroyed by some sort of mining or industrial development or at the will of resource agencies.

The Court turned its back on any safeguards for protecting Indian religious freedom from government infringement. In a rather Ponchus Pilot (Pontius Pilate) fashion, the Court washed it hands of any responsibility of continuing Earth Based Spirituality and ecologically centered paradigms of Native People. In this denouncement, the Supreme Court states that any protection for Sacred Lands "…is for the legislatures and other institutions."

Post Supreme Court Decision

To my amazement, the reaction of the Native Peoples of Northern California was somewhat compliant with a decision that would destroy their cultural identity. The level of passivity and the need to maintain an economic and social status quo had diminished any outrage that may have been provoked by the GO Road decision. Many Tribal members had grown accustomed to the American society and favored their conformity to an assimilated lifestyle. Prior to the devastating Court decision, there were several meetings convened to discuss strategies and plot out actions that would be implemented in response to such an adverse Court ruling. Community members voiced their passions of resistance and direct actions, which sometimes included the ultimate sacrifice of "laying their lives on the line." A decision that would destroy an area that was central and indispensable to our spiritual existence was paramount and would mandate formidable resistance. However, after the GO Road decision, many of the same young "radical" tribal members reneged on their rebellious positions and advanced a more cooperative posture. Needless to say, their previous commitments proved to be only strident rhetoric, but among the core group, we knew that road construction had to be stopped.

In the years that followed, we continued to conduct ceremonies to heal our people and to heal the Earth. The engagement with Chimney Rock and the High Country would be strengthened, and the spiritual resistance to the U.S. Forest Service's construction of the GO Road would grow. Other Tribal Nations whose Sacred Places were similarly situated, and were now threatened with immediate destruction, expressed their adamant support to any direct action necessary to protect sacred lands. Although it seemed apparent that significant numbers of the local Yurok, Tolowa, and Karuk Native communities could not be mobilized in sufficient numbers to stop the GO Road construction, we were confident that larger numbers of Native Peoples from other Tribes would lend support and join our resistance.

Just as community organizing on a regional and national level was beginning to gain strength, the U.S. Congress, in 1992, passed legislation to establish the Smith River Recreation Area. The legislation not only preserved a pristine region of the Smith River, but also included a provision that would incorporate the six-mile strip of land initially set aside to construct the GO Road into the Siskiyou Wilderness Area. With this legislation, the plans to construct the GO Road would be stopped and our sacred lands would be preserved in perpetuity. This was a major victory for Native Peoples in Northern California and for a unique Earth Based Spiritual Theology. However, the legal precedence established in the GO Road case would still adversely impact Sacred lands throughout the Nation. Also, it should be noted that the decision to include the closure of the GO Road in the Smith River Recreation Area Bill was absent of significant consultation with Native Peoples, and it proved effective in quashing all community organizing that would lead to direct action or a consolidated resistance to oppose the genocidal Supreme Court decision rendered in the GO Road Case.

Throughout the 1990s, we joined with several national Native, environmental, and religious organizations and created the American Indian Religious Freedom Act Coalition. The Coalition, comprised of over 200 Tribes and organizations, was spearheaded by the Native American Rights Fund, the Association on American Indian Affairs and Seventh Generation Fund. Together, we drafted a bill that would comprehensively restore, preserve, and protect all aspects of our Spiritual/Religious beliefs and practices. Concurrently, the U.S. Senate Committee on Indian Affairs convened regional hearings throughout the nation and received input directly from Native Cultural Leaders on the need for such comprehensive legislation. We made several trips to Washington D.C., provided testimony at many congressional briefings, and strategized with Constitutional Law Scholars at several leading universities. The Comprehensive American Indian Religious Freedom act was reviewed and scrutinized by Native Spiritual Leaders, Congressional Advisors, and legal scholars; however, the opposition to our proposed legislation was very strong. Lobbyists financed by the many corporate arms of the extractive industry dissuaded congressional opinion, and our legislation never advanced beyond committee review.

The work of the American Indian Religious Freedom Act Coalition was not totally in vain, as our Coalition was successful in securing legal protection for the sacred use of the medicine, peyote, by members of the Native American Church. Later, in May 1996, President Clinton issued an Executive Order to Protect Sacred Sites (Ex Order 13007) directing all federal agencies, "…to the extent practicable and allowed by law," to allow Native Americans to worship at sacred sites located on federal property and to avoid affecting the integrity of such sites. Like the first American Indian Religious Freedom Act of 1978, the Executive Order to protect Sacred Sites was only a well-intended policy statement of the Government, and could not be legally enforced to stop destruction of our most sacred lands.

With the proposed legislation of the Comprehensive American Indian Religious Freedom Act, we hoped to broaden the legal scope within which our spiritual practices could be legally reviewed under the Free Exercise clause of the First Amendment. Even more specific to sacred land protection, the proposed legislation requested the legal ability to stop the destruction of places within national forests and on federally owned or managed lands that are sacred and recognized as such by Native Peoples. We were seeking a legal "cause of action" that might open the doors of the American judicial system to recognize our rights to freely exercise our Earth Based Spiritual practices. Knowing quite well the built-in institutional bias of the American judiciary, we only sought to be on a level playing field to litigate First Amendment Protection for all First Americans.

In retrospect, as we now consider the adverse and profound impacts of the GO Road decision on Native Spiritual beliefs, we better understand the pernicious intent of the GO Road decision. We now know that if it is allowed to mature we will quickly see the vanishing of an Earth Based Paradigm that could reverse the destruction of the Earth and, concurrently, the escalation of the human potential to destroy all that is sacred and perhaps all life on Earth. In concluding this analysis, we can only assume that the decision in GO Road was less about Native Peoples and our right to practice an Earth Based Theology, and, instead, was a decision to promote the free and ravenous access to publicly "owned" lands by the extractive industry. The sacred lands of Native America were like thrones in the trail of corporate greed and had to be removed.

{CHAPTER 11}

Rising to the Tolowa Dee-ni' Language Challenge

Loren Me'-lash-ne Bommelyn

THE TOLOWA DEE-NI' LANGUAGE (DEE-NI') IS A MEMBER OF THE DENÉ LANGUAGE FAMILY FORMERLY KNOWN AS THE ATHABASKAN LANGUAGE. The Tolowa Dené are a member of the Oregon Pacific Coast Dené (OPCD) language family subgroup. The OPCD language family spoke a mutually intelligible language along the Pacific coast that covered a territory from Wilson Creek in California, north to Flores Creek, and east to the Applegate River drainage in Oregon, across eleven river drainages. The OPCD was surrounded by three language stocks: the Penutian to the north and east, the Hokan to the east and the Algonquian to the south. These languages are either still currently spoken in North America, or were spoken until recent times. The area of northern California and southern Oregon is one of the most multilingually diverse areas of the world. Four of the eight North American Language stocks are embodied here: The Dené stock spoken by the Tolowa-Chetco-Tututni, Hupa, Mattole, Bear River, Wailaki, Umpqua, Coquille, and Siletz; the Hokan stock spoken by the Chimariko, Yana-Yahi, Karuk, Shasta, Pomo, and Washo people; the Algonquian stock spoken by the Yurok and Wiyot; and the Penutian stock spoken by the Wintu, Takelma, Siuslaw, and Coos.

The grammar of each stock is unique and separate from each other, each having its own worldview in describing life and its relationship to the universe. The proximity of these peoples allowed them to form multilingual communities held together by economic exchange, exogamous intermarriage, and ceremonial practice.

Dené branched out into dozens of daughter languages across North America. Dené languages are spoken on the West Coast, on the Great Plains, in Alaska, throughout the American Southwest, and in Mexico. The Dené language population has well over 700,000 members today. The Tolowa cognate for the term Dené is Dee-ni' describing a citizen of an exact location.

The pre-historic Dee-ni' population is estimated to have been ten thousand citizens. Their population plummeted following the California Holocaust that began in 1851. At its terminus in 1856, approximately 2,000 Dee-ni' survived. 1,834 Dee-ni' were driven off to the Coast Reservation at Siletz in the Oregon Territory, while others were imprisoned on the Klamath River Reservation in 1857, leaving fewer than 200 Dee-ni' in their aboriginal homeland. Eventually, the Dee-ni' were incarcerated on the Hoopa Valley Reservation in 1868. The 1910 census counted 121 Dee-ni' in California and 383 Dee-ni' in Oregon.

The Dee-ni' were protected under the Xaa-wan'-k'wvt Treaty negotiated in 1855. Because of this treaty, they gained the 44,000-acre Smith River Reservation in 1862. The U.S. Congress annulled the reservation in 1868. The Tolowa Dee-ni' were driven to the Hoopa Valley Reservation (HVR). Some Dee-ni' escaped the reservations, and these people managed to eke out a shrouded existence on the fringes of Euro-American immigration and colonialization in the homeland. On May 20, 1862 Congress approved the Act to Secure Homesteads to Actual Settlers on the Public Domain that opened limited lands to Dee-ni' for re-settlement in their homeland off the reservation. On January 18, 1881, an 80-acre allotment was secured at Nii~-lii~-chvn-dvn along the Smith River.

Euro-American citizens in Ukiah sympathetic to the economic and physical distress of California Indians encouraged Congress to pass legislation to acquire isolated parcels of land for homeless California Indians. Between 1906 and 1910, a series of appropriations were passed that provided the funds to purchase parcels. The 163-acre Smith River Rancheria was purchased for the benefit of the Dee-ni' in 1906. The Euro-American settlers expected all Dee-ni' to relocate to the Rancherias, yet some of the Dee-ni' laid low in the back-wood

environment. Today, the Smith River Rancheria is the Tolowa Dee-ni'
Nation Reservation (TDN).

I was born in 1956 to day-sri Jim and Eunice Henry Bommelyn. Dad
was a Wintu man and Mom was a Tolowa woman. The term day-sri
serves to apologize for saying the name or names of the deceased that
was traditionally prohibited. Both were of Karuk ancestry as well. Dad
may have been Chimariko as well. Because of where we descend from
and where I was reared, I am a Nii~-lii~-chvn-dvn Dee-ni': A Dee-ni'
citizen of the Nii~-lli~-chvn-dvn village. This is a suburb once governed
under the Yan'-daa-k'vt Yvtlh-'i~, the Yan'-daa-k'vt Policy. I am an
enrolled citizen of the greater Tolowa Dee-ni' Nation.

Nii~-lii~-chvn-dvn is a small community of Dee-ni' who survived
the Dee-ni' Holocaust by living among the Yaa-xvsh-chu, the Big Foot,
in the coastal mountains. They endured the abuses of the Boarding
School colonization and the sterilization era of the 1920s, and lived
through the Termination Period until the Restoration of the Nation in
1983. Historically, the fish dam was erected there, and tobacco was culti-
vated. Ceremonies were held there until they were federally prohibited
during the 1920s. The Nii~-lii~-chvn-dvn Dee-ni' grew a large garden
and orchard and raised cattle, pigs, and chickens. They gill-netted the
river, eeled in the upriver falls, clammed the ocean shores, dried surf fish
on the beach in the summer, and hunted deer and harvested the hills
for acorns and huckleberries in the fall, all while speaking the Tolowa
Dee-ni' language.

Auntie Laura was born at Nii~-lii~-chvn-dvn in 1908. At Around
twelve, she was seized by the Bureau of Indians Affairs (BIA) and sent
to the Sherman Institute in Riverside, California. She was punished
for talking Dee-ni' and was forced to peel a 500-pound bin of onions.
Due to the pungent stench, by the end of her punishment her snot hung
in her lap and she could no longer see. She could only feel the onions
with her hands and the knife to finish her chastisement. In complete
desperation, she and four girls planned their escape from the institution.
Each of the girls were from a different reservation located across the
state. Laura's home was 800 miles away at the opposite end of the state.
For several days, the girls snuck the counted and guarded food rations
from the commissary. Then, one night, they cut the window screen and
slid down knotted sheets to freedom into the night. They traveled at
night and hid during the day from the Federal Agents who pursued
them. Arriving at each girl's reservation, all the girls were cared for,

recuperated, and then the rest of the girls continued walking on north. Finally, one year later, Laura and a Pomo girl reached Ukiah, California. She stayed there and managed to contact her mother, my Grandma Alice. Grandma Alice hired a car and rescued her. Finally, Auntie Laura was once again home and safe, deep in the virgin redwood forests of Nii~-lii~-chvn-dvn on the Smith River.

I was born into the Federal Termination Era. Indian termination was the policy of the United States starting in the mid-1940s until it ended in the mid-1960s. Termination was shaped by a series of laws and policies with the intent of assimilating Native Americans into mainstream American society. Assimilation was not new. The belief that Indigenous people should abandon their traditional lives and become "civilized" had been the basis of policy for centuries. But what was new was the sense of urgency, that with or without consent, tribes must be terminated and begin to live "as Americans." To that end, Congress set about ending the special relationship between tribes and the federal government.

In practical terms, the policy ended the U.S. government's recognition of sovereignty of tribes, trusteeship over Indian reservations, and inclusion of state law applicability to native persons. Senator Ben Nighthorse Campbell, a Northern Cheyenne from Colorado, spoke of assimilation and termination from the native standpoint:

"If you can't change them, absorb them until they simply disappear into the mainstream culture....In Washington's infinite wisdom, it was decided that tribes should no longer be tribes, never mind that they had been tribes for thousands of years."[1]

The Smith River Rancheria (SRR) was terminated locally in 1960. The Termination was finalized at the federal level with the publication of that notice in the Federal Register on July 29, 1967. The Nii~-lii~-chvn-dvn Dee-ni' warded off the BIA termination efforts with gun threats and remained intact. They then formed the Ne-le-chun-dun Business Council (NBC) in 1976 to confront termination and support the Nee-dash Ceremony. Nee-dash is the Dee-ni' World Renewal Ceremony for Genesis. After restoration of SRR under the Tillie Hardwick Case in 1983 NBC transitioned into the Tolowa Nee-dash Society.

The Tolowa Dee-ni' endured under the Del Norte Indian Welfare Association where I grew up. The Association had begun in 1929 to continue the tradition of gathering together and supporting one another.

The Tolowa Dee-ni' held their meetings and events in K'vsh-chu Hall, located adjacent to the terminated rancheria. I learned to dance there. I heard our language and our history. I felt safe at the K'vsh-chu Hall.

As a child, I heard the elders say these three words at a feast: tee-sii-ghvs, tee-sii~-ghvs, and tes-ghvs in a conversation. I knew it meant to "be hungry," but why were there three different words? I asked them what it meant, and they sternly said, "It means hungry!" and I retreated momentarily. And thus, my linguistic journey began. Mom and Dad encouraged us to speak Dee-ni'. They took every opportunity to get us to spend time around our aunts, uncles, and the elders. In addition, Mom was a genealogist who visited the elders regularly. She addressed our law of not speaking of the dead. If a person named the dead to a family member, he would be fined and paid in cash to resolve the transgression. At times this transgression could cause a fist fight. Mom ensured them it was all right, and that she was not going to fine them as they feared. These visits taught me to have deep respect and love for our elders. Some of the elders were tri-lingual; they spoke Tolowa, Yurok, and English. And some spoke Karuk as well. Some My grandfather Billie Henry spoke those languages and Portuguese. Yurok elders played a linguistic game with me. They would d ask me questions in Tolowa and challenged me to answer them in Yurok.

Most of all, when it came to ceremony, the elders said, "If you don't do it right then don't do it at all. If you do it wrong, you will make it worse." They said, "When you make something, make it good like it will last for generations." Never say, "Aw, it is good enough. Always do the best you can." Day-sri Uncle Ernie said, as his Mom, Grandma Alice said, "If you can tell me that an ant climbs up a fir tree out on a limb to the tip and back to the trunk and onward to the tip of the tree, maybe you can talk Indian." Day-sri Sam Lopez would say, "If you are going to be a singer, you'll need to speak our language. I asked, "Why?" He'd say, "You're gonna have to talk Indian to compose your own songs!" So, I learned the language. All the while it was pondered by our community, "How can we write Dee-ni'?"

During the 1950s and 60s, the passing of each elder made more eminent the loss of our tribal knowledge, history, and language. The Association started a concerted effort to find a way to write and record the language. During the 1950s, speakers wrote Dee-ni' with the English alphabet. However, this seemed impossible. English does not have the necessary sounds and letters needed to write in Dee-ni'.

Being a language advocate, Mom was appointed by the Association in the late 1960s to research methodologies to write the language. In 1967, she read a language article in the *Times Standard* newspaper describing the Hupa writing their language with support from the Center for Community Development (CCD) at Humboldt State University. Because Hupa and Tolowa are related Dené languages, Mom knew Dee-ni' could be written with this new alphabet. She contacted Tom Parsons, the director who was sponsoring the writing efforts going on at Hoopa California.

Hupa was being documented with the innovative single sound Uni-fon Alphabet. The Uni-fon Alphabet was a relic left over from an effort to make a worldwide writing system for weather tracking data across the globe. This alphabet was modified to include the two additional sounds necessary to write Dené. The Circle-H and the Gargle-H were added. Immediately, Tolowa Language Classes began with the elders and the community at Del Norte High School in Crescent City in 1969. For the first time, the Tolowa Dee-ni' witnessed their language being written on the chalkboard. Betty Green, a Nii~-lii~-chvn-dvn Dee-ni', became the official scribe. Shortly after, the Yurok and Karuk communities adopted the Uni-fon Alphabet as well. The first Uni-fon electric typing element was designed and paid for by the CCD.

Each Wednesday, Mom picked me up from Redwood Elementary in Fort Dick. I was taken to the high school where as the elders directed the writing of Dee-ni'. Day-sri Amelia Brown was born in 1869 and lived for 110 years. She was an herbalist and a basket maker who did not read or write. Day-sri Sam Lopez was born in 1886 and lived to be 91 years old. He was the Nee-dash Ceremony Headman, Lead Singer and Scripture Orator. Day-sri Ella Norris was born in 1895 and lived to be 87 years old. She spoke Tolowa, Yurok and English. Day-sri Gobel Richards was born in 1900 and lived to be 83 years old. He was a singer and a Scripture Orator for the Nee-dash Ceremony. Many additional L1[2] speakers assembled to work on language documentation as well. L1 speakers are those individuals who spoke native languages as their first language. We documented the villages and which families descended from them. We collected genealogy, noun lists, and verb conjugations. Amelia gave detailed ethnographic descriptions of what life was during her time. She knew survivors from the Dee-ni' Holocaust that obliterated the landscape between 1851 through 1956. Eighty-percent of our population perished during the Holocaust. She teared up as she shared the descriptions of the massacres and debauchery they survived. At home, Dad shared about the massacres along the Trinity River of our Wintu ancestors. The world was set ablaze in our minds as our people perished under the bullets and blades of the Dragoon Squads paid by the State of California to accomplish its charge of genocide. Along the Trinity the Blue Coats imbibed in the debauchery as well.

I dove deeper into my work because I wanted to pray in Dee-ni'. I also heard people say, "I wish I had listened to my grandparents better. I thought they would live forever. Now they're gone and who can I ask?" I was determined to remember what was shared with me. I visited Amelia and asked her questions. During one of our visits, she said, "I wish you knew the old people. There were old people when I was a girl, and they could tell you anything." I was amused as, I thought, she is 105 years old! Then, for a fleeting moment, I saw a vision. A tunnel through time as the aged spoke to the young—and, when that youngster was old, they spoke to the next generation, who spoke to the next generations, all the way back until the beginning of time. Back to Genesis at Yan'-daa-k'vt, our axis mundi. I spent a lot of time with Amelia. My interest and inquires would give her a headache, something she never shared with me. Once, Amelia's daughter, day-sri Berniece Humphrey, told me when Mom and I pulled into the driveway that Amelia would say to her, "Ch'a', ghii 'ii~-ghvn xuu ghalh. Shsi's 'ii~-ghee-ts'ilh-te." ("Again, that thing is-coming. My-head is-going-to-ache.") Secretly, that Christmas, I strung Amelia a dentalia necklace, and she secretly crocheted me the edges of a towel, a hand towel, and a washcloth set. We both chuckled as we surprised each other with our gifts.

I would go for tutelage with Sam Lopez. We'd sing and talk Indian. I'd follow him as he sang. One time, he abruptly stopped singing and said, "I know what is wrong with you. You're trying to sound like me. You must use your own voice. Sing my songs using the voice God gave you." At the end of our session, he'd ask if I wanted some ice cream. I'd decline by saying say, "Duu." I needed to train. And then another time I said, "'Ay~." The tilde represents the nasal feature for the Dee-ni' vowel. It is written following the vowel rather than superscript above the consonant as in Spanish. He happily got up and went to his chest freezer and opened the lid. "What kind to you want?" he asked. There must have been a dozen different flavors in that freezer. I chose maple nut. After that, we shared ice cream before Mom picked me up from our tutelage sessions.

As I approached graduation from high school in 1974, I knew the language well enough to receive a state Eminence Credential. Because of my young age and the expectation for us to be the first generation to attend college, college became a reality. All agreed I needed to complete a teaching credential at Humboldt State University (HSU). The culture shock of a riverine kid at college was severe. I had no knowledge of Euro-American culture, its norms, or its vocabulary spoken by the students from Los Angeles. At the end of the school year, I returned home for a year and worked in the Title IV Indian Education Program. I returned the following year with more understanding of the Nuevo Euro-American culture, customs, and terminologies I needed to survive in the Whiteman's world of HSU. I graduated with a secondary teaching credential with an emphasis in Bilingual Bi-Cultural Education for Tolowa in 1980 and returned home to find employment and let the Dee-ni' teacher Bernice Humphrey retire.

Following my return home, Bernice and I facilitated the completion of the first edition of the Tolowa Dee-ni' Language text in 1983. I compiled an expansive second edition of the language text in 1989.

I was met with opposition as I began teaching for the Del Norte County Unified School District in 1980. To entice the school district, the Center for Community Development at HSU paid my salary for the first six years; I taught with a descending contribution each year. The intent was that HSU would pay for Dee-ni' to be taught, and the district would pay for other instruction and program management. When I attended the new teacher reception, the superintendent asked me, "Why are you here?"

At the school site, my administrator asked me, "Why do you want to teach a dead language?" The superintendent and school board carried the same sentiments toward my work. I was denied access to paper and pencils from the school site. The Head Secretary of the high school charged, "Go get your pencils from the Indian Ed program!" Over time, I won over the old guard. While the rest of my new teacher cohort enjoyed the normal permanent teacher status at the end of their third year, I was made a permanent employee at the end of my sixth year by the retiring superintendent.

Lena and I married while at HSU, and our daughter Tayshu followed in 1979. When she started preschool, her teacher reported she did not know her body parts. Tayshu knew them in Dee-ni' and her teacher said about herself, "I need to learn them." When our daughter started kindergarten, she came home and announced, "I need to speak English." I went into my bedroom and secretly cried. Our sons Pyuwa and Guylish arrived in 1981 and 1983. We continued speaking Dee-ni'.

The arrival of the computer era in the 1980s made the use of the pencil written Uni-fon Alphabet out-modeled. Software was unavailable for Uni-fon. The Macintosh Computer Company developed special Uni-fon programs and installed them in a limited set of Apple computers at HSU. The Uni-fon Alphabet had nine letters that were not available on a standard keyboard, so the new Practical Alphabet needed to be keyboard-friendly. The new alphabet needed to type the barred-L, the barred-I, the barred-U and the vowel nasal-hook. The Hupa, Yurok, and Karuk language programs abandoned Uni-fon for versions of the Roman alphabet as well. The Tolowa Dee-ni' language program converted to the Roman Lettered Practical Alphabet in 1993, with great anguish to the Tolowa community.

Then I discovered, to type the Practical Alphabet, the barred-L, the barred-I, the barred-U and the vowel nasal-hook letters. They were not available on all typewriters. The new Practicable Alphabet eliminated typewriter use entirely. I managed to get the pocketbook, *Now You're Speaking-Tolowa: The Dee-ni' People, Their Language* published using the Practical Alphabet in 1995.

I wanted to attend graduate school to study grammar and phonology in order to accurately describe Dee-ni' and to remedy the issues surrounding the computerization of Dee-ni'. The school district granted me a two-year sabbatical. I started my linguistics graduate program at the University of Oregon in 1995 and completed my master's degree in 1997.

A phonemic sound study for Dee-ni' was completed by the Linguistics Department and I in 1995. The study prompted the revision of the Practical Alphabet to the Tolowa Dee-ni' Alphabet (TDA) in 1997. These renovations allowed the TDA alphabet to be produced from the keyboard. The Taa-laa-wa Dee-ni' Wee-ya' text was printed in 2006. This update has been successful and productive in all the technologies that followed, from the iPad to cell phone texting to the printing and the use of visual media.

The creation of new nouns to meet the on-going changes in contemporary life is a constant task for the language committee and myself. The development of new words is accomplished with phonological shifting, grammatical composition, onomatopoeia, and Dené to Dené borrowing and calquing. Currently I have entered over 18,000 words in the online Dee-ni' database at weeyadvn.com.

Not to forget students who excelled, but after teaching Tolowa in the classroom for 34 years and with the failure to produce new fluent speakers, we started the work to redirect our approach. The language staff was sent to New Zealand and Hawaii to understand how their language efforts are successful. First, all the Islanders speak one language. Secondly, immersion instruction is present from preschool through twelfth grade. "Immersion" means speaking the language verses talking about the language. Thirdly, the language was taken back into the home to give it a nest. A Language Nest supports the language beyond the classroom, gives it prestige among the users, and moves the language from the abstract to the concrete for authentic communication.

Today, Teacher Credentialing, Dee-ni' curriculum development, and instruction in the classroom and Headstart have continued. Dee-ni' is present in offices, at ceremonies, in songs, and in the cultural NDN-tivities, meaning "Indian-ativities" The Dee-ni' program assists the learners in recognizing what their Language Policy is and how that affects their learning and use of Dee-ni'. Humans acquire an unconscious bias for their mother language. These bias and concepts impact the use of other languages and can be problematic, especially in the U.S. where Americans have accepted monolingual speech as normal and expected. While wanting to speak their heritage language, many Indians suffer from the repressive perception that it is not okay to speak their language. The examination of these biases helps the language learner to overcome the maladies inhibiting them from learning and speaking their language.

The Language Program has embraced the Language Nest methodology. The Nation provides curriculum, coaching, and practice. The most powerful tool is to teach the learner to be a Language Hunter. Citizens, alone or in small groups, work toward vocabulary expansion and database usage. They also source document study, listen to recordings, and work toward focusing their learning around meaningful communication for their own lives. Charter School discussion continues as a possible model to embrace and support our culture, history, and language. How can we support a deeper functioning Dee-ni' while facing state funding mandates that all instruction shall be in English?

The Nation hopes to uplift and strengthen our spirits as a lucid, transcendent, whole-hearted Dee-ni' community. By addressing the deep wounds held within our collective memory, our communities may heal these wounds to thrive verses to survive in a marginalized lifeway. The Dee-ni' must be free and emboldened to know they are a first world people in their Nation and within our larger American Nation. The return to a clearer Dee-ni' worldview, illuminated by language, sits at the core of our re-emergence. To emerge from the ashes which were heaped upon our homelands and on the hearts and in the minds of our people, our race will be able to push back on the enduring policies and practices of colonization in order to loosen the detrimental unconscious behaviors we practice, and instead write new ones to resume living. As one of my mentors, K'ay-lish (Sam Lopez) once said:

> Dan'-t'i nuu-k'wii-daa-naa~-ye' shu' ghvtlh-xat.
> Long-ago our-ancestors well they-lived.
> Xwii-day lhan ghii~-li~.
> Everything much-of-it there-was.
> Ghii srii-dvt-ni~k hii shaa~ duu-day nays-'a~.
> The lazy they alone nothing owned.
> Mee-wi srii-nis srtaa~ ghee naa-ghaa-deslh-nvsh.
> Every day food about they-worked.
> Nuu-k'wii-daa-naa~-ye' xwii-day yaa-winlh-ts'it.
> Our-ancestors everything they-knew.
> Mvn' yvslh-sri~.
> Houses were-built.
> Me'sr-xat yvslh-sri~.
> Gill-nets were-made.
> Xee-nvs yvslh-sri~.
> Canoes were-built.
> Ch'ee-t'a'-'a yvslh-sri~.
> Salmon-spears were-made.
> La' shaa~ yvlh naa-ghaa-deslh-nvsh.
> Hands alone with they-worked.
> Hii wee-ni dii xaa-ghi srxii-xay nu'-nee-tr'vn' naa-ch'aa-ghit-'a.
> That reason this new generation to-you-all we-are-talking.

Heritage Language learning and speaking are a horrendous task. There are challenges at every turn. Social exclusion, English only policies, English mother language fears, and the lack of funding challenge the task. One should mention our intergenerational poverty and the adversity it casts upon the proposition speaking one's heritage language. Folks in poverty struggle to survive while speaking English, let alone to take on an extra-legal proposition of speaking a now exotic language. The native speech communities have dried up and reconstructing them seems insurmountable, and it may be?

It was just a generation ago our language flourished, but now that is gone. I missed them as they passed on. Mom was the last L1 Dee-ni' speaker. I have held to the dream that we can see and know our world through the eyes of our language. I find envy in other languages such as English and Japanese that still own their right to express and know their worldview from their ancient dream-time till now. We are reduced to express our worldview through new languages of the conqueror like English and Spanish.

Each Indian Nation or tribe struggles with rebuilding their languages and identity. People are at a loss of hearing, learning and speaking their ancient knowledge. Disagreements over orthography and dialect at times blinds us and our desire to know and speak our languages.

We are at the final stage of the last glowing coals of our languages left by the fire of our timeless beautiful languages. Many populations are resurrecting their languages from texts and recordings. Now is the time to shovel our coals together and rekindle our fire before cold ashes replace them.

In contradiction to this end I am deeply saddened as my Nation has begun the dis-mantling of our Waa-tr'vslh-'a~ (Culture) Department. With the omission of the department from the 2019 budget will deliver the final blow. Perhaps our languages need to build a new path of resurrection. Conceivably a 501c3, a charter school with state English only policies, or some unknown foundation funding can assist us.

I reach inside for strength. I recall the account of Test-ch'as, a tsunami event. Some millennia ago, a massive earth quake and tsunami obliterated the seacoast. A harbinger, the Dog, spoke to us in Dee-ni'. He warned it was coming. The dutiful packed provisions and their necessary belongings and departed to the mountains. The tvt-ch'vs (tsunami imperfective form) rammed into the coast at Chit (Harbor Oregon) and knocked the tip of 'En-may (Mt Emily) loose and carried it to Elk Valley north of Crescent City. The survivors returned to Chit. Chit was completely erased away clean. The great house terraces and stone fireplaces were gone. Over time the Dee-ni' rebuilt our nation from the devastation. By the European Invasion we had returned to ten-thousand citizens.

I find and get solace here within our Indigenous knowledge. We are a small number of Dee-ni' desirous of language and cultural continuance. If our ancestors did it, perhaps... we will as well.

Endnotes

1.   George Horse Capture, Duane Champagne, Chandler Jackson, Ben Nighthorse Campbell, Ben. "Opening Keynote Address: Activating Indians into National Politics". *American Indian Nations: Yesterday, Today, and Tomorrow*. (Rowman Altamira, 2007) 2–3.

2.   First language speakers.

CHAPTER 12

Tribal Water Rights: Klamath-Trinity River

Michael W. Orcutt

MY NAME IS MICHAEL ORCUTT. I am a descendant of Chilula, Hupa, Karuk, and Yurok People and an enrolled member of the Hoopa Valley Tribe (HVT) located in the Klamath-Trinity River basin in Northern California. During my career, I've had the opportunity to serve as the Director of the HVT's Fisheries Department for over thirty years. Through this time, I've witnessed the Tribes of the Klamath basin evolve and build tremendous technical and scientific capacity, to the point where Tribal capabilities far exceed anything that either State or Federal agency programs possess. I will attempt to document the struggles and victories that the HVT have been able to accomplish through the exercise of its Indigenous—and, some would say, its inherent—water rights given by the Creator.

Early Career

My story and career in fisheries began when I was a sophomore at Hoopa Valley High School and was recruited by the local Hoopa Bureau of Indian Affairs (BIA) Area Office. At that time, the BIA managed the timberlands of the Hoopa Valley Reservation (HVR). The reason that I was selected was that I was a Hoopa Valley Tribal member and a stand-out math student, and they wanted someone to work with BIA foresters doing what was called "regeneration surveys." I was extremely fortunate to be given such an opportunity. I worked there for three summers, until I graduated high school in 1976. After graduation, I worked at Hoopa Tribal Forestry as a forestry technician doing an array of tasks, even firefighting when necessary. Then, Gary Rankle and Tom Payne from the United States Fish and Wildlife Service (USFWS) met with the Hoopa Valley Tribal Council (HVTC) and Hoopa Forestry Director Lawrence "Jip" Latham, who both recommended that I be hired for a position with the USFWS. I was hired, and I worked under the joint supervision of USFWS and HVTC staff as a fishery technician.

I became involved in Fisheries at a time when the "fish wars" were occurring on the Lower Klamath River. The "fish wars" were actually Tribal people who believed in their inherent rights, as Klamath Indigenous people, to harvest Klamath River salmon. In the late 1970s, their brave and meritorious actions ultimately established and reaffirmed the fishing rights of both Hoopa Valley and Yurok Tribes on the Klamath-Trinity River. Thus, the start of my career was coincidental with the exercise and reestablishment of tribal fishing rights on the Klamath River in Northern California.

It was during this time that the Bureau of Indian Affairs was tasked with managing the tribal trust resources of the Klamath River, and they started to contract out for various functions, such as law enforcement and biological expertise. They contracted with the USFWS to provide the biological expertise necessary for them to properly manage the tribal trust fishery resources. It is worth mentioning that this was during the time when, because Tribes of the Klamath River were actively exercising their fishing rights, our local congressional representative Doug Bosco [D-CA, 1983-1990] was openly claiming that the Klamath River salmon were being depleted by the overharvesting of fishing by Klamath River Tribes. Further, he was also suggesting that Congressional action was necessary to deal with the "Indian over-fishing problem." This issue will be discussed later in this chapter.

It would also be remissive on my part if I didn't mention that, when the BIA began to provide for the regulation and management of the Klamath fisheries, it did so with an iron-clad fist. For example, when the initial conservation closures were imposed on the Klamath tribal fishery, the closures were met with tribal resistance, which often led to armed confrontations between Federal BIA enforcement officers and the Indian people who were simply exercising their inherent rights to fish for Klamath River salmon. The BIA had imposed conservation closures of the Klamath Tribal fishery because not enough fish were reaching their natal spawning grounds. Indian people were being arrested and jailed for doing something that they had always done for millennia. Like many other places in the Pacific Northwest, the federal government was using the Lacy Act (1900) and other conservation laws to arrest, prosecute, and, in some instances, incarcerate Indian people for the simple act of exercising their fishing rights. The federal government was using the Lacy Act prohibitions against transporting, selling, or acquiring fish taken or possessed in violation of Indian Tribal law or State law See 16 U.SC. See 3372(a)(1) &(a)(2)(A). There are examples like the Sohappy Case in the Columbia River, where David Sohappy, a Yakima Indian, was sent to federal prison for five years for selling 345 Columbia River steelhead that he had harvested. It is with proper respect that we acknowledge the courage and fortitude of those Klamath tribal people who stood up for the preservation of their fishing rights, even in times of extreme adversity.

Some of my first fishery jobs were to survey local streams on the Hoopa Valley Reservation, where I worked for the USFWS for nearly a year before I enrolled at American River College in Sacramento, California. When I first began college, I was somewhat ill-prepared to take some of the required courses such as chemistry, zoology, biology, and other science-based courses, in part because these types of science courses were not offered at Hoopa High School. However, I was fortunate to have grown up around some notorious fisherman and old-timers and, because of that, I understood the streams and forest much differently than did most of my fellow scientists. I continuously challenged and pushed myself, so my strong work ethic coupled with traditional knowledge provided a unique management perspective for me. I was proud to have graduated college, in part because there were only a handful of Native Fishery biologist in the Pacific Northwest at that time, but, more importantly, because I saw that Native People needed a seat and voice at the table.

In the beginning, though, getting me out on the front lines as a representative of the Hoopa Valley Tribe was very challenging because I was so shy by nature. I am eternally grateful for some mentors along the way who were always supportive and encouraging to me. My first boss,

Robert Hannah, was an extremely bright and capable scientist, and I was very fortunate to have worked under him. Another mentor, lifelong friend, and colleague is Danny Jordan, who was on the Hoopa Valley Tribal Council. He advocated that the Hoopa Valley Tribe hire me as I neared graduation with a Bachelor of Science Degree in Fisheries Biology from HSU in 1982. I would also like to acknowledge that, throughout my career, even when I was learning the "ropes" (often the hard way), I always got positive support from our elected leaders, the HVTC.

Danny was one of the first HVTC members to become actively involved in the management of the Klamath River Fishery, which, at the time, was being managed by multiple state and federal jurisdictions. As an example, ocean recreational and commercial fisheries were managed under the Magnusson Stevens Act (MSA) by the Pacific Fishery Management Council (PFMC). The PFMC managed federal ocean waters off the coasts of California, Oregon, and Washington, from three to 200 miles offshore, while the States (Resource management agencies) managed the ocean fisheries from zero to three miles off the coast. The State of California also managed the in-river recreational harvest of Klamath origin fish stocks. At the time, because neither Hoopa Valley nor Yurok Tribes had the capacity or authority to manage the Indian fisheries, the Department of Interior (DOI), through the BIA, was managing and regulating Klamath tribal fisheries.

The HVT took one of their first steps into the arena of management of the Klamath River Tribal fisheries with the appointment of Danny Jordan to the PFMC's Salmon Advisory Sub-Panel as a representative of Klamath River Tribes. One of the earliest issues that needed to be dealt with was the development of conservation standards for Klamath fall Chinook salmon (e.g., how many salmon were necessary to replenish the Klamath River fish population). Once a conservation standard was established, a determination of the harvestable surplus of Klamath origin salmon could be made. Since fall Chinook salmon have the largest run of Klamath-origin salmon harvested by tribal and non-tribal fisheries, the first major conflict over the rightful harvest of Klamath River-origin salmon came from non-Indian commercial and recreational fisheries. One of the earliest management "facts" that was established was that most of the Klamath-origin Klamath fall Chinook salmon were being harvested by non-Indian ocean fisheries before the fish could return to the river to reproduce. Code-wire-tagging data (small microscopic tags implanted into the fishes' noses) from Trinity River and Iron Gate fish hatcheries indicated that upwards of 80% of the Klamath River-origin fall Chinook salmon were being harvested in non-Indian ocean fisheries before ever returning to the Klamath River. It was likely based on this fact that Congressman Doug Bosco chose not to legislate management of the Klamath Indian fishery, and instead chose to introduce two bills: PL 98-541, the Trinity River Fish & Wildlife Restoration Act, and PL 99-552, the Klamath River Basin Fishery Resources Restoration Act. The latter legislation, PL 99-552, established federal advisory committees to negotiate the annual allocation of Klamath salmon amongst tribal and non-tribal fisheries.

The 1986 Klamath Act provided a forum for "negotiations" about the allocation of Klamath Basin fall Chinook salmon. Some of the earlier agreements (1985) allocated a 70:30 split between non-Indian and Indian fisheries. It was not until 1993, when the Interior Department issued its Solicitor's Opinion (see Memorandum from John D. Leshy (M-36979), Solicitor of the Department of the Interior to the Secretary of the Interior (Oct. 4, 1993), pp. 3, 15, 18, 21 (1993 Solicitor's Opinion), *cited with approval, Parravano*, 70 F.3d at 542), that this changed. In his legal opinion regarding the federally reserved fishing rights of Hoopa Valley and Yurok Tribes, Solicitor Leshy concluded "…that the entitlement of the Hoopa Valley and Yurok Tribes is limited to the 'moderate living standard' or 50% of the harvest of Klamath-Trinity Basin salmon, whichever is less.'" This published legal opinion established a clear and legal entitlement to the harvest of Klamath origin fish stocks for Hoopa Valley and Yurok Tribes. Subsequently, the Department of Commerce through the PFMC formally adopted this legal opinion as "applicable federal law," so that today the allocation of Klamath River fall Chinook salmon is routinely divided on a 50:50 basis between tribal and non-tribal fisheries. A non-Indian commercial fisherman, Pietro Parravano, representing ocean fisherman, filed a lawsuit challenging the legal opinion, but Cert was denied by the Supreme Court (1995).

HVT Strategy Shift: Build Larger Fishery Resource Shares for All

During Klamath salmon negotiations between tribal and non-tribal fisheries, it was becoming increasingly apparent that rebuilding the Klamath-Trinity River fishery was going to be a major factor in resolving the long-term disputes over Klamath River salmon allocations. The HVT's strategy began to evolve, shifting to the identification of factors that were causing declines in Klamath-Trinity fish populations. One of the major factors was determined to be the over-diversion of water from the Trinity River. An emerging body of scientific information from the Department of Interior suggested that, since the operation of the Trinity River Division (TRD) began in 1964, and on through the early 70s, nearly 90% of the Trinity River flows were diverted into the Sacramento River for use in the Central Valley Project (CVP). Conversely, Trinity River fish populations had suffered an almost inverse reduction in size, losing 80-90% of their pre-TRD-levels of abundance. It was based upon this finding that Congress enacted the 1984 Trinity River Fish & Wildlife Restoration Program with the specific goal of restoring Trinity fish populations to pre-TRD levels of abundance.

Based upon similar findings, and in conjunction with the 1984 Trinity River Restoration Program, (PL 98-541), Interior (USFWS), initiated a 12-year, in-stream flow study, to also determine what actions were necessary to restore the Trinity River fish populations to pre-TRD levels of abundance. Although several factors delayed the study completion, by 1992 Congress had codified the need to determine actions necessary to restore Trinity fish populations through PL 102-575, the Central Valley Project Improvement Act (CVPIA). Section b (23) of the CVPIA added the requirement that any Trinity River fishery restoration actions necessary to restore the Trinity River fishery needed to "…meet the trust responsibility to the Hoopa Valley Tribe." Even more important was the requirement that the restoration action (e.g., fishery restoration plan) have "…concurrence of the HVT." Without this added requirement, implementation of the Trinity River Fishery Restoration Plan would have been at the discretion of the Interior Department. Further, the CVPIA required that, if the HVT "…concurred with the Trinity River Fishery Restoration Plan"—later called the 2000 Trinity River Record of Decision (ROD)—the Trinity River Fishery Restoration Plan should be "implemented accordingly." The 2000 Trinity ROD is based upon a joint 1998 USFWS-HVT in-stream flow study report that recommended a suite of fishery restoration actions, including the reallocation of nearly 250,000 acre-feet of TRD water for the restoration of the Trinity River fishery in order "…to meet the trust responsibility to the HVT." Later, we would realize that this single action was probably one of the largest redistribution of water supplies within the state of

California.

The HVT offered several unique additions during the development of 2000 Trinity ROD including the inclusion of a geomorphic flow requirement intended to re-contour the Trinity River channel between Lewiston and North Fork Trinity River, and also the stipulation that measurements of Trinity River Fishery restoration would not be just by fish numbers or yield. Rather, measurements would be evaluated based upon healthy Trinity River attributes. Of course, CVP water contractors Westlands Water District (WWD) and the San Luis and Delta Mendota Water Authority (SLDMWA) were not satisfied. They chose to litigate the 2000 Trinity ROD, ultimately losing the case in 2005 when the Ninth Circuit Court of Appeals ruled that nothing stood in the way of the "…full implementation of the 2000 Trinity River ROD," and that the "…restoration of the Trinity River fishery was unlawfully long overdue." Further, the 2000 Trinity ROD represented a reduction in the diversion of Trinity River water to the Central Valley Project, from about 73% to about 53%, with the corresponding fishery restoration flows increasing from 27% to 47%.

The HVT also assisted the Interior Department with the securing of additional Trinity River flows to avert a 2002-like fish kill on the Lower Klamath River. In 2002, the largest adult fish kill (over 70,000 adult Chinook salmon) in North America occurred primarily because of low flows, elevated temperatures, and a disease pathogen called *Ichthyopthirius multifilis (ich)*. In response to potential fish kills, Trinity River Division (TRD) water has been released numerous times since 2002, averaging approximately 35,000 acre-feet when preventive flow releases have occurred. The TRD and its impoundment of Trinity River water is part of the Central Valley Project (CVP) which enables the diversion of TRD water into the Sacramento River for hydropower and agricultural uses. Klamath basin scientists have developed scientifically based instream flow increases from the Trinity River to offset the likelihood of another large scale fish die off in the lower Klamath River.

The HVT was instrumental in securing additional water under authority of the original 1955 Trinity River Division (TRD) Act (PL 84-386). Interior and HVT both defended Bureau Of Reclamation (BOR)'s actions to release additional Trinity River water. These actions were contested in litigation brought by WWD and SLDMWA, who argued that the CVPIA and 2000 Trinity ROD capped flow releases at the specific volumes contained in the 2000 Trinity ROD, and that no additional Trinity River water was authorized to be released. However, as federal defendants and intervenors, HVT prevailed in February 2017 when the Ninth Circuit of Appeals ruled that the Interior and BOR had authority to release additional flows under the 1955 TRD Act, Section 2, proviso 1: the "fish preservation and propagation provision" to protect salmon migrating through the lower Klamath River. As to the disposition by federal Courts of Section 2, proviso 2—Trinity River water to be released annually for "Humboldt County and downstream water users"—the Courts chose not to resolve whether BOR could use this water for the protection of migrating salmon through lower Klamath River, even though BOR had used that specific authority previously in 2015. At that time, WWD and SLDMWA had contested the use of that authority in the Federal Eastern District Court, which later dismissed the case without prejudice, (they chose to withdraw from the existing case, but can relitigate the case in future) primarily because of the Ninth Circuit Court's ruling on the proviso 1 authority to release Trinity River water to protect Lower Klamath River migrating salmon. Note that, because of the HVT's legal research and advocacy, Interior published a Solicitors Opinion (M-36979) finding that the 1955 Act Section 2, provisos 1 and 2, represent separate and distinct authorities to release TRD water, even though BOR had combined the two provisos for nearly fifty years.

So, legally, the proviso 2, Humboldt County and downstream water users 50,000 acre-feet TRD water contract with BOR, represents additional water that can be used for beneficial uses, including fishery protection or economic development—which is what the original legislative history identified as the intended purpose. Accordingly, over half of managed TRD water is dedicated to fishery restoration (2000 Trinity River ROD) and to the preservation and propagation of Trinity fish populations (Lower Klamath River augmentation flows and Humboldt County's 50,000 acre-feet contract with BOR). Under authority of the 1955 TRD Act proviso 1 and 2, this amounts to over 645,000 acre-feet of managed TRD water—well over 50% of the inflows into the Trinity River reservoir—being available for restoration and preservation and propagation of the Trinity River fish populations. The average annual inflow into Trinity River reservoir is 1.2 Million Acre of water.

History of Hoopa Valley Reservation Creation and Relevance to Tribal Water Rights

Western water laws, including those adopted in California, are based upon a system of prior appropriations, the concept of first-in-line is first-in-right…which simply means that the first person using water for beneficial use has the first right to the use the water for that purpose. In the case of Indian Tribes and creation of their reservations, the 1908 landmark case *Winters V. United States* is where Indian water rights were first recognized by the Supreme Court. This case established the Winters Doctrine, which stated that when Congress reserves land for an Indian reservation, Congress also reserves water sufficient to fulfill the purpose of the reservation. In the situation of the Hoopa Valley Reservation, created by executive order in 1864, this means that the HVT has the oldest claim to waters of the Trinity River, since the HVR was created for Indian purposes, including hunting, fishing, and gathering.

Tribes have many options to protect their rights, including seeking a full-blown, in-stream adjudication of their reserved rights such as was done with the Winters Case. This case involved the adjudication of the Milk River in the state of Montana—an adjudication that is still not finalized after over 100 years. There are some inherent impediments to the approach of adjudication, including that it is very costly and time-consuming, and also that adjudication must be done in a State Court proceeding.

Even so, many tribes across the United States have taken this approach, including the Klamath Tribes of Oregon in the Adair (1983) case, which is close to being completed by the Oregon Court system. In the situation with the Trinity River, the Hoopa Tribe has not made a claim for Trinity River water based upon its senior Indian water rights through an in-stream adjudication (quantification) because of the above-mentioned impediments, which are often very time-consuming. Instead, we have sought to make federal reclamation laws consistent with federal trust responsibility requirements.

Tribal Self-Governance to Develop Technical Capacity

The HVT was one of the first five original demonstration tribes to utilize the Amended Indian Self-Determination Act (PL 93-683) to use Tribal self-governance to develop Tribal capabilities. Until the early 1990s, the implementation of Klamath and Trinity River monitoring and restoration work was being conducted largely by California or Federal government agencies. In the early 1990s, the HVT became a "self-governance demonstration project tribe," which meant that other Interior Department agencies that were conducting programs for the benefit of "Indians" were eligible for the development of self-governance compact agreements between Interior and tribes. Federal Program activities that had been previously managed by other Interior agencies including USFWS and BOR were now eligible for tribes to contract with the federal government. These agreements were later called Annual Funding Agreements (AFA), and they allowed for Indian tribes to negotiate funding agreements for restoration work—including work being done under the Trinity River Restoration Program administered by BOR.

In the early years of the AFA negotiations, the HVT leveraged meaningful participation in programs that California and federal resources agencies had previously been conducting largely void of tribal involvement. For example, the California Department of Fish and Wildlife (CDFW) annually operated fish counting weirs on the upper and lower Trinity River to assess fish populations. CDFW had plenty of experience conducting this kind of work, and usually only had to make minor "cost of living allowances" when it made its budget request to BOR. Fish counting was exclusively CDFW domain and represented job stability for its employees. I vividly remember some of our earliest AFA negotiations where we were regularly being dismissed by CDFW staff and seemed to have reached an impasse because of this. BOR's Mid-Pacific Regional Director Roger Patterson, along with BOR's designated AFA negotiator, told CDFW representatives that BOR would not be renewing its contracts with CDFW until the HVT's AFA negotiations were completed. Within two weeks, CDFW contacted us and BOR, and we reached agreement on the placement of HVT staff at both weir sites, where our presence remains to this day. Today, we call the two weir sites "co-managed" projects, meaning they are operated jointly by HVT and CDFW.

HVT Fisheries Department growth and expansion was largely facilitated by its reliance upon the self-governance laws and regulations where, today, we regularly compact over $4.0 million in TRRP funding annually and employ over forty people full time or seasonally.

Comprehensive Management of the Entire Klamath River Basin

The HVT has remained a consistent advocate for the comprehensive and responsible management of the entire Klamath River basin. The HVT was made painfully aware of the need to have a healthy and functioning Klamath River basin with the 2002 adult fish kill on the Lower Klamath River. Many of the fish that perished were Trinity River-origin fish that never reached the HVR. For the record, HVT has always been supportive of the removal of the PacifiCorp-owned hydropower dams, and the benefits of improvements to Klamath basin water quality, and of the reintroduction of fish into the upper Klamath River basin. However, we've been opposed to tying PacifiCorp dam removal to water allocation agreements such as the Klamath Basin Restoration Agreement (KBRA), which expired in December 2015. With the expiration of KBRA, and the emergence of the Klamath Hydroelectric Settlement Agreement (KHSA) that was signed by California, Oregon, DOI, and PaciCorp representatives in April 2016, the issue of removal of PacifiCorp-owned dams on Klamath River remains with the Federal Energy Regulatory Commission (FERC). FERC needs to approve the transfer of ownership of the PacifiCorp owned hydro-power dams to a non-profit entity—the Klamath River Renewal Corporation (KRCC)—for the potential removal of the hydropower dams by 2020.

With possible removal of the Klamath dams, much work needs to be done to improve the health of the Klamath Basin, including: 1) Development of an overall management structure; 2) Improve water quality in upper Klamath basin; and 3) Allow for tribal participation in Klamath fish introduction plans inclusive of determining the fate of Iron Gate Hatchery. Since the expiration of PL 99-552, the Klamath Basin Fishery Restoration Act in 2006, there has been no coordinated Klamath Basin management structure in place. The HVT has offered its Klamath Basin Joint Directorate and independent science-based structure as a template for managing Klamath River basin resources. With regards to improving upper Klamath Basin water quality, the

HVT developed a proposal that was offered to the EPA. This proposal builds off the HVT's Treatment as State under the Clean Water Act (CWA) to work with Oregon and California to identify water quality problems in the upper Klamath River basin, and to recommend actions to improve this water quality, which is key to any long-term water balance in the Upper Klamath River basin. A very apparent reality is that, even with removal of PacifiCorp-owned dams, fish cannot migrate through the Keno to the Upper Klamath Lake reach of Klamath River because of poor water quality conditions.

Finally, the fate of Iron Gate Hatchery (IGH) needs to involve Klamath Basin tribes as active co-managers, since IGH produces millions of fall Chinook salmon. If PaciCorp Dams are removed, the lost fish production from IGH will need to be mitigated in some manner. Moreover, the future fate of IGH will need to be assessed within the context of fish reintroduction above Keno Dam and Upper Klamath Lake. Presently, because of an Oregon law, only the Oregon Department of Fish Wildlife and Klamath Tribes staffs are working on a fish reintroduction plan, so it is critical that the technical staffs of the lower basin tribes be involved with the fish reintroduction plan. Much work needs to be done, but for tribes we have no other choice, and we have no other option or river to depend upon.

{CHAPTER 13}

Fish Wars on the Klamath River

Walt Lara Sr. & Kishan Lara-Cooper
Featuring Testimonies by Robley Schwenk & Frank McCovey

A letter to the Sacramento Bee (August 19, 1978):

> The Department of Interior and the U.S. Fish and Wildlife Service are interfering with rights of a sovereign dependent nation within the United States and its people who possess the right of internal self-government and self-determination.
>
> The proper procedure for any closure of the river was clearly set down in the regulations developed by the Indian community. In section 258.11 of those regulations it states in part, "…In order to adopt any recommended emergency regulations the biologist-in-charge, through the Bureau of Indian Affairs, shall call for a meeting and a vote of the Indians of the Hoopa Reservation. Four meetings are to be held for the purpose of hearing the recommendations of the biologist-in-charge and for discussion of them." These meetings were never held.
>
> The reason given for issuing the order to close all Indian fishing below the Highway 101 bridge was to conserve the resource. It was pointed out at the meeting, however, that the water is not being released from the Lewiston and Iron Gate dams in

sufficient amounts to cool the waters of the Klamath. The water being held back causes water temperatures to rise which in turn effectively stops the salmon from moving upstream.

In the meantime, nothing has been done about the intensified logging activities in the Klamath River. Nothing has been done about cleaning up the spawning streams or placing fish ladders on those streams clogged by logging debris and gravel.

Promises have been made to the Indian people that steps would be taken to conserve the resource by closure of the off-shore troll fisheries and promises have been made to limit or close the sport fishing on the Klamath River below the 101 bridge. Promises have been made for many things including resolving of the Jesse Short case so that an interim or otherwise functioning governing body could be formed to regulate and conserve the resources of the Hoopa Indian Reservation.

We, as Indian people of the Hoopa Indian Reservation are tired of promises and tired of actions by others to take away or diminish rights reserved to ourselves when the reservation was established. It must clearly be understood that our main concern is conservation of our resources for ourselves and our children's children. However, it must clearly be understood that we cannot allow anyone or any government agency to arbitrarily impose laws upon us in which we, as Indians of the reservation, have had no part in promulgating.

—*Walt Lara, President, Klamath River Indian Wildlife Conservation Association*

THE KLAMATH RIVER RUNS EAST TO NORTHWEST THROUGH THE YUROK RESERVATION BOUNDARIES. From the beginning of time it has been the life source of the Yurok people both physically and spiritually. I learned from an early age of the relationship between humans and the spirit of the river. The river represents "time" in the Yurok prayers. The river assists us in the cleansing of the world, spiritual baths of our flower dance girls and medicine people, and continuance of mankind. It brings us together in space and in time. Without water, we have no connection to the universe or the dimensions beyond.

I learned of the spirit beings within the water, Kemas (a serpent), and the oral history around fishing. I learned of the life cycles of the fish, the importance of treating salmon with respect, the first salmon ceremony, and the tides of the water. But most of all, I learned the respect one must have on or near the water's edge. For example, if a person calls out to you for assistance from across the river, or is in need of a ride across the river, you must accommodate that person in a "good way" even if that person is your enemy. You are responsible for the safety of that person. This act is out of respect for the river while you're on the river. Unkind words, unnecessary yelling, or fighting is against "Indian Law."

Our houses are built with the door opening toward the river. It symbolizes our spiritual connection to water. The flow of the river seldom deviates from its original path—although earthquakes, logging practices, drought, and the cultivation of growers diverting the tributaries have all affected that path.

It is our belief that when someone passes on, his/her spirit goes out the river toward the west. If a person from a village up river passes on while down the river, that person's body must travel home by boat with the person's head pointed downriver. As you're traveling up the river, you are supposed to go on the opposite side of where you would normally travel because a spiritual journey is the opposite of a human journey. There are also spiritual rocks along the river that we go behind (not in front). When the boat reaches the Blue Creek side of the river, the body is then turned so that the person's head is pointing up the river, and continues as such until the boat reaches the village destination.

I share all this information to emphasize the complex nature of our relationship with the river. Our beliefs around the river and ocean are serious. They are not a playground for water recreation or careless practices.

When I was fourteen years old, my brother and a couple other guys were eeling on the south side of the mouth of the Klamath River. Merkie Oliver (awok) and his uncle, Clarence Peters (awok), were crossing the mouth from the north side, coming toward us in a canoe in order to eel on the south side of the river. A breaker capsized the canoe and washed Merkie and Clarence toward the mouth of the River. We could see their heads bobbing in the water now and then. We, the boys and I, stood helpless along the shore, and there was a lot of panic among the fisherman on both sides of the River. Kenneth Franks (awok), a decorated war hero, lived just up the river at Resighini. He was a boat racer who traveled to places like the Colorado River to compete, and he owned a KG9 motor speed boat. Witnesses to the capsizing frantically summoned him to come and assist. Kenneth opened up the motor toward the mouth of the river. Meanwhile, those that stood on the shore searched continually for the two men. We could no longer hear their cries but, miraculously, Merkie's feet hit bottom right out in the center of the mouth of the river—the current of the river had created an island underwater. As their feet dragged in the sand, the two men anchored themselves and stood on the dune waist-high in water. As the tide went out, it exposed the island. This all happened within an hour and a half. We could clearly see that they were standing there waving their arms. Kenneth eased toward their location. As a boatsman, he could find the eddy and the safest route with ease. He edged along close enough for the two men to wade toward him. They quickly climbed aboard the small racer and Kenneth headed up the Klamath River, zipping past all the on-lookers including myself and my comrades. The two rescued men, dripping wet, held on tightly to their eel hooks and waved them in the air as they passed. This was a miracle for a fourteen-year-old boy, one that I will never forget. These men continued to live in harmony with the Klamath River for many years. Merkie was a famous fishermen and was never too far from the river on any given day.

When my grandfather, Jimmy Marks (awok), heard the story it brought back traumatic memories for him. He had lost his son, Harvey (awok), at the mouth when Harvey was trying to rescue a careless boater. My uncle Harvey was the father of five children and was a fishing guide on the Klamath River. My grandfather walked the beaches for many months in hopes that his son had washed ashore. He had no tolerance for careless acts on the river and continually shared traditional teachings regarding safety and respect of the ocean and river.

Over the years we have lost many lives to the River and witnessed a few rescues. Several years later, my son, Walt Jr., was summoned in the midnight hours from his bed. Two young boys and their father had set their net too close to the mouth and a breaker had capsized their boat. The boys were strong enough to swim to shore, but their father, who was weighted with boots and fishing gear, was not. The father held tight to the anchored net in the cold water. Walt Jr. had to dock his boat a few miles up the river at the Glen boat ramp, but once he got on the water he opened up the motor full board. The father, in telling his story, said that he recognized the sound of Walt Jr.'s motor and knew that he would live.

We as a community have witnessed the power of this spiritual body of water, and through traditional knowledge and a responsibility to it, we have survived. From time immemorial the River has nourished our people, has identified us as a people, and has provided an intimate relationship to the world around us. In this chapter, with the help of Robley Schwenk and Frank McCovey, I will share a small glimpse of the fish wars on the Klamath River, which occurred all along the Klamath and Trinity Rivers. It should be known that each person involved made a valuable contribution to the collective effort to preserve our fishing rights. In some ways, it felt like a ceremony in that each person played a critical role and worked together without any formal rehearsal. Efforts were made by Margaret Carlson (awok), Donna Martin (awok), and their team at Ah-Pah and Willie Colegrove (awok), Peter Masten (awok) and their team in Hoopa. This is a living history and I encourage anyone living near this site to talk to community members about their role in the Fish Wars on the Klamath River.

From my perspective, the Fish Wars began when I was about ten years old (circa 1945) when Dewey George (awok) and Hector Simms (awok) got arrested for fishing at Snake Rock. According to the State of California, Yurok people were only allowed to fish up the Klamath River at Tecta. We were allowed three fish per day. Anyone who lived at the mouth of the Klamath River would have to travel by boat fourteen miles up the river to catch three fish and then paddle all the way back. For many elders, children, and disabled community members, this was not only a hardship, it was nearly impossible. Consequently, people like Dewey and Hector would fish on the reservation down the river from Tecta with the risk of getting arrested.

From the moment of Dewey and Hector's arrest all the way until the fish wars battles on the river about 32 years later, the State of California continuously harassed us for fishing. Many of us who would fish to sustain our families, grandparents, and children had to hide our fish or nets in order to avoid harassment and arrest. Then, in 1969, Raymond Mattz made positive change for Yurok people. He was fishing with Jim Hodge (awok), Chuck Donahue (awok), Hank Johnson (awok), and Jack Mattz[1] on the reservation below Tecta and was caught. Raymond claimed all five gill nets as his own and was cited for "illegally" fishing. Raymond took the case all the way to the Supreme Court in Washington, D.C. alleging that "the nets were seized in Indian Country…and that the state statutes prohibiting their use did not apply to him."[2] The Mattz

v. Arnett case was decided on June 11, 1973. Justice Blackman delivered the opinion for a unanimous court:

> Our decision in this case turns on the resolution of the narrow question whether the Klamath River Indian Reservation in northern California was terminated by Act of Congress or whether it remains "Indian Country," within the meaning of 18 U.S.C. 1151. When established, the reservation was described as a "strip of territory commencing at the Pacific Ocean and extending 1 mile width on each side of the Klamath River"…we conclude that the Klamath River Reservation was not terminated by the Act of June 17, 1892, and that the land within the boundaries of the reservation is still Indian country…[3]

The Mattz v. Arnett case decision acknowledged that the Klamath River below Tecta to the mouth was also reservation. We (Yurok people) ascertained that we had retained the right to fish on the reservation. As it was now decided by the Supreme Court that the Klamath River was reservation,[4] we had all the confirmation that we needed to continue fishing on our homelands.

For the next five years after the Mattz v. Arnett decision, there were multiple incidences on the Klamath River of state and federal officers harassing Yurok people. Many of these incidences were triggered by tourists, sports fishermen, and citizens of Klamath who did not support Yurok fishing rights. We developed the Klamath River Indian Conservation Wildlife Association (KRICWA) to advocate for our retained right to fish. Robley Schwenk, a Vice-President of KRICWA, and I traveled to Washington, D.C. to meet with the director of the Bureau of Indian Affairs (BIA) and California's congressmen. Walt McCovey Sr. sponsored our trip. The BIA argued that Yurok people did not have the right to fish because we weren't an "organized" tribe (being "organized" meant that we had to have a governing body, a constitution, bylaws, and financial credibility). This was not accurate. As descendants of allottees, we retained the right to fish on the reservation and on our traditional lands whether we were organized or not. In the meantime, we (KRICWA) elected Susan Masten to work as a liaison with the BIA.

During the year of 1978, the harassment by state and federal officers increased dramatically. Life-threatening situations occurred and the violence of the Fish Wars hit its peak. One night, many Yurok people were fishing up and down the river. Federal officers ticketed two teenage boys, James Donahue and John Donahue (awok), for fishing. At the time, James had a broken leg with a cast. Before any of us could do anything, the federal officers wrapped the gill net around the boys' boat and dragged the boat, with them in it, out the mouth where the river meets the ocean, gave them a ticket, and released the boat into the mouth where it tipped over. The two teenage boys struggled in the water, managing to make it to shore alive.

I cannot express the feelings of helplessness and anger that I felt as I witnessed this inhumane act toward two young boys. It seemed that the officers had no regard for human (Indigenous) life and were trying to set an example by attempting to drown two of our own. It reminded me of the time of the Gold Rush when Indigenous people were put into slavery. They were required to find a quota of gold each day. If they were unsuccessful, settlers would cut their hands off to teach a lesson to all the other Indigenous people that they had best meet their quota. This method of instilling fear was a common practice during times of genocide and still continues today. This is why it is so important that our young people understand that fear is a natural human response to oppressive acts, but we can't let our fear guide us. Instead we must call on the strength and power of our ancestors that lives within us. Although I felt fearful for my son Walt Jr. who was heavily involved and my daughter, Lorraine who was in a boat with Becky James that day; I took great comfort in knowing that our elder, Geneva Mattz (awok) prayed for our safety.

After the incident, we held a meeting at Margaret Keating School in Klamath, California to talk about the continuing persecution from the federal officers, the racism of the local townsmen, and the false statements from the newspapers. As a community, we decided to continue to fight for our right to fish. So, we went back down to the river and put in our gill nets. Before long, the federal officers arrived with boats full of weapons. I have invited Robley Schwenk and Frank McCovey to share their testimonies. Robley was a Vice-President of KRICWA, a Yurok fisherman, and an advocate for Indigenous rights. Robley was an avid writer, spokesman, and negotiator. Frank McCovey was a Yurok fisherman who fished the Klamath River every day of the Fish Wars. Frank put his life on the line to protect our inherent right to fish.

Robley Schwenk

My grandmother used to wake up and pray for the health of the river every morning from her deck. The Klamath River has always been the bloodline of Yurok people. I have lived in Requa (at the mouth of the Klamath River) since I was a young boy. When I was about nine years old, I remember looking at the geese fly above the river and telling myself that I wanted to live at Requa forever… and I have. I remember spending everyday on the river as a child. I used to swim in the slough. My grandma used to say "go down the dock there and ask them for a fish head." We would do that and bring her back some fish heads. She liked those fish heads to eat.

Prior to the Fish Wars, one of our biggest obstacles on the river was the tourists. The Klamath River was world-renowned for its Steelhead; it was once called "The Steelhead Capitol of the World." People from all over the world would travel to Klamath to fish and enjoy the river view. They would stay at the Requa Inn or across the river at the camps. There have been a number of movie stars that have stayed at the Requa Inn over the years. I never felt like the tourists liked to see Indian people fish. The tourists would be at the river all day and wouldn't even catch a single fish, and there we would be bringing in dozens. Most tourists were really opposed to Indian fishing rights because they didn't understand that we had retained rights for hunting, fishing, and gathering on our reservation. They started writing their congressmen in Washington D.C., and the next thing we knew, officers were on the river. My friend Corkey Simms named these men, "the feds." We didn't know if they were actually federal officers, what their titles were, or who had sent them.

My most prevalent memory of the Fish Wars was the federal officers coming down the river in a boat. They were whooping and hollering, slapping their hands on their mouths, like stereotypical "Indians." This behavior was a norm for them and a way to intimidate or belittle us. Sometimes we would already be down at the river; other times we would go down to the river after they showed up. Each time, they would harass us and tell us that we needed to stay off the river. We would remind them that we had the right to fish. In one interaction, they grabbed Walt and the other officer pulled a pistol on me and said, "I told you that you're not allowed to fish here anymore." At that moment I thought that I might be killed in the next few minutes. It's hard to describe how I felt.

It should be remembered that we (Yurok people) didn't have weapons during the Fish Wars; only the "feds" had weapons.

Another memory of the Fish Wars was when Frank McCovey and his brothers were fishing on the river. The boys had cameras and were taking pictures of the "feds" harassing people. So, the "feds" ran into their boat and sunk them. Walt, who was kind of a hero throughout the Fish Wars, jumped from boat to boat to save them. I was so upset to see that kind of violence happens to a person for no reason, other than to destroy evidence.

We knew that we needed fish to survive; fishing is a part of our livelihood and is our inherent right. So, we (Yurok people) resisted and continued to put our nets in the river. We knew that we had the right to fish on the river because it had already been proven by the Mattz v. Arnett case, where the Supreme Court had ruled that the reservation extended one mile on each side of the river, clear to the mouth. That entitled us to fish. But the state still wasn't recognizing that, and neither was the Bureau of Indian Affairs.

One of my jobs in the Fish Wars was to keep the public aware of what was happening on the Klamath River. We formed a grassroots organization called the Klamath River Indian Conservation Wildlife Association (KRICWA), which was a subsidiary of the Requa Indian Community Association (RICA). We utilized both organizations as a form of resistance. I was the secretary of RICA and one of the vice-presidents of KRICWA. Some of the key players in formulating and operating these organizations were Jackie Webster, Walt Lara, Barbara McQuillen, Ethel Blake (awok), Mollie Ruud (awok), Pearl Peters (awok), Ted Jake (awok), Albert Gray (awok), Glenn Moore (awok), Bud Ryerson (awok), Dewey George (awok), Howard Ames (awok), Frank Ames (awok), Babs Nova (awok), and Walt McCovey Sr. (awok), to name a few. We had a newsletter that we sent out every month. We contacted senators and lawyers, and developed fishing regulations. We had a board made up of highly respected people of Requa and Klamath. RICA was a member of the Inter-Tribal Council of California and Tri-Counties. When the Fish Wars began to escalate, our Chair, Walt Lara, contacted the Secretary of Interior, Cecil Andrus, to request action and invite him to the Klamath River. Then we sent traditional runners up the river to invite a representative from each village to attend the meeting with Secretary Andrus. After Secretary Andrus's visit, the "feds" left and the harassment decreased, but we continued to advocate for our fishing rights.

Overall, my memory is that there were a lot of Indian people resisting. A lot of occasions when people got their boats ruined and tipped over. I feel lucky that nobody was killed. I think that my grandmother's morning prayers for the health of the river over the years kept us all safe during that time.

It's important for the next generation to be aware of this history. Our young people should think about things like why we only ended up with a mile on each side of the Klamath River when our natural homelands extended south to Little River passed Trinidad, California and north to Damnation Creek, approximately ten miles north of Klamath, California. Most importantly, remember that nobody gave us fishing rights. Fishing rights were retained by the people of our tribe!

Frank McCovey

I grew up along the Klamath River. We would walk down to the river at daylight or dark, rain or shine. As a young person, I was taught to respect everything, such as the trails and the river. My elders told me that when you walk on a trail you must give thanks to the trail. If you walk along and you don't have good respect, the trails will turn over and you will fall down and break your leg or sprain your ankle or something like that.

When I was a child, I learned to never waste a fish and to always give a lot fish away. All my life, I have been free with my fish. I will find the nearest old person and share because that it what our people do. I learned a lot from my dad, Grizzly Ike. I always used to watch him hang nets. He made his own net needles, oars, dip nets, and eel nets. He also taught me how to smoke fish. He had a special brine and method to cook it. We fished in the ocean and in the river for salmon, steelhead, trout, sturgeon, and surf fish. My dad was a famous guide at the mouth of the Klamath. When I was in my twenties, I began hanging my own nets. I have been kippering (smoking) salmon for fifty years now.

The Fish Wars started in the spring salmon time and lasted until the end of summer. We were told by the Bureau of Indian Affairs (BIA) that we no longer had a right to fish with a gill net. However, the BIA didn't have any proof that we couldn't fish. So, my cousins Chet, Mindo, Boo Boo, and Hoddie all went fishing. We didn't catch anything, but we continued to fish every day. For several months, Yurok people came and went but I fished every day until the Bureau of Indian Affairs (BIA) asked me, "What is going to make you quit?" They told me that I wasn't allowed to fish but they couldn't show me in black and white why I couldn't fish.

When I went to college, I learned that they didn't ratify our treaties. I understand that in our history, the federal government called all of the headmen from surrounding tribes together to meet in Hoopa. In the midst of negotiations, the cavalry shot them. Out of the thirteen headman that attended, only two escaped. After that, when the cavalry wanted to talk to the headmen, villages would send a spokesman. So then, the cavalry began to solicit their own spokespeople from villages. They would say, "You're the spokesperson; get over here and sign this." That is how I understand that they got their treaties signed.

In regards to the Fish Wars, I remember the day when things got really heavy and the battle actually started. My brother Richard was into cameras, so he took a whole bunch of pictures of the BIA violence on the river. I always thought it was odd that when he went to pick up the developed pictures at the photo store, they were gone. Anyway, I was fishing in my boat, a sixteen-foot Kundeson Craft with a sixty-horse Scotat Water motor, right next to my net. The BIA blazed down the river toward me and tried to pull my net out of the water and into their boat. I pulled the net back into my boat, and then they ran their boat into mine. A federal officer sprayed me in the face with mace so that I couldn't see, and two or three of the federal officers jumped into my boat and put handcuffs on me. Blacksnake and my brother, Richard were there to defend me. I also remember Lincoln McCovey, Puzzy Dowd, Joe Henderson, Punky Whipple, Corkey Simms, and Paul James being there. There were about seven federal boats and 40-50 Indian boats in the area. I hollered to the officers to put a life jacket on me because I had big boots on, and I thought I was going to sink like a rock because they were sinking my boat. They stuck a life jacket over my head. My handcuffs were on really tight and my hands went dead. I kicked my feet as fast as I could. I knew how to swim. I had been swimming in the river all of my life. But I was handcuffed, maced, and had big Buffalo boots on. Blacksnake pulled me out of the water and put me in Punky Whipple's boat. After that, I was arrested for fishing and taken to Crescent City.

Although we were all fishing by ourselves, there were four of us that were arrested: my brother, Richard; my cousin, Joe Henderson;

Figure 4: Joe Henderson being taken up the river in a federal boat after being arrested. Courtesy of Del Norte Triplicate, September 2, 1978, vol. 99, no. 68.

my cousin, Paul "Toe" James; and myself. We stayed in jail for two days. Apparently, fishing on the reservation was considered a federal crime, so we were supposed to appear in court in San Francisco within 48 hours. Since the "feds" had no way to transport us there, they tossed us out of jail.

In the end, when the BIA asked me "What's going to make you quit fishing, Frank?" I told them that I would stop fishing when off-shore (the commercial fisherman out in the ocean) quits fishing. I also told them that I wanted an opinion poll to see what our people wanted to do. At that time, the BIA was pushing for the Yurok Tribe to become an organized tribe. They argued since we weren't an organized tribe that we didn't have the right to fish. So, I wanted to hear whether our people wanted to become organized or not. We had the opinion poll in Klamath, California. Many community members like Molly Ruud and Pearl Peters volunteered to organize the poll. The results found that the majority of the people didn't want to organize until the Jesse Short[5] case was finished. I gave my word that I would follow through with the will of the people. So, I walked away from the BIA and I continued to fish.

›››

These two testimonials are important in that both Frank and Robley are descendants of allottees who had the right to fish despite not being from an organized tribe. They are both Indigenous people of the Klamath River who represent Indigenous families and the philosophies of a way of life that has been in existence for thousands of years. Their

Figure 5: Walt Lara meeting with the Secretary of Interior, Cecil Andrus. Courtesy of Times Standard, September 8, 1978, vol. CXXV, no. 246.

participation in the Fish Wars was out of responsibility to the future of our people. Throughout their lives, they have held true to our spiritual beliefs, our relationship with the river, and our way of life.

Once the federal officers had handcuffed Frankie McCovey, the violence on the river escalated. I remember running across five or six boats to get to him. It was clear that there was no regard for our status as sovereign nations, our retained fishing rights, or our safety and well-being. So, we began to retaliate. Since we had no weapons, when the federal officers pulled guns on us, we used our oars to defend ourselves. We dismantled the motors on their boats so that they could not get away. We planned to wrap a net around one of the federal boats and drag it out to the ocean, with the officers aboard, as they had done days earlier to the two teenage boys. We had the boat circled and were all ready to move when I made eye contact with Ted Jake (awok), a respected Yurok elder. He and his elderly friend had clinched their hands onto the sides of their boat as it rocked from the vigorous waves caused by the confrontation. I could see that his boat was full of water and he did not have a life jacket on. From the intense look in his eyes, I was suddenly reminded of the teaching of our ancestors: out of respect for the spirits of the river, it is against the law to fight, holler, or have negative feelings while on the river. So, that is how that confrontation ended. We ceased and decided to handle this matter in a way that was more conducive to our Indigenous philosophy. We pulled our boats off the river and we contacted the Secretary of Interior for a meeting.

There is so much more to be shared about the Fish Wars. I encourage anyone who can to reach out to community members in the Klamath area to hear their testimonials. Readers, please remember that the tactics used in the Fish Wars by the Bureau of Indian Affairs were not new tactics. Many of the strategies have been utilized against Indigenous peoples since the time of first contact. Nor have these methods dissolved. For example, the treatment of Indigenous people protecting lands at Standing Rock echoed alarming similarities. Furthermore, many of the issues continue to hold true. For example, in the letter that started this testimonial, I drew attention to off-shore commercial fishing, the environmental impact of logging, and the lack of release from the dams. The Fish Wars are not over and the advocacy is ongoing. We are vulnerable to uninformed administrations, diversions of resources, and shifting legislation. Therefore, it is important to learn from previous generations so that you can continue the efforts to protect our water, salmon, resources, and environment for future generations.[6]

Endnotes

1. Chag Lowry. "Living Biographies: Lavina Mattz, Ray Mattz, Marvin Mattz." *Indigenous Living Biographies.* Recorded in Klamath, California, 2000.

2. Justice U.S. Supreme Court. Mattz V. Arnett, 412 U.S. 481 (1973). Accessed September 21, 2018. https://supreme.justia.com/cases/federal/us/412/481/

3. Ibid, 412, U.S. 483-505.

4. It is important to note that during this time period, the Hoopa Valley Indian Reservation included traditional Yurok territory along the Klamath and lower Trinity Rivers. Today, this "extension" is now referred to as the Yurok Reservation.

5. The Jesse Short, ET AL, v. The United States Case began in 1963 and concluded in 1993. The case was brought by "Indian residents of what was then the Hoopa Valley Indian Reservation to address disparities in the way that funds derived from natural resources on the reservation were distributed." (Yurok Tribe Website, Retrieved November 15, 2018).

6. This chapter is a part of a larger book project to be published in the future.

"In the Spawning Ground"

Brian D. Tripp

"IN THE SPAWNING GROUND" ©
A PRAYER · POEM BY BRIAN D. TRIPP

I AM FROM THE SPAWNING GROUND · ITS
THE ONE THAT WE ALL KNOW · AT ONE
TIME · OR ANOTHER · WE ALL SWAM FROM
THE SAME HOLE · THATS WHEN MY WATER
BROKE · THATS WHEN MY FATHER SPOKE · HE
SAID · WHEN I WAS YOUNG · I WAS TOLD · KNOW
HOW THE WATER TASTES · KNOW WHICH WAY
IT FLOWS · FEEL THE WIND · KNOW WHICH WAY
IT BLOWS · LEARN FROM THE ANIMALS · THE
BIRDS AND THE BEES · SAY A PRAYER · FOR THE
HOME GROUND · THE RIVER · THE ROCKS · THE
MOUNTAINS · THE OCEAN · AND TREES · ALWAYS
GIVE · MORE THAN YOU TAKE · ALWAYS WORK
HARD · FOR THE PEOPLES SAKE · DON'T TELL
LIES · DO THINGS RIGHT · SING YOUR OWN
SONG · AND YOU WONT GO WRONG · SO
WHAT I KNOW · IS WHAT I OWE · TAKE IT ·
USE IT · THEN PUT IT BACK · IN THE GROUND
WHERE IT WAS · BEFORE IT WAS FOUND ·
THEN GIVE IT WATER · AND LET IT FLOW
GIVE IT LIGHT · MAKE IT BRIGHT · LET IT
GLOW · WITH LOVE · WITH RESPECT · THAT
WAY · THAT DAY · WE ALL CAN GROW ·
YO·TWA   YO·TWA   YO·TWA

PART 3

Songs to be Sung Again: Testimonials of Resilience and Beauty

Through ceremony, regalia, and art; Indigenous knowledge is revitalized and preserved. Thus, awakening the inner spirit leading to a pathway of healing.

{CHAPTER 14}

Songs of "Those Within"

Callie Lara

INTRICATELY SHAPED ABALONE SHELLS ADORN THE PRAYER ITEMS OF THE INDIGENOUS PEOPLE OF THE HOOPA VALLEY. Their song vibrates across the river from the dance grounds, creating an energy that speaks to ninasa:n (the world) in prayer. The shells slapping together with the song of a waterfall continues to echo off the mountain while dancers stomp the ground and harmonize with the rhythm of the world in ceremonial songs. Clam shells, bull pine, cedar, and juniper berries rustle against each other, mimicking the wind as it beats against the timber that surround the valley floor. Materials are bound together with the natural fibers that flourish within the historic boundaries of my home. The spirit of wildlife, birds, otter, deer, and spiritual beings of the forest and river contribute to the sacred prayers of an ancient people; all the while the patterns of the universe hover just above. "Shea ninas:an," I am present in this moment, we continue prayer as root is fed into the fire, a beacon between human beings and the dimensions of this world and time.

This is my inspiration. I am a regalia maker. I am a member of a society of individuals dedicated to the preservation of our ceremonies.

Figure 6: Callie showing her granddaughter, Tasahce Se:wenah how to work with maple bark. © 2019 Dorothy Gage. Courtesy of Dorothy Gage.

We understand the formulas of an ancient people. There are many stories to be shared of the purpose that keeps us connected to the world, to our environment, and of the spirit animals that carry our prayers. Our ancestors have guided us in the revitalization and restoration of our traditional way of life. I am among many contributors of regalia, ceremonial prayer items, who have survived the colonization and the attempted annihilation of a people. I am Natinixwe (spirit being on a human journey) from Jimekenehutch, Tsewelnaldin, Medilxwe, and the far-off lands of Oklahoma. My ancestors from these places live through me. Me che nai kiwil dichwin il, those within come out and are born again. Alice Pratt ne:en,[1] a ceremonial practitioner, began her prayer in this way, referring to our ancestors, our DNA and our genetic memory. Through this concept, historical accounts, and personal events, I will share my story in hopes to give a glimpse of an ancient people. I will begin with my grandmother, Emma Hitchcock Norton. She was an enrolled Cherokee tribal member and grew up the oldest of five sisters in Tahlequah, Oklahoma. Her grandmother, originally from North Carolina, survived the relocation infamously known as the "Trail of Tears" at twelve years old. My grandmother Emma met my grandfather, Jack (Hupa) at Haskell Indian Boarding School. They became educators and made their way back to Hoopa where they remained. My grandmother Emma didn't like to talk about the historical events of her people, but she did share with me a skill in the intricate ribbon work stitching of her grandmothers. I became very comfortable with needle and thread at an early age. This is important to me because it is the only connection I have to my grandmother, Emma's people.

I was born and raised in the Hoopa, the center of our world. I was fortunate to be surrounded in the Hupa culture and traditions. Materials that are abundant to our home were placed in our small hands. We—my sisters Holly, Patti and I—learned to twist and braid in hopes to become seasoned weavers; we peeled and stripped roots and maple bark into fine strands and strung shells and beads into necklaces that reflected the life of the ocean. As children we were told, "let your hands do it." I believed it and let my heart and mind follow.

At eleven years old. I made my first xoji kya, ceremonial dance dress, of the Hupa people. I had a cousin named Joelle, attending Berkeley University at the time, who had access to nicely cut abalone from a button factory. In the 1960s, these unique materials were hard to come by. Joelle brought them to me during her summer break. The 1960s had a renewed confidence and interest in the rebuilding of regalia. The sons and daughters, seeking traditional knowledge, used modern threads and materials that were available. That was my mother's generation. Her parents had survived the boarding school era, where traditional ways of doing things were discouraged. My mother's generation bred a new generation, my generation. Although unpopular, we spoke out, protested, and began to reclaim our truths. We rejected the injustice, foreign Christian teachings, and educational institutionalization that swept across Indian Nations and impacted what had been a traditional way of life for almost one hundred years.

For some, higher education presented itself as a way to "beat institutions at their own game." Education was important in "waking up our people," and continues to be an important tool in the preservation of our way of life. With that said, it is also important to embrace the traditional teachings not taught in a classroom but through our ceremonies, prayers, and elders.

I was guided by my grandma Nancy and Grandpa George, in the concepts of the K'y win ya ton ya:n ma ah'winew (the way Indian people do things) that held our people together. This gave me the confidence to complete my first xoji kya. Probably somewhat archaic or clumsy in design, it was completed with the haunches of the deer hide wrapping around the hips, with a two-inch pleat in the fold of the hide. The pleat is not only significant to the structure of the dress, but holds a spiritual significance as well. The shells, beads, fringe, and an apron add to the song of the dress. As a child, I completed the dress over the summer, learning the basics of regalia making. "Always work with your materials in a good-way; never take from the environment more then you need; put your things away while in mourning," were lessons shared by everyone. I learned that your feelings could be passed on to your dress or regalia piece. I gifted this first dress to my Grandma Nancy Nixon. Her contributions to our prayers and people impacted me greatly. It was important to her that we learn as much of our language as we could, participate in ceremony, and understand the philosophies of the Hupa people. She loved to tell us stories: lessons of coyote, the little people, big foot or the Kixinai, (the ancient people). These stories were and are timeless in meaning. She performed the duties of the medicine for the Hupa ceremonies, the Brush Dance, Jump Dance and White Deerskin Dance, during the late fifties through the early 1970s.

Fifty years later, I watched the morning sun bounce off the abalone

Figure 7: "Ning a'awhte ning q'ina xw a'unte" (I am you, you are the other me) Dresses that Callie made for her grand-daughters. © 2019 Princess Jintcon Colegrove and Maiya Rainer. Courtesy of the Ka'm-t'em Photography Project.

shells of the first dress I had made. My first instinct was to offer to remake the dress; however, this dress represented my beginning and a connection to the voices of my grandmothers, "let your hands do it."

Over the years, I have completed nine ceremonial dresses (taking six months to a year to complete each dress) for daughters and grand-daughters, as well as assisted others in the process. Although I have contributed numerous prayer items to our ceremonies, I have never completed a piece alone. There have always been helpers—whether they were gatherers, weavers, carvers, storytellers, hunters, researchers, or elders—that have worked alongside me, forming and shaping my perception.

In the early 60s, my husband Walt, Chris Peters, Dewey George, and other elders of the community were reviving the ceremonies of the Yurok people. Walt's grandmother's generation were not allowed by the U.S. Government to perform their ceremonies, and his people hid regalia pieces in attics and other places in fear of it being taken or misused. Indigenous people of the north coast were the surviving children of parents and grandparents that witnessed regalia leaving their homeland by the wagonloads. Families also lost regalia to collectors (private and from institutions), those that benefited from the hardships such as illness, death, or land issues inflicted on our people.

The stories of village massacres in the pursuit of gold, land, and the artifacts of our people were fresh in their minds. Therefore, the revivification of ceremony became a conflicting time for them to bring regalia out in fear that regalia could be stolen, taken, or that those leading the dances might not be doing the dances correctly. However, it is our belief that if you don't do right by the regalia, meaning not allowing the regalia to dance, it will come back on you, "eat you up." Regalia has to dance, to sing! Regalia has a spirit and must be respected. I grew up in a time when old people would tell their stories of dresses or regalia pieces crying from closets and attics.

The Hupa people never had an absence of ceremony. At times it was done in secret and other times publicly. It was uncommon for our people to dance for non-Indian entertainment. And there was a short time that we were ordered by the powers-that-be occupying Fort Gaston in the Hoopa Valley to hang an American flag on the dance grounds in order to have a ceremony.

Over time, trust began to build among the people in the revitalization of ceremony. More and more families brought their things out, and regalia makers began their contributions to ceremony. Dances are now filled with new and old regalia.

For many years, I have spent my seasons gathering and preparing materials, always with an understanding of the piece or its unique relationship to ceremonial prayers. Through whiŁ diniŁ' ay (my mind stretching out from me), I would visualize a design and begin to create. However, at a certain point the piece takes on its own life or spirit and begins to direct me. It becomes itself. There is resistance in trying to manipulate the outcome. When a piece becomes itself, it is a powerful moment. It is when a dress or regalia piece speaks. This is when a regalia maker becomes humbled. The bond, thoughts, and prayers of the work become stronger. For this reason, I have not been able to make a piece for sale nor monetary gain. How could I sell a prayer? I believe the difference between a regalia maker and a jewelry maker is that a jewelry maker has the freedom to creatively blend materials from all over the world and to express their interpretation of their world. A regalia maker is accountable to the prayer of the k'ixinai, the environment, and the K'iwinya'nya:n . We use materials that are referred to by our people as "blessed materials," chosen by the k'ixinai to represent a spirit to the dance, such as the woodpecker for his relationship to his family; the gentleness of the deer; the tenacity of the porcupine; the environmental consciousness of the humming bird, or the prayer of an abalone. Although binding materials have changed over the years, the blessed spirits have not.

I sometimes hear comments such as, "if we had the material of today back then, we would have used it!" I believe this comment deserves clarification. Using modern binding material such as glues, threads, etc., does not change the importance of a spirit such as a woodpecker or albino deer, beings we were taught to use in prayer by the k'ixinai. Having access to beautiful peacock feathers, for example, in this day and age does not make a peacock a blessed animal of our ancient prayers. We've learned the prayer of each "blessed material" through our stories that are passed down from one generation to the next, prayers given to human beings by the k'ixinai. From the beginning of time, our natural environment has taught us to be better human beings. Although there are those that seek to find ways to improve or modernize our regalia, our acorn soup, and/or our formulas in ceremony, we have a responsibility to learn the purposes and protect the lessons of the k'ixinai. In this way, we reclaim what has been taken and we listen to our genetic memory. Therefore, regalia used for sports mascots, Halloween costumes, or for the entertainment of the non-Indian community are very hurtful and offensive, not to mention a constant reminder of the historical oppression of a people. There is no argument to justify the mocking of ceremonial items.

Ella Johnson, ne:en, my stepfather's mother, a Yurok woman, was a basket maker. Growing up, my stepfather would take my sisters and me to Weitchpec, where she lived, every Sunday morning. While he chopped her wood or did minor repairs, we washed her dishes and did light housework. Grandma Ella would work with her basket materials and tell us stories. Once, I noticed the materials she was working with were different from the ferns or spruce roots I had seen her weave, and I asked her about it. She was pulling strips from a long piece of maple bark. I sat with her awhile and we talked about k'Ło kya, the apron or bark skirt. We made plans for me to gather with her on her next outing. Time went by and we never made the trip. For years, I wondered about that process and tried to envision the complete technique. Much later, Loren and Lena Bommelyn had completed a bark skirt, which had not been done in years, and encouraged me to make one. Other opportunities came up to gather bark, and I began to perfect my work.

They, referring to elders, would tell us to enter the forest in a good way and introduce yourself and leave a gift for the to:n (spirit beings of the forest). We were also told not to look directly at the little people of the forest. We believe that they are from another dimension of the world; if one appeared to us, we were to look away. They would also say, "to:n are keepers of the forest that will leave you alone if you acknowledge them and leave tobacco or something shiny like silver or copper as a gift," and also "leave the forest exactly how you find it!" After witnessing my Grandma Ella care for her materials and my Grandma Nancy's stories, I knew not to treat materials as scraps. I was reminded over and over as a child that I was a guest in the forest and must respect the creatures and spirits within it.

One morning, in the springtime, I was gathering maple bark in the mountains. I parked the truck along an old logging road and made my way down into a ravine, where I had been watching the growth of a small maple forest. The leaves of the maples were open wide. The water was obviously flowing along the cambium layer. The dirt was moist and rich as I slid down about fifteen feet with my small tool kit. Once I got to the bottom I introduced myself to the forest. While patting a handful of the soil on my right shoulder, I whispered my name, my family, and my purpose there. I breathed deep to allow the energy to flow from my spirit. It was quiet, the morning sun illuminated through the open spaces along the canopy of trees. I squinted through the rays of light searching the forest floor. The fragrance of fir, maple and madrone was refreshing. Alders shadowed the maples, and in the dense light it was important to follow the trunk of the trees high above to distinguish the difference in leaves. I found the tree: six inches in diameter and healthy enough to have a strip removed without damaging the tree. I knew that maples were very durable. In previous years, over an eight-year period, I had the opportunity to journal the life cycle of the maple forest, and the measurements and progression of what I will call a wound, from a strip I had taken from a tree. I found that within six to eight years, the bark will close over a wound as the tree continues to grow.

I began to work, tapping lightly on the bark, listening for the slight pop and squish noise the bark makes as it separates from the trunk. It is a good indication of the water flow just under the bark. Often the tapping brings in the woodpeckers that will answer tap for tap, probably looking for a mate. I'd made my first incision when I noticed a movement just above my forehead, about thirty feet in the distance. I looked in the direction of the movement. A very long, tawny tail with a wide hook on the end slowly swung back and forth like a pendulum. My eyes followed the length of the tail upward, where a panther lay along the wide branch of the tree. I guessed that she was six foot long or better. As she licked her wide paw, her yellow eyes watched me with interest. There is something quite eerie about panther eyes, and I was close enough to see the long hairs along the flat brow of her forehead. She did not hold her head erect nor were her ears flattened, so I knew I had not been hunted but had probably wandered into her space. Remembering to relax, which has taken practice, I dropped my tools into my container and carefully backed away. Once I reached the dirt road above, I fought the urge to sprint toward the truck, not wanting the cat to hear the shuffling of my feet. Sitting in my locked truck, I could appreciate the rituals of our people, acknowledgment of the to:n, being aware of my energy and remembering I am a guest in the forest.

Another example is while gathering bear grass. I had entered the high mountains in a good way but stepped in a hornet nest. The bees gushed from the ground and swirled around me like smoke. I whispered again my purpose and backed away. The hornets covered the front and back of my sweatshirt and crawled along my cheeks and across my mouth. I felt the weight of the swarm across my shoulders. Once I reached the truck, my niece Tasha slowly removed my sweatshirt. Her tears flowed the whole time but she did not panic. She said she did not even breathe. I dropped the sweatshirt in the brush and, without a sting or bite, we drove away. They, referring to the elders again, would tell us to wash your face when something unusual, or a "shifting of the world," took place, so we stopped at the first stream.

For me, it would be irresponsible not to teach my people about these things—the lessons, rituals, and techniques—however, there has to be an understanding to protect intellectual properties. It must become one's responsibility to recognize those that abuse and disrespect this knowledge for personal gain. I think my grandmothers would have approved. They were great teachers and had many students.

Among the pieces of regalia I have had the privilege to work with is the me:w nasita:n. But first it is important to say that when a young girl transitions into a woman, she becomes a spiritual being and welcomes her medicine. She is called a KinaŁdung, a girl of puberty. Her medicine is her power, her contribution, and her connection to the celestial beings that will guide her. During her xoq'it ch'iswa:l,[2] ceremonial prayer items are shared with her through dance such as the prayer of world renewal, the prayer of the continuation of mankind, the healing ceremonies, the cleansing ceremonies, and more. She now becomes significant in the sacred things. This is the one time, in our human form, that we bring all these prayers together, since we don't mix our medicines. For example, while one dance is going on, for those ten days we do not mention another ceremony, nor do we use some of the items that are specific to a ceremony with another. Therefore, during a woman's life of menses she would not handle these men's prayer items.

Walt is a ceremonial dance leader among his people. My youngest daughter used to help him with many things regarding dance. She helped him take care of his regalia, and traveled to many dance family homes throughout the year to discuss details of ceremony. For this young girl, it was a difficult transition in her life to step back, no longer his assistant. As a young woman she learned to appreciate and understand her medicine.

Once a woman goes through menopause, she no longer carries that particular medicine. During this time in her life she will work with men's prayer items in the construction, repair, or gathering. I began working with men's ceremonial pieces in this way after this transition in my life.

Hai me:w nas:sita:n, the ceremonial Jump Dance headdress, reflects the layers of our universe in its construction. Our world is layered in dimensions. Within these layers exist spirit beings, time and space, and worlds beyond. During ceremony, these layers overlap, and all exist within the human realm. Our prayer items not only act as communication between us and the k'ixinai but also keep us grounded in this world. Hai K'ise:qot, a head piece that drapes down the back, is adorned with a prayer painted in intricate designs for the K'ixinai that are standing behind the dancers. Blue jay, dove, and other tail feathers of blessed birds are intricately tied at the bottom of a k'ise:qot to enhance the delivery of the prayer and to sweep the energy following the dancer as he moves in a spiritual way. An eagle feather sits above and carries the vibration of the prayers out and beyond. I have had the opportunity to create and recreate many of these things. Each regalia piece has a specific and unique purpose. A regalia maker understands and becomes accountable to the prayer.

In the process of revitalizing the Flower Dance for the Ner-er-ner people of the coastal Yurok tribe, my family spent many years interviewing and researching information regarding the details of the dance. For our people, the Flower Dance was one of the first restrictions Indigenous people had by the non-Indian community. Walt's Grandmother, Josie Marks, had left him with a lot of information, and his mother invested her knowledge in her granddaughters. It therefore became their goal to restore the dance. My job was to make the traditional regalia necessary to complete the prayer. I also studied, interviewed, and participated in Hupa Flower Dances, and viewed collections from a variety of sources for information regarding the construction of Flower Dance items. Over several years my husband and I worked with woodpecker scalps. I traded for the deer belly of hides and other materials. Once, a friend negotiated the belly of a deer hide for the canning of his deer meat. Another gave me a beautifully brain-tanned hide if I promised to make something nice for girls to wear. Yadao Inong, a young Yurok man, was just learning to brain-tan hides, and it was perfect. My son-in-law, Sam Cooper, intricately carved the redwood and ocean spray sticks for the top of the Jump Dance head piece, It took about a year to complete two me:w nasita:n.

Shortly after this time, I had the privilege of repairing a large dance collection of me:w nas:sita:n. During the many months it took to repair eleven headdresses, and through discussions with ceremonial keepers, I was able to identify which pieces were made by the same maker and approximate timelines of constructions. During the late 1800s and early 1900s, natural materials of sinew, iris string, and sturgeon head glue were used to bind the layers of a me:w nasita:n together. Brain-tanned hides formed the head dress and flaps. The durability and flexibility could not be matched with more modern materials that were later used.

During the 1920s to 1940s, a cotton twine replaced most of the iris string in the construction of these pieces, but sinew was still used abundantly. It was important to me to maintain the integrity of the design and constructions. All pieces removed to be replaced with newer materials were returned to the caretaker, down to the smallest feather or piece of thread. Since these precious items had been in and out of the spirit world, carrying the prayers of our people for many generations, the old materials would be returned to the spirit world through fire. This was the most significant time in my life of regalia making. It is a treasured experience.

Figure 8: Kameron McCovey, Teh-sa'a:n-xwe Cooper, Sagep Blake, and Peter Blake wearing me:wh nasita:n and necklaces made by Callie Lara. © 2019 Gary Colegrove. Courtesy of Ka'm-t'em Photography Project.

While I was in the process of making a third me:w nasita:n, I repaired another collection. Over the year, I worked with the five headdresses. In this collection, gauging by the materials used in it, was one of the oldest pieces I've come across from the 1800s.

In the summer of 2018, during the Jump Dance of the Yurok people, I stood waiting for the dancers to come up the river from Catep village, toward Pecwan where the Sragon Dancers were dancing. Until recently, Joe Jerry's Dance Camp had not come out for approximately ninety years. Although it was talked about often over the years to bring this side out, the dance-makers waited for a leader or leaders with the right characteristics to lead this camp, and also to have enough regalia to support this revitalized camp. Six years previously, Jake Blake and Frankie Masten, both young men, had been selected. It was one of the most beautiful sites I was privileged to witness. In the distance, I could see the eleven feathers atop the dancer's heads, gently vibrating in the wind. The dancers walked in single file. The Me:wh nasita:n (headdress) shone a brilliant red in the afternoon sunlight. Adorned in old dentalium necklaces, faces painted, and wrapped in xoji-teh (deer-skin blankets) they moved with careful steps. Walt, the mah-chi-qal (one who walks in front) moved toward the dance house with his cane guiding his steps. Each dancer mindful of his purpose. Some silently mumbled in prayer. As the line passed, I saw the things I had made. I was overwhelmed at the beauty of the kisiqot, beads, blankets, and young men who wore them. At the end of the line, Jake and Frankie followed. I smiled quietly to myself. Four of the me:w nasita:n I had worked on for a long period of time were among them. The gathering, care and attention given to the spirit animals and materials was worth the many years in prayer with my ancestors.

Although I'd like to continue with the stories of whiŁ diniŁ ay, I will end with saying that knowledge of our ancestors is not always easy to find, and shouldn't be. There are so many lessons in the process of regalia making. A regalia maker understands the complex network in our world. We often open ourselves up to historical trauma, struggle to maintain the integrity of our way, and have a continual struggle to qualify ourselves and our traditions. For me, there has been healing in the making of prayer items, genetic memory vs. epigenetics. I am a regalia maker with a passionate relationship to the implicit nature of our environment and to the timeless prayers. When I look at ceremonial regalia I see myself, my people, and our way of life. I am reminded who I am. "I am you and you are the other me" Le Red. We as "spiritual beings on a human journey" continually seek those within that come out and are born again.

Endnotes

1. A word to refer to the deceased.
2. In the Hupa language translates to "on her they beat,",referring to her Flower Dance where they will beat in time on her with sticks.

{CHAPTER 15}

Íhuk: A Time of Renewal, Transformation, and a Journey Towards the Future

Lyn Risling

SHE STOOD BLINDFOLDED, FACING THE EAST TOWARD THE RIVER AND MOUNTAIN, SURROUNDED BY A CIRCLE OF FAMILY AND RELATIVES. It was right before first morning light. Her mother approached her from behind and began to rock her back and forth as a special very old Íhuk song was sung. At the end of the song, her uncle, who stood in front of her, removed the blue jay feather tav covering her eyes. She was now a new person, no longer a girl. She looked out into the world for the first time as a woman.

She opened her eyes after days of being blindfolded, and fasting on only acorn water, and getting up at dawn each morning for her ritual bathing at a nearby spring. Then she would gather ten loads of wood and stack them behind her yavureekrívraam (menstrual house). After another ritual bath and short rest, she would be led to a special area to build her rock pile that represented her future life as a woman. She said a prayer for luck with each rock she carefully placed on her pile. As she performed her tasks, she was always accompanied by her woman helper who shook a deer rattle to let others know to look away from the girl. All of her tasks were done for "making her luck" and were done with

Figure 9: "First Íhuk." © 2007 Lyn Risling. Courtesy of Lyn Risling.

prayers she had learned in the Karuk language.

After her jobs were completed, the girl would be prepared for the morning dance, dressed in her maple bark skirt, eyes always covered by her tav. She would be led to the dance grounds where singers were waiting to start the dance. The girl was the central part of the dance as she stood and danced in front of the line of men singers and dancers, while the women singers stood to the side with their dance sticks that kept time with the beat of the songs. After the beginning songs, the girl danced back and forth as the men behind her did the same, always facing the east with their backs to the fire. Finally, all the people who had come to the ceremony formed a circle and danced around the girl as each man and boy took turns turning her in the middle. They all sang and danced to "make luck" for her during the ceremony and for her future as a woman.

Always isolated from others except her helpers, in a special camp set up for her, the girl was allowed visiting later in the day by women close to her such as aunties and grandmother. They shared their experiences, advice, and words of wisdom about being a woman.

The dance would happen again each night and in the mornings and afternoons. After her tav was removed, the girl would run ten times from her camp area to the dance grounds and pray to the morning star to the east. At the end of her run, she would be prepared for the last dance in her new ceremonial dress and necklaces.

This new young woman was my daughter twenty-one years ago. It was a time of transformation and renewal. It was a transformation of my daughter into womanhood and time of renewal of the Íhuk, a Karuk coming of age ceremony for girls, that had been dormant for over 120 years.

The idea of bringing back this ceremony began at least five years before it became a reality. I had already begun, years before that, to make a ceremonial dress for my daughter. Then my good friend Julian Lang, who later became my partner and husband, introduced me to some very old recordings of Íhuk songs and other Karuk songs that had not been sung or listened to by most people for many, many years. Like the ceremony, these songs lay dormant. Julian had spent many hours and months learning these songs and then, as he shared and taught many of them to me, a seed was planted that would inspire us to bring back this ceremony for my daughter and others.

At first it seemed like an overwhelming task, since we had no one to guide us that had either experienced or seen an Íhuk ceremony. In prior research, Julian had discovered ethnographic materials that had been written by linguists and anthropologist in the early 1900s from Karuk informants. Some of this information touched briefly on the Íhuk ceremony. Through my own research I uncovered more bits of information, but not a complete picture of the ceremony. But slowly we began to piece together a vision of what the ceremony might be like. We went to museums and studied Íhuk dance items that were no longer being made, and consulted elders for any knowledge they might have concerning the ceremony.

We contacted another Karuk family whose daughter was a friend of my daughter about bringing back this ceremony for both of them. After they agreed, we began working closely together toward that goal.

Julian and I gathered family relatives together who were closely connected to us through other Karuk ceremonies and who were interested in helping bring back the Íhuk. We held practice sessions to teach and learn the old songs. With Julian's knowledge of the Karuk language, and from our research, we began to learn some Karuk language connected to the ceremony.

We included my daughter whenever we could in gathering materials for dance regalia. Through trial and error, we began to learn how to make Íhuk dance regalia such a maple bark skirts, dance sticks, and a feather Tav. Fortunately, we also had relatives and friends who helped and shared with us in our efforts. I continued working on my daughter's ceremonial dress and she helped make necklaces. We took my daughter out to gather acorns for the ceremony and we taught the girls how to process and cook acorns. My daughter began to practice fasting for several months.

Although there were a lot of uncertainties about what we were doing, with lots of prayer and help from others, slowly but surely, things started coming together as the girls reached their first menses. We decided to hold the ceremony at an old village site where Julian's grandmother had come from and where Íhuk ceremonies had taken place long ago. Over the weeks prior to the ceremony, we cleared the grounds where the dance would take place and eventually set up camp. We prepared the girls and did final preparations for food, water, and the grounds.

We called upon the Spirits of the place and our ancestors to be with us and give us guidance. As the ceremony unfolded, we began to feel their presence, but also discovered that the ceremony had a Spirit and power of its own. We had to adapt to unexpected challenges, but experienced magical moments as well. The old Íhuk songs came alive again and filled our hearts.

After the end of the Íhuk ceremony, we had so much to reflect upon. We kept our daughter in seclusion for several days afterwards. The

Figure 10: "Rebirth into Womanhood." © 1997 Lyn Risling. Courtesy of Lyn Risling.

ceremony, from the beginning stages of preparations to the end, had taken us through a journey of transformation and rebirth. Through her experience, my daughter faced her own challenges and found her strength and power through prayer and believing in herself. Although she would yet to comprehend all that she went through, I knew the experience had changed her and I believed it would have an impact on her for the rest of her life.

After a little while, and after much discussion about this amazing experience, Julian and I asked ourselves, "So, what next? Where do we go from here? Is that it?"

A story our ancestors told about the Íhuk came up in our research. It tells of how the Íhuk began with the Deer People up in the heavens and how it was given to humans. We learned that Íhuk is the Spirit of Deer Girl who had the first ceremony to bring luck to her as she turned into a woman up in the heavens, the home of the Deer People. We also learned that the Karuk people living along the Salmon River would hold a "Spring Dance" every year to celebrate the return of that Deer Girl Spirit. When she returned to Earth, she would travel to ten villages along the river, stopping at each, where the people would hold a ceremony in which a chosen girl from their village would represent that Spirit.

After much thought and discussion, our next goal became to bring back the Spring Dance to the village site, where we had held the Íhuk. After contacting a family that had a daughter of the right age, and lots of preparation, we were able hold the ceremony. Since then, we have had a Spring Dance or an Íhuk almost every year to the present. It has been an amazing journey of new experiences and learning throughout each ceremony, as we work with different families every year. Many of the families continue to share these experiences with us by helping, dancing and singing for each new young woman to make luck for her.

Through their experiences, these young women have learned about the importance of ceremony and culture to our families and communities, as well as to them personally. They have grown into strong women, most going on to college, working to serve their communities, and participating in ceremonies and other aspects of their culture. Because of their active participation, I know that many of these women will take active roles and responsibilities to support the continuation of our ceremonies and culture.

As I look into the future, I see our youth facing new challenges, different from those of previous generations. I feel hopeful in knowing that many seeds have been planted in them through the work of those who worked hard to restore many of our traditions, language, and ceremony, as well as our sovereign rights to practice these. They can learn not only from their own experiences, but also from knowledge of the past, and they can receive guidance from their ancestors to help keep our cultures moving forward for many future generations to come. We must always remind ourselves that we come from resilient peoples, with cultures and beliefs that were in balance with the natural world that sustained them for thousands of years. Our ancestors believed in renewing the Earth through prayer, ceremony, and song. As these beliefs continue to be renewed, the generations ahead of us will experience their own transformations and rebirth into the future. This is something we must all work towards to keep our world in balance.

CHAPTER 16

Being of the Same Mind

Julian Lang

Kíri koovur íimkun kumáheesh xas pámita vaa nímaahtihanik.
"I wish you folks could see what I have seen." (An old Karuk
expression said when words cannot express how one feels.)

MY LIFE CHANGED IN THE FIFTH GRADE. It was when a
non-English speaking brother and sister joined our classroom from
Guadalajara, Mexico. Curious about them, I began learning Spanish.
In the sixth grade, my mom brought home a series of booklets on
learning the German language. Obviously I had a knack for languages.
Looking back I see that I was also being introduced to other cultures
from lands which were very different from our American culture. One
day it dawned on me: A culture was residing within me, one that was
equal to the German, Spanish, and American cultures. It was my own
indigenous Karuk culture. I had come to see that Karuk people possess
the same aspects of culture that I was learning about in my foreign
language studies, including a distinct language, a long shared history,
art and music, a spiritual belief system, laws and a political structure
to govern ourselves and our lands. I realized that the knowledge in my
Karuk grandmother's head was as important, if not more important
(to me at least), than the knowledge I was learning at school. Realizing
this made me a happy Karuk Indian boy from Katimiin. Still I needed
more. I needed to hear more stories about my people.

Years later, at college, I discovered that when an Indigenous people, like the Karuk people, possess their own laws, history, language, religion, political structure, and lands, this is, in fact, the pillars of what today we call "Tribal Sovereignty." It can be shown that Karuk People have lived here in a sovereign way for at least 10,000 years. The neighboring Yurok, Hupa, Tolowa, and Wiyot peoples can assert this same fact about themselves as well. If added together, we collectively possess 50,000 years of combined knowledge and experience directly relating to living on this land.

At the heart of this vast knowledge is what is sometimes called "Original Instructions." From the earliest generations to those of us living in the present, our ancestors passed along certain knowledge which prescribed and directed us to regularly gather together to sing, dance, pray, and cast off all our bad feelings and thoughts. We were told to follow the ancient recipe designed to bring good fortune to our people, to our land, and to enable us to pass on good medicine to the sick, the weak, and the elderly. It is a process that will bring our own personal lives back into balance. We are told to follow these instructions year after year.

Long before Plymouth Rock, Christopher Columbus, the Oregon Trail, or the Gold Rush of 1849, our culture was guiding us to remain connected with our Original Instructions. It was a protective power to help us in our struggles and to aid us against threats to our very existence. A recent condition is making this ability to connect with our instructions more difficult: language loss. A person can gain insight into our culture by physically "doing": we can learn to build, to make, and to sing and dance. But to fully understand the Original Instructions, we must hear them spoken in our Indigenous languages. The words lead us directly to those who came before us and to their testimonies, confessions, histories, and creation stories. To be honest, all that we know today came to us from elders who spoke only their original languages and who received their instructions in their particular language. Each of our local tribes has its own Indigenous language. Its importance can't be stressed enough.

I have had the honor of helping to bring back and re-establish many ceremonies of our region as a worker, a singer, a dancer, and a language speaker. I had the honor of sitting and discussing the intricacies and histories of our ceremonies with elders for many years. These days, I bring the knowledge they shared with me to the ceremonies. During the 1990s I helped to re-establish the Íhuk ceremony up on the Salmon River. The ceremony is held just upstream of the old village of Vunxárak, my grandfather's birthplace. At the time of the Redick McKee treaty signing in 1851,[1] my grandfather's great-grandfather signed his X on that treaty for the Karuk People of our area. My great-grandmother, who lived to be over 107 years old, spoke often and proudly of her grandfather's role as a leader and dreamer of the people. She told us that our village, Vunxárak, was a dance site for the Íhuk ceremony. This ceremony is called the Flower Dance in English, and is held when a girl becomes a woman. It is once again an important occasion among all of the local tribal peoples to come together and make luck for the girl's future and bless her transition into womanhood.

The impact of bringing back this ceremony proved to be important in many unforeseen ways. By relighting the ceremonial fire, the land itself is able to hear the prayers of the people once again. The ritual act of feeding the earth is resumed. The extended families and descendants of the village's ancestors are beckoned back and reconnected with their ancestral place. Family oral histories are heard once again. Kinship ties are restored. Most importantly, the Original Instructions are being honored again.

We will receive many gifts by the return of ceremony: the dance makers gain new and sometimes startling insights into the purpose of the ceremony; the family of the girl for whom the ceremony is being held restores itself in a ceremonial way; the community witnesses and actively participates in the age-old symbolic ritual to transform a young girl into a woman through dance and song; and, once again, tribal adults and elders are able to sing and dance with their young people.

I don't know if it's funny or sad, but it's not uncommon to return home after having poured one's heart and soul into preparing for and conducting a ceremony only to find that the outside world, society's world, seems awfully pitiful and spiritless. It seems best to stay disconnected from the drama, from television, from everything for as long as possible so as to keep connected with one's feelings of contentment. We refer to our ceremonial experiences as a time when "the spirit enters us," and we become aware of what we call "power of the ceremony." When you live with the ceremony from the point before the people arrive to the time after everyone leaves, you will receive your own personal message. It will be a message from the mountains that is only for you. It will likely be more of a feeling than something as simple as a verbal message. And if you remain disconnected from society and nurture this message, it will take root inside you.

I can tell much more concerning this Indigenous ceremonial experience, but I won't. Let me say this instead: YOU will become whoever you are after experiencing your own ceremonies. The more time and effort you put into it, the more distinctly you will define yourself. And remember it's not about YOU but others. For elders, the ceremony is healing. For adults, it is power to provide for one's family and for others. For kids, it is a blessing. For the Earth, it is love.

Endnotes

1. Robert F. Heizer, Eighteen Unratified Treaties of 1851-1852. Between the California Indians and the United States Government, Archeological Research Facility, Department of Anthropology, University of California, Berkeley, CA, 1972. http://digitalassets.lib. berkeley.edu/anthpubs/ucb/text/arfs003-001.pdf.

CHAPTER 17

Utilizing Art to Preserve Our Way of Life

Dr. George "Pordie" Blake

MY MOST PROMINENT MEMORY AS A CHILD PARTICIPAT-ING IN CEREMONY WAS SITTING WITH OTHER LITTLE BOYS DOWN IN THE FRONT OF THE DANCERS NEAR THE FIRE, AS ONLY CHILDREN DO. Jimmy James was singing the last song to finish up the Deerskin Dance, an esteemed appointment. Jimmy was a Yurok man with a strong spiritual side. He was singing with everything he had. His voice echoed, in essence bounced, beneath the canopy of oaks as he sang. We turned around to look at the line of people watching the dance behind us. We were struck by the crowd of people standing there with tears running down their faces. We knew that something special was happening, and it bonded in our minds and our hearts to this day. There are moments in life that never leave you, and you almost don't want to speak of it because words can't describe the feeling, as if it was a moment frozen in time.

As a regalia maker, canoe maker, elk antler carver, and contemporary artist, I have had the opportunity to contribute to the preservation of our ceremonies and our way of life through art. My contribution is a result of forging relationships, friendships, and giving due respect to elders. I had an intent desire to learn and acquire knowledge. In high school, I lived with my Aunt Lila and Uncle Frank. My uncle's dad died, making it my uncle's responsibility to lead a Deerskin Dance and Jump Dance camp. They didn't have much regalia or baskets due to losses, so, when I was living there, Auntie worked on a lot of baskets and Uncle fixed and made regalia. That was when I began carving acorn spoons, as a way to offer help. I also remember seeing Grandma Nancy prepare the acorns for the dances. She was the medicine woman and had a role in all of the dances. That was her job for many years. Those experiences shaped my attitude about my place in our culture.

One of my most influential teachers was Dewey George. Dewey was a Yurok elder from Sregon (a Yurok village) who was known for his vast understanding of the culture. He was a canoe and regalia maker. He was a man who unwittingly gathered knowledge just by living it. He

Figure 11: George "Pordie" Blake dressing his boys in regalia. © 2019 Princess Jintcon Colegrove. Courtesy of Ka'm-t'em Photography Project.

paid close attention so he had knowledge to pass on when people were interested. Dewey's sister and my mother were life-long friends. So, I spent a lot of time observing him and getting acquainted. Learning opportunities came up when I least expected it. For instance, when we were fishing, I marveled at his techniques. He fixed a fish-stripping table right at the edge of the water. I had never seen that done before, and I couldn't believe how simplistic the design and how fast he could process a surplus of salmon. I learned a lot by spending time with him and being there at the instant when information would come up. A lot of the time, knowledge is only shared at precise moments. When I had a specific question, I would go and visit him. You have to make conversation with elders when you want to learn from them. In order for them to recall information, you have to stimulate their thinking. Dewey contributed a lot. I know that Walt Lara and Chris Peters were always with him during that time too. Dewey was a teacher. When he was dying, I went to see him. Before going, I was aware that he was uneasy about passing. He told us about his dream. "Today, I went and laid down and I had a dream," he said, "I went up and I could see the gates. The grass was so pretty and green." He started to cry as he spoke of it. He stopped talking, composed himself, and said, "I saw these little angels over there. And it was my job to teach them how to fly." His dream settled his troubled spirit in the dying process.

In 1975, Beanie, my cousin and ceremonial leader, bought a log big enough for a canoe from the coast and had it hauled home. He asked Dewey to come up to make a boat. He invited me to bring my chainsaws to help Dewey, but it was too hot for Dewey and he only stayed for a short time. I sawed all day, and it was so exciting that I wanted to put lights up so that I could work after dark. That was the first boat that I completed. Since then I have made many boats, although I have never kept count. At a deep place in my life, I wandered from the crowd at the Deerskin Dance to photograph canoes as the afternoon sun shone on the river. I looked on at seven boats at the water's edge. The first was made by Dewey George, the second by Hanes Moore, and the remaining five were canoes that I had made. As an artist, I acknowledged that I'm not getting rich or famous, but I must be doing something for my people. After that, I had an occasion to make a special prayer for the Yurok, my father's people, to don their own canoes made from their own wood. The next year, I found myself helping with five canoes from logs that the Yurok Tribe had acquired. I thought that was a special thing.

Homer Cooper was another person that had a lot of knowledge. I will always remember when I wanted to learn about bow making and I told that to my elder friend, Francis Roberts, while I was driving her down to Johnson's (a place near the village of Watek). I didn't realize that she was a cousin to Homer from Pecwan Creek. She immediately took me to his house. We walked up on the porch, knocked on the door, and he hollers "atlumah" (come in). I watched her walk over where he was sitting, clear across the room. He stood and they engaged in dialogue back and forth in Yurok. Finally, when the conversation stopped, he looked up at me and grinned with the biggest smile, revealing some missing teeth. I could tell that he was delighted that I was interested in bow making. That was the beginning of our friendship that lasted until he died.

Homer told me a story about how he wanted a bow when he was young. An elder in Pecwan was making bows for the older boys, and Homer decided, "I'll go ask Mama." The bow maker told him, "If you can get me a knife and a wet stone, I will make you a bow." Homer got the knife and wet stone from his mother and he got his bow, joining the ranks of the older boys. At twelve years old, he said that he worked like a man; his mom took him out and put him on a ranch in the Arcata bottom. One day, he came back to his room in the barn and his bow was gone. Somebody stole it. That bow was his prized possession.

Homer taught me a lot about the sinew-backed Yew wood bow. The art of making sinew-backed bows was a lost art for Hupa people. The last known Hupa bow maker, James Hostler, died with the knowledge. So, I spent a lot of time researching and learning about bow making. There are key components to making a sinew-backed Yew wood bow: the proper collection and application of sinew, the gathering and preparation of sturgeon glue, and the making of arrows. I sought out people to connect with, and came together with others by chance.

There is an art to gathering sinew properly from the deer. There are ways to take sinew off the deer that makes nice long pieces for stitching things together, for regalia, and for tying arrows. It's a process of taking the sinew off over the joints; one of them even goes through the joints. I have been teaching my son and others how to do this, so that as they hunt they can start saving it. Once you dry sinew it will last for a long time. I was told that one of the finest sinew-backed bows in the world was the Turkish bow, and they also used sturgeon bladders and sinew like us.

Figure 12: George "Pordie" Blake sharing a sinew backed bow. © 2019 Princess Jintcon Colegrove. Courtesy of Ka'm-t'em Photography Project.

A doctor and friend of mine, Charles E. Grayson, held a world record in flight and owned one of the foremost private archer's collection in the world. His information was vital to the command of some of the things that the old masters were telling me about sinew application. He told me once that the Hupa arrow was meticulously done. He said that it is one of the finest arrows that he found in the world, and only an Aleutian island otter arrow could compare to the Hupa arrow.

I connected a bit with Hanes Moore in an ill-fated event.[1] In our solemn search on the Klamath River, we happened upon a sturgeon. I asked him to show me how to extract the bladder for glue and he obliged. Although bittersweet, that was an important juncture. Homer then showed me how to stew it up with the skin and parts of the fins. He would cook it until all the fat raised to the top to be scraped off. A long time ago, they used to chew it, spit it, and put it on a piece of sinew.

I studied and practiced making bows and arrows for many years until

I felt like I got it right. When Homer was in the hospital before he died, I took a bow to him, sort of hiding it behind my back. He said, "Whatchu got behind you?" When I gave it to him, he laid it on his lap and stroked it from the center all the way out to the ends, slowly. Then he got a big grin on his face and he said, "That's the way I remember them as a boy." I finished college, but that moment was graduation for me.

I was a disturbed youth, and when I was in the military service my mind would race, such that I would sit up until daylight pondering out the window and playing my guitar. I saw the sun come up that way about every two weeks while I was there. Music and lyrics resonated with me, and I tried to imagine and made it my life goal to have "a satisfied mind," as the song by Joe Myas had eloquently described.

Now, there are things that I've come across that are above religion. They're miraculous, and so sensitive and painful that it bears thinking about for a moment. A friend told me of her family who was interned to a camp in Ohio during World War II. Eventually, two siblings came to the West Coast, and the parents stayed in Ohio. My friend told me of her father visiting both her and her brother in a dream the night her father died. He was true to character, giving instruction on how to live their lives and carry on without him. When I heard that story, I said, "That's my theory, that he's greater than religions, ain't nothing to do with a religion." That was a spiritual thing that happened from the maker. That was so amazing to me.

There have been times in my life that I've been spiritually riveted, particularly by song. Words don't give you an understanding when you're dealing with something so special; language doesn't describe what's happening. What we're seeing, feeling, and experiencing—we can recognize there's spiritual meaning in it. We have the opportunity not only to touch something almost unattainable here, but to embrace it. I've seen some of my children, especially my third daughter, embrace their gifts, unexplained by religion, with dreams and premonitions. That astounds me and brings me comfort. For my descendants I would say to pursue your understanding with your maker, with God.

Endnotes

1.   The author wishes to keep the details of the "ill-fated event" implicit.–Ed.

{INTERLUDE}

"I am a Visitor of the Forest"

Callie Lara (2017)

I am a visitor of the forest. I travel gently into an environment
sacred to the dwellers.
The brown and gold bracken crunches underfoot.
Twigs and limbs are tangled like webs before me.
Along the perimeter of the trees bear grass shoots sprout up.
In the distance timber circling open prairies allow the day to
cast light on the vegetation spread across the ground.
Above me, the dense canopy vibrates the whispering of the
trees from one to another. Down the ravine, I hear the songs of
flowing water trickling over the rocks.
Rays of light shoot through the limbs, like spears spotlighting
the beauty of the landscape.
I smell the aromas that guide the inhabitants, the burst of a
budding orchard, ferns, lichen, bark, and the decomposition of
the forest in the cycle of life.
I feel the presence of life all around me.
I hesitate at the sound of a large creature lumbering through
the brush or the stealth of a feline moving along the branches.
Small animals scurry along the forest terrain in their social
practices.
Woodpeckers fall silent as I pass but then quickly alert the
residence of my presence.

All that is the forest gives to the prayers of the world.

I am most humbled by the magnificence of the spirit being, the little people, in the mist.

A labyrinth to another dimension of the world I am forbidden to travel.

At this moment, all that I have described falls to the back of my consciousness.

Easily my spirit transcends and time unifies us.

Although only for a moment, I have participated in a phenomenon of time and share the breath of the forest, I am the captive.

I cry out, "I am a visitor of the forest!"

PART 4

The Basket Travels: Testimonials of Awakening and Next Steps

Each person is valuable and can make an essential contribution to the protection of the natural environment and preservation of Indigenous knowledge. Like pieces of a puzzle, we must work collectively as a whole. As such, this section addresses sovereignty, education, and action.

CHAPTER 18

Letter to a Young Native: Sovereignty is Action

Shaunna Oteka McCovey

Ai yu kwee' Young Native,

I BEGIN THIS LETTER WITH A HARD TRUTH. One that is not sugar-coated or dressed in niceties to soften the blow because you do not deserve that. You deserve to know, upfront, the reality of our situation, so you will be well armed when the day comes and you must stand up for your people and for your tribal nations. So here it is: Tribal governments in our present time are not truly sovereign governments. Native American nations and tribes have not been true sovereigns since before the white intrusion.

Prior to contact, being a sovereign meant the right to self-govern, and not just the right but the inherent right. "Inherent" means we were born sovereign and that our sovereignty was not granted to us by the United States Government. Each tribe, village, nation, band, pueblo, etc. had its own way of governing its people, its own tribal laws, and its own way of protecting and taking care of tribal homelands. For the sake of clarity, I will call inherent sovereignty *true sovereignty* for the remainder of this letter.

Tribal government today exists because the United States Congress passed the Indian Reorganization Act of 1934 (IRA), which allowed us to form replicated versions of the U.S. Government. Mini-governments, constitutions and all (and you should know that those tribal constitutions were not written by tribal people). Maybe it was a good thing—to let people who were traditionally self-governing govern themselves. Then again, maybe it wasn't. The structure of government that was required by the IRA completely ignored our traditional ways of living and being as distinct and sovereign peoples. All of this begs the question: if we are not true sovereign nations, what are we? I'll attempt to explain.

We are quasi-sovereign. "Quasi" means *apparently, but not really* or—*kind of.* This is, unfortunately, the official definition of tribal sovereignty that we are stuck with—sovereign, but not *really* sovereign. Quasi-sovereignty allows tribes to regulate their people in various ways. Tribes can determine membership, make laws and ordinances that apply only to tribal people, have some limited jurisdiction over lands, and have other powers similar to states. While there are some aspects of sovereignty interlaced into the everyday workings of tribal government, those aspects are given by the U.S., and what the U.S. is giving to tribes is the ability to act as smaller Federal governments within the larger Federal Government structure; hence my previous reference to mini governments. That is not true sovereignty. Tribal governments function because Federal funding is passed through to tribes, and that funding rarely increases. Each year Congress passes an appropriations (money) bill that gives a specific amount to each Tribal government. The funding is used to run programs like, education, social services, etc. So, Tribal government operations are dependent on funding from the Federal Government. That is not true sovereignty. A tribe does not exist in the eyes of the Federal Government without federal recognition, without the U.S. Government saying it exists. That is not true sovereignty. You may argue that tribal nations are owed this funding and federal recognition because of treaty rights, because tribal lands were given up, because federal Indian case law dictates it, and you would not be wrong. Many tribal people feel this way, but again, this is not true sovereignty.

The most frightening aspect of quasi-sovereignty is that the United States Congress can take away our right to govern ourselves with the stroke of a pen. It is as easy as passing legislation that shrinks our reservations, or terminates entire tribes, or attempts to exterminate our culture by relocating us to urban areas or sending our children away to boarding schools. All of this has been done in the past, and the past is brutal. It should never be repeated.

Now that we have established that the Federal Government sees us as quasi-sovereign, I wholeheartedly believe that now is the time in the course of our history (and this letter) for us to think about sovereignty differently. While we must acknowledge the characterization and try to understand this view (because we are stuck with it), it is our responsibility to make the word "sovereignty" meaningful to us. We can make sovereignty mean what we want it to through *action*. How do we do this? We do it every day in the way we navigate the world. We do it through our actions as individuals, as human beings in the very unique situation of being blessed to be Native to this land. We do it because we fiercely believe that we are special and that we are powerful. When we, both individually and collectively, express these attributes, we create our destiny. The world is ours to make and remake. It always has been. We just got a little sidetracked.

You see, sovereignty much more about perspective. I understand this may be a bit confusing because we often hear about our tribal governments "asserting their sovereignty" in different political arenas. When we "assert" our sovereignty, we feel empowered and our perception is that we've been heard by the Federal Government. This, however, is not always the case. Sometimes when we "assert" our sovereignty, nothing happens. We are told by the Federal Government that we are sovereign, so many of us mimic the words without really having a true understanding of what that sovereignty means to us and to those who call us sovereign. Our perspective of our own sovereignty and another's perspective of our sovereignty can be very opposing. I want you to know is there is a clear difference between *assertions of sovereignty* and *exercising one's sovereignty*. An assertion is simply using words to say we are sovereign, but exercising sovereignty is done through action. And as we all learned in middle school, actions speak louder than words. I want you to think of true sovereignty as a muscle. You simply cannot tell it to grow. You must exercise the muscle if you want to see the growth.

Now I want to explore ways in which true sovereignty means action. ***Sovereignty in Action Means Leadership***.

I am a red man. If the Great Spirit had desired me to be a white man he would have made me so in the first place…It is not necessary for Eagles to be Crows.—Sitting Bull (Hunkpapa Lakota)

You are an eagle. You were born with sovereign wings and white tail feathers to steer you in the four directions and in the directions of the river: up the river, across the river, down the river. Sitting Bull wasn't from the rivers, he didn't eat salmon and eels like we do, but he was a great leader and he had the right idea. He speaks a profound truth: we were born Native for a reason and we were born to think and act for ourselves. We had our own ways of being, our own languages and lands, our own distinct societies practicing religious and spiritual traditions that were completely unique to us. That is true sovereignty. I use the quote from Sitting Bull as an example of exercising individual true sovereignty, which is what a leader must always do. When he made this address in the mid-1800s, he stood as a leader of his people, tall and proud to be a unique person from a distinct culture. He was proud to be different, to have different values and a different way of looking at the world than the white men he addressed. And, if you notice, he made a slight dig at the white men by calling them crows, which are clearly not as majestic or as powerful as eagles. His action was to stand and claim his Native heritage, and at the same time tell the white men gathered there that he was not going to be like them, and neither were his people.

A leader must have integrity. A leader must be strong enough to stand against the tide of uncertainty. A leader must be smart enough to know when to act and when to strategize. A leader must look at the whole picture. A leader is a visionary who has the best interest of the people at heart. Most importantly, a true leader must be humble. Humility allows a leader to be open and willing to listen to everyone's input. Real leaders do not make decisions by themselves.

The sad truth is, we are lacking this in Indian Country. There are many good leaders who are working to find new ways to exercise sovereignty, to lead their tribal governments in the right direction. There are even more good leaders out there who are not working for their tribal governments, but elsewhere in Indian Country, and the private sector. And there are just as many (if not more) leaders embezzling money from their tribes, misappropriating funds, or abusing their positions of power for personal and familial gain. Every week brings a news article telling the same story: the Tribal Chairman or Council Member or Board Director or even the Head Start Program Manager took money from the tribal coffers to benefit his or her family or personal business. These people are not true leaders. Instead, they exemplify exactly what a leader should not be. When you steal from your tribal government, you steal from your tribal people. That is never okay. Yet is happens all too frequently.

You must remember that leadership is a gift given to you by your people. It comes from your community. Whether it is given via traditional means because of your place in ceremony, or given in non-traditional means related to the job you do or by a vote of the people, leadership is not something to be taken lightly. Good leaders will always *act* in ways that express true sovereignty. ***Sovereignty in Action Means Responsibility***.

As a young Native person, you were born into a world of great responsibility. You are asked to move through this life as a representation and reflection of the beauty of your people. You are responsible for the health, welfare, and well-being of your family, your people, your community, and your tribal government. You are responsible for being a good citizen and for being someone who contributes to your tribe, your community, and to society as a whole. This may seem like a lot of responsibility, and some of you might argue that this is too much to ask, but I say to you this is true sovereignty in action. I implore you to do the very best you can to be responsible and to act responsibly because your people will be better for it. They will be stronger for it.

If you are a dance person or attend ceremonies, for example, it is your responsibility to be part of remaking the world, putting it back into balance through song and prayer. You do this not only for your own people, but for every living being—person, plant, animal, etc.—who occupies space on this Earth. This is the most unselfish act imaginable. And you are unselfish when you exercise your true sovereign right to practice your traditions and strengthen your culture.

I wish to point out, however, that responsibility does not rest solely upon your growing shoulders. It should be alive in every decision made by your tribal government and those whose job it is to represent you. Responsibility means that in the face of adversity, tribes must act in whatever way necessary to prevent the worst from happening. But more importantly, it means that all tribal people, as individuals, act in ways to protect those things that need protecting. To exercise our true sovereignty is our individual responsibility as well as our tribal government's responsibility.

Being responsible means being a good tribal member. It means being a good human being. It means participating in tribal government or other governmental and community arenas. It means using your voice when change is needed. It means not necessarily relying on your elected representative to represent you—because they often will not. Their views may differ from yours on certain issues, which is why you need to be your own voice. Or, form a collective voice of tribal members with the same concerns. Exercising true sovereignty means making choices. And we must always choose responsibility over everything else. ***Sovereignty in Action Means Taking Care of the Earth.***

We humans have screwed things up. We have not taken our responsibilities seriously, and many of us who have grown up in poverty think that we do not have to recycle! You do have to recycle. It may be a silly example, but it is a significant one. It is your duty no matter the financial or other circumstances you find yourself in to take care of our planet. Taking care of the Earth means tending to it, protecting it. It means giving back all of the blessing the Earth gives so that something remains for the future. It means being thankful for what is provided. It means standing up to those who would assault the very thing that sustains you. The prolific Native scholar Vine Deloria said, way back in 1973, "In this land God is Red." What he meant was that our traditions, our ceremonies, and our religious practices originate from this land, from our sacred places. In order to remain distinct cultural people, we must protect those places, for they give us the power, the medicine, the songs, and the prayers to continue. And this, dear young person, holds true for every tribal person in every tribal nation—collectively, we must all take care of the earth. I give you two examples, now, of true sovereignty in action.

Some of you may not remember the fish kill of 2002, but it is seared into the memory of those of us who fully experienced it. It was devastating. Low river flows combined with high water temperatures created the perfect climate for a disease called *Ich* to spread at an astonishing speed. Upwards of 65,000 salmon died (most tribal people believe the numbers were higher) in the lower Klamath, which means they did not have a chance to spawn. We suffered one of our greatest tribal losses. What did we do in response? We mourned the loss and then we *acted*. The Yurok, Karuk, and Hupa tribes began negotiations with federal agencies and other river stakeholders to remove four dams on the Klamath River. The dams held back the water needed in the river to prevent the fish kill. Tribal people protested. Tribes with past disagreements put them aside to come together for the river, for the salmon, and for the people.

Another example, and one which you most likely remember, is the tribal action at Standing Rock in North Dakota. Native people and their allies came together to protect the sacred waters of the Standing Rock

Sioux Tribe from an oil pipeline. In these two instances, we as tribal people chose to drop our shields and our arguments and join together to take care of what takes care of us. The people at Standing Rock stood, without arms, with only their bodies and their words, against a militarized police force and a giant corporation. That is what we, as people with sovereign hearts, must do in times when action calls us toward something greater than ourselves.

Now, young Native, you may have noticed that the dams still presently stand and the oil pipeline was built, but do not be discouraged. Taking care of the Earth is not a one-time occurrence. It is from birth to death, from daybreak to dawn—it is your life. What you have to understand is that things take time. Battles are won and lost. Patience is a requirement whether you want dams coming down or pipelines diverted. You have to be invested in the change you seek. You have to be willing to work hard for something that you may never see come to fruition. It is a tough thing to process—the idea that I may never see the end result of my actions—because the society we live in is instant. Information can be instantly accessed through our smart phones. Problems are solved in an instant on 30-minute television programs. We are all about immediate gratification, but real change takes time and work, and taking care of the earth is a forever job and an unending responsibility. Your responsibility. My responsibility. Our responsibility.

Sovereignty in Action Means Preserving Your Culture. Cultural preservation is of utmost importance when it comes to exercising true sovereignty. You must act in ways that protect and preserve our heritage, our traditions, our language, our songs, our stories, and our natural environment. It is important that you remember everything that makes up our culture is interconnected. This knowledge allows you to see the world in its entirety and to see that you cannot protect and preserve just one aspect of our culture; you must preserve and protect it all. For example, if you are going to protect the salmon, you must protect the river. To protect the river, you must protect its headwaters and the watershed from which it is born. That watershed is part of a larger system of mountains and valleys, and they must be protected as well. Another example of interconnectedness is our language, which is connected to our songs, which are connected to our stories. These three woven together teach us about our history, but they also provide important lessons that we must apply today and take with us into the future. The loss of any one of these means we lose a huge part of our culture. And that means we become less of who we are as Native people.

I also plead with you to recognize that cultures evolve and change, and truly sovereign people know when change is necessary. Nothing is static. We must all be willing to evolve as human beings and, at the same time, find ways to keep our culture intact. How do we do this? We find the balance. Balance, as you may already know, is essential to the preservation of our culture, and seeking balance every day is the work we must do.

The history of interaction between tribal nations and the United States is terrible. Awful. Repugnant. Unjust. Attempts to destroy our culture have caused tremendous dysfunction and pain in our communities. We sometimes call the pain created by the past "historical trauma," which many of us have carried into the present day. But I want to say to you, young Native, we have to let go of that pain. We must never forget what was perpetrated against us as, but if we do not learn how to forgive, if we choose to remain angry and hobbled by our pain, we cannot move forward. You see, pain keeps you stuck. Pain will keep us stuck in the past, traumatized by our history, our hearts hardened. We do not want that anymore. We do not deserve it. Let us send their historical trauma right back into the past where it belongs. Let us make our sovereignty something different, make it something stronger, because we have the final say. We give ourselves our true names—we are The People. The People Upriver. The People Downriver. People of the Pines. True People. Principal People. Elk People. Strong People. Peaceful People. Mountain People. The ultimate truth is: we define us.

What we have been doing is making do. We are good at adapting to unnatural circumstances. It is why we are still here, why we have survived everything meant to kill us. We are also very good at our own self-destruction. We are good at being jealous of one another, of only looking out for our own immediate family and not our community and people as a whole. These are traits we have learned over time as a result of the breakdown of our traditional ways of living, of our culture.

Young Native, I could call you the future of our people, but what "people" would we be without our culture? And I could say the future depends on you, but what "future" do we have without our culture? What I am saying is, for us to be truly sovereign, we must act in ways that perpetuate our culture. If we do not do this we will disappear. We will drown in the dreaded melting pot where money is our God and all of our salmon come from farms in the ocean.

Your choice is really quite simple. You can make do or make change through *action*. Action that is guided by your true and sovereign heart. Now tell me, what will you choose?

Very Truly Yours,
SOMc

{CHAPTER 19}

A Time of Reflection: The Role of Education in Preservation

Adrienne Colegrove-Raymond

EARLY ON, IN EXCHANGE FOR LAND, TRIBAL LEADERS SIGNED TREATIES THAT SECURED EDUCATION AS ONE OF THE PILLARS OF PROTECTION FOR FUTURE GENERATIONS. Since contact with White settlers, Native Americans have had to strategize on how to best educate their youth for the sake of preservation and planning for future generations. Unfortunately, for many Native Americans, the educational system has been, on many accords, a negative experience and, in many cases, profoundly unresponsive to their needs. Students struggle to engage in a system once utilized as a genocidal attack of forced assimilation. Today, education remains a focal point for most tribes and it is often touted as one of the keys to tribal economic development, environmental sustainability, and protection of resources. This has been a challenge, because most tribal communities have been left spinning from the effects of contact. Now that the dust has somewhat settled, they are finally in a position to reflect on the experiences of their ancestors and to establish how they will move forward.

My father always shared a favorite saying: "You have to know where you come from, in order to know where you are going." This saying is in alignment with Native American ideology of honoring and learning from ancestors while at the same time planning for future generations. I have utilized this advice over the past twenty years to develop culturally relevant college recruitment plans, preparation models, support programs, and educational plans. It is through this lens that I reflect and guide students on why education is important and how it can actually be a tool for cultural preservation and tribal existence.

Growing up on the Hoopa Valley Reservation was the greatest gift from my parents, as it was from there I received my nurturing and grooming, and where I developed my sense of belonging. It provided me with an unmatchable grounding that has carried me through the most difficult challenges of life's journey. Learning and discovering was an intrinsic part of my early educational experience and cultural upbringing. At an early age, I remember sitting in on political, cultural, and social conversations. My opinion was not only solicited, it was also embraced and, at times found to be of value. Learning was very important to me, and my environment was perfect for college preparation. Attending college was never an option; the only question that I had growing up was, what college would I choose?

Interestingly, it was when I stepped onto a college campus that I began to question my own insights and intelligence. And, most profoundly, it was there that my cultural and spiritual value systems were negatively challenged. It was also at the university that I learned that Native Americans are considered a disadvantaged minority group. And, to my dismay, I discovered that Native Americans have the highest rates of suicide, alcoholism, diabetes, etc. My excitement for learning began to diminish in the classroom, where my cultural wealth was dismissed by conflicting value systems and worldviews. I have shared this experience with many of my family, friends, and colleagues, and to my dismay, their educational struggle was much the same.

I am certain my own skepticism was influenced by the experiences of my grandparents during the Indian Boarding School era of the 1920s. Boarding schools were established as part of the War on Indians in the State of California. At an early age, like most of their peers, both of my grandparents were forcibly sent to boarding school, removed from their homeland and families. My grandmother attended The Sherman Institute in Riverside, CA, over 700 miles from home, and was forced into a system designed to separate children from traditional life to become "civilized" by assimilation. As was the case for Native students in

Figure 13: "Dad at Takamildin."[1] *Courtesy of Adrienne Colegrove-Raymond.*

boarding schools across the Nation, she was shamed and disciplined for her cultural upbringing. It was there my grandmother learned English and was punished for speaking the Hupa language. This punishment came in the form of not being allowed to go home and being farmed out for domestic work during the summer months for wealthy families in the Riverside area. Nearly all Native students are descendants of those who have had similar experiences. And yet, my grandparents encouraged all of their children and grandchildren to value education. They put a lot of pressure on all of their children to do well in school.

What a seeming oxymoron! How could they promote a system that was oppressive and culturally destructive to Native students? My grandmother stated it very clearly: "I learned early on that we need to learn the White *system*, not their *ways*, because it is then that we will beat them at their game." She never lost her cultural training, medicine teachings, prayers, basket making skills and language. Her husband, my grandfather, was a logger, cultural dance leader, cattleman, father, fisherman, and regalia maker. To avoid boarding school, my grandfather jumped train and went AWOL for many years, where he had ample opportunity to travel to many parts of the Western half of North America. He was forced to interact with some of the most oppressive and racist groups. For his very survival, it was essential that he observed non-Native communities. From this experience he learned that there was great power in education. He often said, "One day we will have our own Indian lawyers, teachers, bankers, businesses, and such. And, we will manage our own tribe."

Historically, as typically presented in stories, our ancestors were very adept at interacting with other tribes and non-Natives to enhance knowledge and skills. Tribes near the Hoopa Valley inter-married, participated together in ceremonies, and traded with one another. They did this while maintaining their distinct languages, cultural rules, and knowledge. I am told that my great-grandfather spoke Hupa, Yurok, Karuk, and English. Certainly, this was the norm to navigate the different groups for their economic system of trade.

The generation of tribal leaders that were raised by boarding school attendees were subjected to conflicting cultures, and yet they carried the fire within them to fulfill intergenerational responsibilities. The people of this generation were the forerunners of navigating the balance of education with maintaining traditional knowledge, language, and culture. They were advocates of both the Indian Education Act and the Self-Determination Act. They fought the "Fish Wars" and established landmark legislation that has solidified the rights of Native Americans, such as the American Indian Religious Freedom Act, the Native American Graves Protection and Repatriation Act, the Indian Child Welfare Act, and the Native American Languages Act. They lobbied to increase allocations for Native American students seeking higher education to continue to protect and retain traditional value systems.

My father, the second eldest of six, graduated at age sixteen from Hoopa High School in the 1950s. He had been successful in high school and was prepared to attend college. However, the $50 scholarship that he received wasn't nearly enough to pay for the tuition, books, and housing. This was the experience of many Native Americans of that era. Funding for college wasn't available as it is today. So, he enrolled in the Navy branch of the military, where he was trained as a cryptologist and assigned to work in Japan for three years. Upon returning home, he quickly became swept up in the Indian Civil Rights Movement of the 1960s, and later became an active advocate of the Indian Self-Determination and Education Assistance Acts of the 1970-80s. He observed the successful tactics utilized particularly during the Civil Rights Movement. Although the nonviolent protest and civil disobedience increased awareness to the cause and issues, he noted that it was the presentation of significant pieces of federal legislation that truly implemented the changes in discriminatory practices. Often, he would reflect on the changes needed to be made in legislation to maintain tribal lands, fisheries, water rights, education, and protection of sacred sites. "We need great writers and presenters, and we need the credentials to protect our inherent rights," he would often say. "It is because we continue to fight, through protest and court, that we maintain our river, land, and culture." At the core of the protection of all our resources, he would often say, "is the First Amendment right securing freedom of religion." Solely it is because we practice our ceremonial dances, as they have been practiced since time immemorial, that we continue to secure our sacred places and protect our water rights. Before my grandfather passed away, he often reflected on the beneficial accomplishments tribes made during his lifetime. He said, "So many worked endless hours for the next generation, and now this next group coming up is starting to give it all back to the Federal Government." It was startling to hear such honest words.

Who better than our own tribal members to manage our resources, educate our youth, promote our languages and culture, repatriate cultural items, heal our sick, build our homes, defend us, and direct our departments? I think most everyone would unanimously agree that tribes are seeking future leaders with all of this in mind. The manner and mindset in which our youth gain their education, and the need to keep in contact with tribal elders and mentors, is crucial.

A college education can be utilized in many different ways. It can assist in developing personal careers; it opens up opportunities; it creates options. It provides a perfect venue for students to learn the art of writing, presenting, and researching. These skills make education a valuable tool for writing grants, lobbying, managing resources and departments, building economic development, revitalizing language, and protecting sovereignty. However, with all of the positive aspects of knowledge, the educational system can also be extremely distractive and the diverse worldviews can become misleading to even our brightest and most talented. Students have to be cognizant to never forget that the American educational system was based on providing leadership skills for a capitalistic society and it was used as an effective form of assimilation. A capitalistic society, where members seek personal wealth with little to no regard for community or the environment, boldly conflicts with tribal value systems. Although tribes within the United States are subjected to this model, effective leadership models within tribal lands—and in support of Native programs across the nation—are based on tribal value-systems.

When educators are unaware or even oblivious to the issues facing Native Americans, it can be difficult for students to draw cultural relevancy from the educational system. Until there is an increase in Native American education faculty, students may find that the burden lies on them to build correlation between what they are learning and their future cultural and career goals. Students can accomplish this by consciously selecting topics for writing and research projects that will provide the skills needed to work for Native American tribes and entities.

Unfortunately, some students can be snared into sharing tribal knowledge, cultural methods, songs, and prayers in exchange for novelty and uniqueness or simply a good grade. This can become a dangerous route. In the end, students often feel culturally taxed. My grandmother often commented that getting too comfortable within the system can cause one to let their guard down and reveal too much information to the anthropologist, archaeologist, professor, and researcher. Sacred knowledge has been passed by oral tradition to keepers who have been selectively chosen by elders. It is a student's obligation to protect and place value on it, as if it were their bank account; few share their financial information with strangers. Students who are mindful of the cultural information written and spoken about demonstrate exemplary practice for tribal professionalism.

Students can effectively learn to challenge the system when curriculum conflicts with tribal values and belief systems. By maintaining close contact with Native American professionals and cultural elders who are aware of the pressing issues facing tribes, students can become adept at balancing the learning with traditional values. Often, students graduate from college and determine that much of the information that they really are going to use actually came from their mentors and tribal professionals.

Returning home to the reservation or working for Native American programs is the goal for most Native students in higher education. Tribes have made an investment in students to build on their strengths and skills in the hopes that these skills and strengths will be utilized for the benefit of the tribal community. Upon college graduation, students may find that easing back into the workplace can be a delicate maneuver.

Students are wise to be cognizant and respectful of the historical knowledge and experience available to them as new professionals. So much of the work of maintaining cultural knowledge, protecting sacred sites, and securing sovereignty has historically been done by tribal members determined to uphold the rights for which their ancestors diligently fought. Although many of these tribal leaders lacked formal college degrees, their intelligence and successful strategies could run circles around the most "educated." Many of these were silent leaders; their names were not in the headlines. They worked, wrote, testified, and protested on behalf of future generations. They weren't "glory seekers;" rather, they fought because it was their duty to establish a brighter future for the upcoming leaders.

Students do well to value the price of land that was negotiated for the right to be educated. With that right comes the responsibility to continue to protect and preserve the cultural value systems and traditional ways that were established since time immemorial.

Endnotes

1.   Willie Colegrove (ne:en) pictured at Takimildin (place where acorns are stirred). To his back is the xonta nikyaw (big house) and he is facing a large family dwelling. This place is the center of the world for Hupa people. Willie found peace and solace in these ancient structures to connect with his past and rejuvenate his personal promise to protect and restore the Hupa way of being. "Education doesn't give entitlement, it gives responsibility." –Ed.

{CHAPTER 20}

Next Steps: The Education System; Inclusiveness, School Dropouts, and Cultural Pride

Jim McQuillen

PUBLIC SCHOOLS ARE A PLACE WHERE CULTURAL NORMS AND VALUES ARE REINFORCED AND PASSED ON. Whether we want it this way or not, culture is taught and communicated in the public schools. Native people need to realize this, embrace it, and have our culture celebrated here as well. We want our community and cultural lessons taught in the public schools alongside the fairy tales of Snow White and the great authors of the mainstream culture, such as Shakespeare and Homer. If we don't have our stories and language reinforced here, our culture will face endangerment or extinction once again. Public schools are also supposed to reflect the communities they serve, and not just the dominate White culture.

Local Native cultural educators and contemporary heroes such as Walt Lara Sr., Chris H. Peters, Abby Abinanti, Callie Lara, Bertha Peters, Loren Bommelyn, Fern Bates, Venola Dowd, Maria Tripp, and Richard Meyers Sr. need to be featured in the local public schools with their life stories and cultural lessons. We need to continue to insist on parity for local tribal cultural knowledge and have that reflected in the public school curriculum. Native students need to see and hear from role models and people who look familiar and who have had life experiences such as theirs. There is so much that can be learned from each culture, both historical and contemporary. We just have to allow the time and space for this learning to occur.

The Yurok language classes taught at Hoopa High School, McKinleyville High School, Del Norte High School, and Eureka High School are examples of what cultural competency can be. These courses were implemented with the help (and threat) of ACLU lawsuits against the local school districts Del Norte & Eureka City Schools, but we will accept these as wins and a small step in the right direction.

The Native language revitalization movement is vital to the cultural education in the schools. It is also vital to helping public educational institutions be more welcoming and culturally competent places so Native students feel accepted there and in society as a whole. Cultural inclusiveness and cultural awareness is so much more than a one or two day professional development teacher in-service training with panels and speakers. It is realized by system-wide reform, by a paradigm shift in the curriculum and course selection where tribal culture, language, and the staff are reflective of the students served by the school system. We need courses in Native American studies in grades 8-12, Native language courses at the K-8 grades, and accurate curriculum which reflects the local culture, history, and identity.

There are so many students today who are hungry for information on the history of the local tribal people. History lessons are necessary to explain how the aboriginal tribal lands were lost through the 1887 General Allotment Act, how familiar relationships and family bonds were systematically broken due to the boarding school era, and how genocidal acts exist here locally in recent history. A trauma-informed approach such as this has potential for community self-awareness and healing, while the absence of these lessons leaves a large gap in under-standing the historical trauma and therefore in self-awareness for the community and its members. But the approach requires information and understanding that these history lessons can offer.

There are many other community groups that have monuments of healing for the historical loss they experienced, including the monu-ments for the Jewish holocaust and the September 11th World Trade Center loss. Tribal people need these same monuments, symbols, and dialog for healing to occur. School curriculum can assist in this under-standing and healing potential.

Curriculum that is Collecting Dust

The wealth of cultural curricula available to K thru 12 teachers often goes unused or it stays on shelves gathering dust. This curricula, housed at the Humboldt State University Indian Teacher and Educational Personnel Program (ITEPP) Resource Center or on the Title VI office shelves, contains model lessons that we desperately need within the schools. There seems to be fear or outright ignorance from the majority of teachers regarding its importance. Teachers often shy away from Native curriculum due to a lack of general awareness of the background information needed to teach the lessons, or just a lack of comfort and familiarity with the material. Native students—like all students—need to feel valued and supported in their learning. Only then can we close the achievement gap and the disparity in test scores as well as the disproportionate graduation rates and attendance problems in the local school districts.

So much more can be taught about the rich contributions of other cultures and American Indians in the fields of history, science, politics, and government, which could lead to classrooms of true inclusiveness and support for Native students' connection to school.

Teachers often want to stay in their "comfort zone," so they teach by the method in which they are most comfortable. Also, they often teach the way THEY were taught when they were students, regardless of changes in our understanding of best practices. There remains a significant and widespread cultural gap between local teachers and the students within their classrooms. This is despite the efforts of curriculum instruction staff and County Offices of Education efforts to offer cultural inclusion workshops and diversity staff training.

More than bows and arrows

Culture is so much more than just holidays, religion, costumes (regalia), and language. It is the everyday living experienced by the students and families. Additional training and feedback for all can help break through this comfort zone for non-Native people, but the best solution is to have Native staff from the local communities come into and be a part of the school staff and teaching ranks. We are in desperate need of additional teachers, administrators, and classified staff who are tribal members and who can be the role model examples for the students to become. Most teachers are White, middle class and speak English only. This profile does not reflect today's classroom student make-up.

In order to recruit a diverse staff, we need to attempt other methods of recruitment. Advertise the strengths of the profession more by highlighting the benefits of the profession, which are so important to Native youth and young adults, such as, "the gift of giving back to one's community," the growing competitive salaries, the ten-month work year, and the ability to influence and shape the next generation. Perhaps by re-starting the Future Teachers of America Program here locally, where high school age students are recruited early and given real experiences to support them into the teaching profession, we can grow our own teachers from within the community.

Ceremony and Resilience

The old ones bring on our tears—tears for healing and tears of pride. The elders sacrificed so much for us to have what we have now. The traditional cultural knowledge was so fragile at one time, and now we have so many young people who want to participate, and so many who find strength and meaning from the local dance ceremonies. Some of the heroes who worked so hard and sacrificed to keep the practices going and secure the dances for new generations often go without recognition. Individuals such as Walt Lara Sr., Chris H. Peters, Ray Mattz, as well as so many other *awok* relatives (those who have passed on) worked very hard to continue to pass on the laws of the people and the ceremonies to help connect and provide an anchor to the next generation.

The dances have returned with great momentum and they are becoming stronger each year, returning back from the brink of extinction. There were years of recovery where there was in-fighting and inter-generational post-traumatic stress that was obvious through the self-destructive behavior, drug and alcohol abuse, inconsistencies, and inner strife. As the recovery shines through over these past three to four decades, the next generation has demonstrated an intense personal and family pride through singing the old songs, having good rhythm, making warm fires, and creating new songs, as well as following our traditional laws.

Today, many relatives and community members enjoy this revival of the ceremonies and active cultural participation. Many family members thrive by actively gathering from the mountains, fishing, just as the ancestors have for thousands of years. Many enjoy the traditional foods, weave the beautiful baskets, and create tools and regalia. But many individuals struggle with this Native lifestyle and balance as they also have to work 9-to-5 jobs, maintain a household, and support their children in public schools. It's a struggle to live and balance the two life styles.

The local dances reflect recovery and revival of the people, and they are a symbol of health and vitality of the people. As the dances and ceremonies have become more stable and consistent, the people have become healthier. A pathway toward recovery from the historical trauma and the brink of genocidal extinction has become clear. People have gravitated toward cultural revitalization, ceremony, and language for recovery. Ceremony and cultural practices provide the answer to and relief for the symptoms of depression, drug and alcohol abuse, feelings of shame and failure, and jealousy.

We see the strength of this recovery in those individuals who live healthy and productive lives with the benefits of cultural continuity. Some of our most successful community members and families, both in education and/or career success, are from families that are intimately connected and active in the ceremonies.

Part 5

Pick Up the Basket:
Testimonials from our Youth

This section is written by three California Indigenous youth who have been identified by community members as actively involved in the preservation of language, culture, and traditions. Each author shares memories of a treasured cultural teaching and describes the role they hope to play in protecting Indigenous knowledge for future generations.

CHAPTER 21

"A Pure Heart"

Princess Jintcon Colegrove (16 years old)

IN THE BEGINNING, THE K'IXINAY ("SPIRIT BEINGS") LIVED
IN THE VALLEY THAT WE CALL HOME, SURROUNDED BY
MOUNTAINS COVERED IN TIMBER. We live along the river that
is the life source of the people. They tell us that the k'ixinay foresaw the
human beings coming in the mist and began to leave. There were a few
that remained to teach the people to care for the world; they taught us
to pray and live amongst all things in harmony.

The White Deerskin Dance is a prayer for the world. My people
have followed the teachings of the k'ixinay from the beginning of time.
Year after year, acorn soup is made to feed the people and the k'ixinay together. The dance begins at the village of Ta'k'imiɫding ("the
place where the acorns are stirred"). The medicine woman and her
helper prepare the acorns farther up the river, across from the village
of xowongq'ut, where the dancing begins. Before daylight, they gather
and heat the acorn rocks. The medicine woman crosses the river in a
canoe carrying the cooked acorns in a big cooking basket. I've heard this
story many times from my grandma Callie, who was the helper of her
grandmother Nancy. This process is a very complex, important part of
the ceremony for many different reasons; for me, it is because it is one
of two ceremonies that we eat with our ancestors. Although we don't
dance every year, we are always gathering and getting ready. Acorns
must be gathered; fish, deer meat, and other foods must be preserved.

Figure 14: "On this day in a good way, I feed the people and the k'ixinay together". Princess Jintcon Colegrove preparing acorns. © 2019 Gary Colegrove. Courtesy of Ka'm-t'em Photography Project.

My family comes out on the Me'dildin side, one of two camps that come from villages on the south end of the valley.

When I became a young woman, my grandma wrapped mixa:ch'e xolen ("Indian root") in my hand and painted me. My xoq'it ch'iswa:l (Flower Dance or coming of age ceremony) happened immediately after. During that time I was considered a spirit being. It was a very important time in my life. I have had many significant events that have formed my life. My highlight was when I was fourteen years old, my family decided that I would make the acorns for our camp at the Deerskin Dance. I didn't question it, because when you are asked to do something for the dance, you do it. I don't know why I was picked, exactly; I was told it was because I am "pure of heart," but I am still figuring out what that means.

In each ceremony, the way of my people stands out most to me. I like to observe the beauty of our people and what each person has to contribute. During the White Deerskin Dance (a ten-day ceremony) we move camp five times. We have what we call "the big truck." It's a big cattle truck that we've had since the early 1970s. My great-grandfather used it, my great uncles, my papa, and my father. Each year, the truck is fired up for this purpose. We load all of our camp supplies in it, and all of the kids pile on top and ride to the next camp. It's the highlight of our childhood; it's an experience that the generations share.

Each day of the dance, I began by spreading the acorn flour on a thin cloth over a leaching basket. I continued to pour water over them throughout the day, until the bitterness is gone and the acorns taste sweet. After I got this started, I went with my mom, my Grandma Callie, and my older cousin Lindsey to the river to search for acorn rocks. I was taught how to find these specific kinds of rocks by looking for the darkest, roundest, and smoothest rocks. Once I found them, I dipped them in the river to see if they turned the dark color I wanted, and if they did, I thrust them against another rock. If the rock broke then it was not a good cooking rock, because it might break in the fire or in the acorns. After I gathered all my rocks, I went back to camp, where my aunties were working. My father's cousin, "Bucky," always had a place cleared for me to work, and kept a hot fire where I placed the rocks in the coals to get red-hot. To acknowledge the way of our ancestors for many generations, I share these details with you.

My great auntie, Cuddles ne:en,[1] always showed me such strength. She sat along the side and watched me work every day. She was our leader in camp, our matriarch; if she liked or disliked how you were doing something, you would know by the way she looked at you. After my rocks were red-hot, just before dinner, I put the leached acorns in the cooking basket and added water. Lindsey got the rocks out of the fire for me with a shovel, and I put the rocks in the basket and continuously stirred them. Keeping the rocks moving is important so they don't burn a hole through the basket. While the acorns cooked, I whispered in the language, "On this day in a good way, I feed the people and the k'ixinay together." Glancing up from my cooking pot, I would see the people working about the camp, eating, and socializing, and I know that I am bound to them. They are the descendants of my great grandparents. Much like my cooking pot filled with leached acorns, the warp and the weft are my ancestors; it is the first weave in my basket. Then all the generations are woven together, one on top of the other, forming my many relatives.

Taken from the fire, I drop my hot rocks into my acorns. The smooth dark rocks are a symbol of an ancient way. The rocks cause my acorns to spatter and spurt in a rolling boil. I stir continually so as not to burn my cooking pot. The blue smoke billows to the heavens. The acorns will feed my family and my ancestors together. These rituals binds us together. That is my prayer. As the rocks cooled and the acorns stopped bubbling, I removed them from the acorns and placed them next to the fire. As soon as I was done, I would take some to my Auntie Cuddles and wait to see her thoughts. She would nod "Good," she would say, and I would go back to finish cleaning up. As I moved through the tasks, I would look over and see my great auntie Doo Doo constantly moving, cleaning, packing, stacking, and making sure that everything was done the right way. My great auntie, Esther ne:en, would always come into camp with a hug and a smile; her hug was always followed by a little chuckle. She would often look at all the acorn eating baskets and tell me stories about her mother, my great grandma, Lila ne:en. She said that at one time, the camp needed more acorn bowls, so Grandma Lila taught her daughters—my Auntie Doo Doo, Auntie Cuddles, and Auntie Esther—to weave baskets, each with a lifeline. Although they were children, they contributed baskets to the ceremony each year. To this day, we use the baskets to serve acorns.

I admire the personalities of all the camp workers, from task masters to the gentle servers, young men in and out of camp bringing wood, propane, fish, or deer meat. As they finish up dancing, the little girls set the table with the clean plates, forks, cups, and juice. My father's mother, who I call Pama, would finish up the cooking. The women would talk and get the food ready, waiting for my father and his father, my Papa, to walk into camp. My Papa is a very quiet man, with a very caring spirit. He teaches us not to judge others and to be accepting; I love that about him. As the two of them walk into camp, several dancers follow behind, black paint smeared across their faces. As they sit down, the women would start setting the food on the table. The younger women would ask the men if they would like coffee. I'd start pouring acorn soup into the baskets and begin to serve, going around the table, asking all the men if they would like some acorns, and running back to get some more. After serving all the dancers I would stand to the side, where the baskets were, and just observe the camp.

I would watch my Grandpa Walt, making his way into camp, talking and visiting with everyone along the way, teasing them, making a joke and laughing. My Grandpa is a Yurok man and highly respected by my father's people. After each dancer was finished eating, I would collect the acorn basket, his plate would be cleared, and a new plate would replace the last, for the next person. I would rinse each acorn bowl and use a soft brush to clean them out, then let them air dry. After the men were finished eating, the women would begin to sit down to eat, and I would begin to serve acorns to the women. After dinner they dance two more times, and then pies, cakes, cookies, and many more desserts were served along with coffee. At the end of each day, every dish in camp was clean. The women would sit around the fire and table visiting as the kids played cards. My mother's face was no longer beet red from the hot fire, and we would finally get ready for bed. Lindsey, who never left my side, and I would get up the next morning and go to the river to gather our rocks and continue our day just like the one before.

For generations, it has been said that "in a good way" we attend the dances. There is so much value in each person. Every contribution is needed. There are three other camps in this dance and each has its own important stories of contribution. We learn so many details of the dance, but the most important is that "in a good way" we attend the dance and, as such, "in a good way" we must attend life.

Within me, I carry the support of my great aunts, the eloquence of my mother, and the wisdom of my grandmothers. Like my father and he like his father, I am a person of few words. We communicate with a look, an expression, a movement, or what we don't say. My mother says we have whole conversations this way. To me it is the purest form of communication, so if this is "pure of heart" I am not unique to it. It is just the way we do things. It is our way. It is K'iwinya'n ya:n mi'awhwhiniw.

Endnotes

1. Translated in Hupa to 'used to be'–a term utilized to refer to the deceased. –Ed.

CHAPTER 22

"It Is Our Purpose"

Donald Moore (18 years old)

I COME FROM FAMILIES THAT ARE VERY INVOLVED IN OUR CULTURE AND CEREMONIES. I have ancestors from the Colegrove, McQuillen, and Moore families that have been very influential to me. Since I was little, I have been involved in my culture, whether it be through the ceremonies or the Yurok language. My earliest memory was following my awok'[1] grandfather Glenn Moore in his yard while he worked on Redwood dugout canoes. He was a beautiful canoe carver; his work is still relevant as his canoes are still used in the Boat Dances and showcased in Washington D.C. I was a little guy yet, so I didn't necessarily work with him, but I do remember being right next to him as he would tell me stories or teach me about the canoe itself. He and my father ingrained in me that the canoe is a living thing, as are our regalia and ceremonial items. I would always ask questions, like "Why are there lines and bumps in there?" They would respond that the canoe has body parts and those body parts keep the canoe alive as our human parts keep us alive. They taught me that there are the kidneys, lungs, heart, and nose that make the canoe breathe so it can live. After following my grandpa around, I wasn't running around with my cousins outside; I would be inside listening to him and my grandma (Dorothy "Dot" Colegrove Moore) tell stories and language or ceremonial teachings. My grandma and grandpa were both amazing people, and because of them I have developed in-depth cultural knowledge.

The McQuillen side of my family has also contributed to my knowledge base. The McQuillens are a big family (mostly girls) that are heavily involved in ceremonies. My aunt Barbara ("Barbie") works for the Yurok Tribal Language Department and has been instrumental in the revitalization of our Yurok language. I'm not the greatest Yurok speaker, but a lot of what I know is because of my grandpa, father, and Aunt Barbie. Along with his sister, my uncle Jim has been a prominent figure in my life and education. Another important cultural sponsor is my uncle Chris Peters. I think ever since I was able to hold a fishing net, I've been his fishing partner. I remember hearing him wrestling around with something outside, when visiting with my aunt Theresa, that would have me putting my shoes and warm clothes on every time to go and help out. I would run outside and ask if I could go with him, whether it be fishing, crabbing, or eeling. One time, I went eeling all night with my cousin, Curtis. It was a slow night (not many eels), it was cold, and we were tired. So, we decided to go home. On our way, we ran into my Uncle Chris leaving Requa, and he says, "Hey Donald, hop in! We are gonna go eeling and put the dip net in." Although I was dead tired, I went anyway because I liked spending time with him. He has definitely taught me a lot about fishing, hunting, and sharing with the community. I am beyond thankful for him.

Another early memory I have was when my dad would bring his drum out, put me on his lap, and sing drum songs. I was around three or four years old, and that had to have been the earliest time I remember hearing my dad sing. From that point forward, I fell in love with my dad's voice. Maybe that's why I love the sound of the drums and the game of traditional cards. Cards is a gambling game based on one's luck and chance that all the local tribes play. I've been playing next to my father for a long time. We have won a few card tournaments together. This past summer, I played in a traditional card tournament at the Sovereign Day celebration in Hoopa. I was singing and drumming a card game song while my dad dealt traditional Indian cards. After the game, "Dang, 'Foofs' (my nickname), that song is smooooth and really got me on a good run." It felt so good to hear. I felt so honored to play cards with my dad and to have him appreciate my song. In the past, I would only sing his songs since that is all that I knew, but a few summers back a song came to me. So, I kept it and practiced it. I didn't get to sing too much that day because we had multiple older, great singers on the team. When my dad hopped in as dealer, our teammates, Cheetos

Figure 15: Donald Moore dancing with his father, Glenn Moore II and his Uncle, Jim McQuillen in the Brush Dance Ceremony. Courtesy of Stephanie Weldon.

and Filmore, looked at me and said, "Go ahead, Foofs," so away I went singing. Just on his turn of dealing and my drumming, we almost won the game. That moment was something I'll remember for a long time. I am usually the one admiring my dad's singing and songs but this time he complimented me and complimented my singing.

Through ceremony, we learn many important lessons. The first thing I learned from the dances (and in general) was respect; not only respect for others but also self-respect. Drinking and using substances around the ceremonies isn't okay and shouldn't be around; that's where respecting yourself comes in. One ceremony that I'm very passionate about is the Brush Dance, a ceremony held to cure a baby or young one that is sick. Both sides of my family are very involved in this ceremony. There are a lot of components that make up the Brush Dance, and a lot to learn from it as well. There are the tribes and families that come and help support, the prayers, the good thoughts that are required, the singers and dancers, the people who bring and make regalia, and the cooks that keep everyone fed. I've been lucky enough to pack medicine four times at the Brush Dances. This means that I was a helper to the medicine woman. I was taught that when you pack medicine for a child or baby, you are supposed to watch over and stay connected with that child for the rest of their lives. Accepting to carry medicine isn't just for show; it is a commitment and a lifelong responsibility. The first time I packed medicine was the summer of 2014, for my cousin Cooney's baby Lillian; the second was in 2015 for Louis Cosce and Tessa's baby Dominik; and the third was for my sister's baby Bennett in 2016. Each of those Brush Dances was at the village of Weyhl-kwel, which is located at the mouth of the Klamath River. Most recently, I packed medicine at the village of Sumeg, which is located in Trinidad, California. I remember when Sammy Cooper and Walt Lara came to my dad's house to talk to me about being the medicine boy for their child. We talked about the importance of having a kind heart, living a healthy life, and being a positive role model. I respectfully accepted the commitment and packed medicine for Tasahce Se:wenah that summer.

Throughout my life, I have learned the value of our elders. Putting elders first before anything or anyone is very important. If you see an elder standing and you're sitting, it's only right to get up and offer them your seat. There is no reason that an elder should have to stand. Another important teaching I was taught was to respect the spiritual life of regalia. The materials that are gathered and hunted to make up the regalia sacrificed themselves so they can live forever and dance forever. Other teachings that I would like to share with future generations is the importance of taking caring of each other. We (Yurok and Hupa people) are hunters, gatherers, and fishermen, and we are good at what we do. In the early part of the year we eel; in the spring time, we fish; in the summer time, we hunt; in the fall, we cut wood and gather acorns and mushrooms; and in the winter, we hunt again. It's vitally important that we share what we have with our grandparents or other elders that we haven't seen in a while. Whenever I catch fish or eels, I go straight to my Gram's and give her some. If I kill a deer, I go straight to Gram's and give her whatever she wants. I also make sure to check on her woodpile so that she's warm. A good way to summarize this is, "Make sure your Gramma's freezer is full, she's always warm, and she's never lonely."

I'm only eighteen right now; my best is yet to come and I'm excited to see what my future brings. These teachings are an important part of my life. It's who I am, it keeps me alive and going. If I wasn't taught these things, I would have no identity, I wouldn't be who I am today, and I wouldn't have gotten to experience as much in my life. I am glad to have been lucky enough to learn from my grandparents, my aunts and uncles, and my parents. They have worked hard to create a better life for me. In turn, I will teach these lessons to my nephew Bennett to ensure he will have the best life.

We have made huge steps as Native people in our communities in protecting our language and ceremonies. There are still many ways that our young people can contribute to this effort. I want to spread knowledge to future kids in order to keep the culture alive and build on it. I want to flood the drugs and alcohol with more cultural teachings. We can stay out of trouble by participating in our culture. We were set here on Earth by our creator for a reason. Even though barriers try to set us back from our purpose, we can persevere. We are strong people, we will come together, and become greater people than we already are.

Endnotes

1.   A Yurok term used to reference the deceased. –Ed.

CHAPTER 23

"I Have a Voice"

Kisdyante Joseph (17 years old)

There is power in my silence, not in my silent pity; watch before acting and actually listen. To make a change you must not be angry before you know everything. In order to make change for the good, you must do it with a good heart" Lacey May Jackson, ne:en.[1] Words I hold dear.

Heyung' Kisdyante Joseph aholye' winwołch. Patricia Joseph aholye'. wita' Tom Joseph Sr., Ne'en aholye'. Hupa, Shoshone, Paiute, and Karuk nawhyay.

I COME FROM THE VILLAGES TS'WELNAL-DING (WHERE THE ROCK STICKS UP OUT OF THE WATER) AND ME'DIL-DING (CANOE PLACE). I am the youngest of ten siblings. I have had the privilege of growing up with a family that knows their culture and native roots. Our traditional ceremonies have influenced my day-to-day life in so many ways. As a little girl watching our community in ceremonies, I experienced the spiritual connection with the world through songs, stories, rituals, and prayers. And later, from the lessons of my transition ceremony or Flower Dance, I was taught that I am a spiritual being on a human journey, self-respect, self-worth, and that my contributions are not only honoring my ancestors but are important to the survival of our future. Through the White Deerskin Dance ceremony,

Figure 16: KinaŁdung, a spirit being in the transition of puberty to a young woman. Pictured: Nijonda Colegrove . © 2019 Gary Colegrove . Courtesy of Ka'm-t'em Photography Project.

which represents world renewal, our community comes together, as one, to pray for the balance between humans and the Ki'xinai (spiritual beings). We also pray that the world replenishes itself. And through the Jump Dance ceremony, a dance for the continuance of mankind, we learn from the animals and nature how to care for our families. Through these ceremonies, I've found my voice to speak and a desire to protect what is sacred.

At my age of seventeen years, my focus is our youth that represents the future of these timeless prayers passed down from our ancestors, and the protection of the world which embraces me. However, the dominant society creates a different way of thinking which I have learned in public schools, such as the Christian teachings of love thy neighbor or be submissive to your husbands. This society teaches girls to be competitive, to be first, the power and control mentality, or to get mine at the expense of others, or victimization. This thinking is the opposite of our way as Indigenous people. For me, I came forth with a dark history ingrained in my veins. I felt the pain of colonialism. It all started with the attempted genocide of my people. I know well the stories of rape and killing of my people, the captured family members that were sent to government boarding schools, the countless fathers killed in front of their children. This left the surviving children and often elders alone to become victims of the victors and elements around them. More and more horrible things happened in these boarding schools. The goal to "kill the Indian, save the man" left devastation for many years. My people were not considered human beings. In these schools, Indigenous knowledge through ceremonies were not allowed. However, through all this, I have experienced the resilience of my people who continued to sing, dance, and speak in our native tongue, sometimes only in prayer. We held on to what was sacred. I still do these things today, in ceremony. As I stomp my heels into mother earth as I dance, I am saying I am here, you are here, and we will not be in conflict with ourselves, but remember how this prayer has survived. These are my roots stretching out for the generation to come.

I have spoken out and my voice will only become stronger. I have assisted in organizing cities to stand against police brutality, and shut down state capitals to stand against the dams so that rivers can flow healthy. Being an "activist" is to stand against what is wrong and stand up for what is right. I come from a long line of activists in my family. It all began with my mother and father meeting during the Fish Wars camps on the Trinity and Klamath rivers in the late 1970s. They were an example to me of being responsible to the world. As I mature, I hope to define my expectations and responsibilities through my actions.

August 15, 2016, a year after my father's passing, my family and I heard the calling to go to Standing Rock, South Dakota. The Oceti Sakowin of North Dakota, people historically gathered together with many tribes in solidarity to halt the Dakota Access Pipeline. It was a very spiritual experience because tribes coming together, numbering ten thousand people, put aside differences to peacefully protest against a pipeline that would be put in the ancestral territories of the Standing Rock Tribes, seriously affecting the environment and people with oil spills and leakage. Our family intention was to operate a dinner camp. We formed the Hoopa kitchen (my tribe from California). There were thirty or more campers in our camp, but within weeks we grew to hundreds. It became the California Kitchen. Support and donations from up and down the State of California poured in. I worked with my family cooking, cleaning, and preparing two meals a day, feeding three and four hundred people for several months. I assisted in the other camps as well, such as the medical center, the learning center, and the commissary. I had the privilege to work with native youth from all over America to become active in the movement. Our goal would continue in our own areas to bring awareness to the plight of environmental protection. We, the youth, attended all the surrounding protests at the Capitol buildings. As part of the seventh generation, it was my responsibility to learn all that I could. My whole life had been in training for my voice to be heard. Standing Rock created a unique space to speak up, to proceed in a spiritual way, and to cry out the injustice. We felt that this was the time and the place to revolutionize an Indigenous philosophy. This was us, stretching our roots into the earth, crying out I am here, you are here and we will not be conflicted with ourselves and remember how this prayer has survived.

There was a time when I stood up and talked at a water board meeting, and I remember asking them, "Does it make you feel good knowing that you are slowly killing my culture?" Throughout my life, it was always those little things that inspired me to make a difference in this messed-up world. Now it is my turn to pass down the lessons and teachings to the next generation. Through my many encounters, I have embraced my niece's (Lacey May ne:en), words to be patient, to hear with all my senses, and to speak with passion. I hope to be a very wise old woman one day, which is the translation of my name, Kisdyante. I wish to share a poem written for me in finding my voice:

The early morning is quiet. A small valley surrounded by mountains and the flora of a dense forest is shadowed by the dark horizon. The full moon illuminates the narrow path that parallels the river below. The soft dirt is cool to her bare feet in the twilight hours. The swish of her bark skirt protects her legs from the tall grass and brush that lines the trail. Not far behind, she hears the foot steps behind her. A kinaŁdung and her attendant run the trail of their grandmothers before them. Perspiration glistens off her nose in the moon light. When she reaches a path that leads down to the river, she slows her pace but moves quickly over the smooth boulders and stops abruptly at the water's edge. The moon is bouncing off the black water. The river is swift and wide. She eases her feet into the cold river. A slight gasp escapes her lips. The attendant, above on top of the path, is quiet and still and looks away. The kinaŁdung performs the spiritual bath of her grandmothers. She has entered the water up to her thighs, and the bark from her skirt dances below the water. Over her right shoulder she scoops the water, then her left shoulder, then over her head. She feels strength. Facing down river, she hears her voice for the first time as she beings to sing her song. The rippling water will carry her song down the river and out to the ancestors. It is odd to her but her voice was stronger than it was yesterday. And tomorrow it will be even stronger.

—*Callie Lara*

Endnotes

1.   A Hupa word used to identify one who has passed on. –Ed.

Closing Statement

Walt Lara Sr.

THIS BOOK SHARES UNIQUE CONCEPTS OF BALANCE AND HARMONY WITH THE HUMAN, NATURAL, AND SPIRITUAL ELEMENTS OF THE WORLD. I was born in 1935, when I was somewhere between seven and ten years old, there was a disagreement at a ceremonial Brush Dance. One of the caretakers of regalia was going to pack up his prayer items and head home because he had been insulted (offended or wounded emotionally). So, my grandfather took off his Stetson hat and sent me around to take a collection to make payment for the insult. I had already been taught the value of maintaining communal relationships and understood that, if someone was insulted, it was important to "settle up" to bring back balance. I also learned that requesting payment was a very serious thing and a person should never flippantly make a payment request. I took the hat around to specific individuals and, when the hat was full of money, I brought it to the insulted party. He accepted and the ceremony continued on with good feelings. I had learned that once a settlement has been made, the involved parties continue with good thoughts and feelings and never speak of the insult again. Settling up was a tool that we used to maintain balance with each other, the environment, and the spiritual energies. The payment could have been minimal; it was the *act* of settling up that was important.

Indigenous people are an orderly people, and have "laws" that govern us to live in balance and harmony with the world. When I was a young boy, my grandparents talked to me about the importance of relationships with our ancestors, our regalia, and our people. We are a people of non-interference. In our way, the energies of the world settle themselves, and it is not an individual's role to "fix" another individual's behavior.

As caretakers of regalia, leaders of ceremony, and/or practitioners of medicine, it is our responsibility to protect the teachings of our ancestors, our prayer items, our burial sites, and our ceremonies. Through this process, we may encounter moments where we want to "right the wrongs," put others in their place, or seek justice. But we must be able to identify whether our desired actions are to protect our Indigenous philosophy...or to protect our egos. My grandparents told me that good things will always come to those who put themselves on the line to protect our way of life, those who are accountable for their words, actions, and behavior, and those who believe in and treasure the energies of the world. Throughout my life, I have carried these teachings at the front of my mind and I have done my best to balance our philosophy, tribal politics, and the outside world. There have been moments when I have been humbled by the energies of the world for my behaviors and there have been moments when I have been rewarded.

In Chapter 6, Dr. Rose Soza War Soldier says that decolonization is a continuance and that each generation becomes more decolonized than the generation before. I believe this. The first attacks on our people by settlers began in my great-grandparents' generation. They struggled to survive the atrocities, and they did. My grandparents' and parents' generations endured the boarding school era. My generation as well continues to suffer from the traumatic experiences of abuse and imposed religion that happened to our parents and grandparents in boarding school. I feel fortunate that I myself never had to undergo the experiences of boarding school. I went to school at the Little Red Schoolhouse in Stone Lagoon. We would walk three miles down and three miles back to attend. My first memory of school was being separated from my grandfather. I remember looking out the window and I would see my grandfather walking home after he dropped me off and I felt like I couldn't move or do anything until he came back. I would just sit there, looking out the window. It made me feel sick to be separated from my grandparents. The best part of my school day was walking home with my grandfather.

Although my schooling was not a happy time, I know that things could have been much worse and the reality of being kidnapped and taken to boarding school was very real. Even so, I have been affected by the genocide and the colonial education of our people. My generation has worked really hard to shift policy, develop grassroots organizations, and preserve ceremony. But we are constantly learning. In my older years, I realize that many of my mentors were influenced by boarding school and imposed Christianity, and that those things also influenced my thinking. For example, for years I used the term "creator" because that is what my mentors would say. But I have always understood that we are not limited to one creator in our Indigenous philosophy.

A brother of mine says that colonization is like weeds within Indigenous knowledge, and we have to pick them out. We have to be able to identify what is Indigenous knowledge and what has been an influence of colonization. I attended a tribal meeting where I heard a woman say that, "Women should not have a say in the ceremonial dances." This really upset me. An example of a "weed" may be evident in our perception of male and female roles. In our Indigenous philosophy, men and women work together harmoniously like the male and female woodpecker. Each has their own distinct role but together they create a balance.

I have had many teachers throughout my lifetime, including Albert Gray (awok), Dewey George (awok), Calvin Rube (awok), Glenn Moore (awok), Howard Ames (awok), Luana Brantner (awok), Alice Spott (awok), Robert Spott (awok), Auntie Florence Shaunessey (awok), Bessie Flashman (awok), Ella Norris (awok), and Bill Reed (awok). As you see, many of them have been female. As a young man, I was selected by them to be a ceremonial dance leader. Throughout my life, I was instructed and guided by them to revitalize ceremony. Together, as a community, we have revitalized the Brush Dance ceremonies at Wehlk-wew, Requa, Sregon, Weitchpec, and Sumeg; the White Deerskin Dance at Weitchpec; the Jump Dance at Pecwan and Chapekw; and the Flower Dance at Sumeg. One of my mentors, Alice Spott (awok), was a caretaker of ceremonial knowledge and had a wealth of knowledge. She never got out front or pushed her way but she gave me direction. One of the youngest women that I worked with was Betty McQuillen (awok), she was a caretaker of her uncle, Bill Reed's ceremonial prayer items. Today, I work with my daughter in the Jump Dance and in the women's coming of age ceremony. This ceremony has been integral in bringing back awareness to the medicine and contribution of women.

I am thrilled that our current generation doesn't know a time when there was absence of ceremony or the use of alcohol during ceremony.

My children's generation is getting closer to capturing the true essence of Indigenous knowledge. They contend that we don't have to utilize another religion to justify the existence of our own; that Indigenous knowledge is valid, valuable, and credible. It makes me happy to hear this and it feels right. I now see in my grandchildren's generation a sense of pride, strength, and identity that makes me feel good about our future. It seems that with every generation, we get closer to being whole again.

It is my sincere hope that the Indigenous testimonials in this book will serve as one more step toward helping Indigenous people everywhere to become whole again. Wok-thow.

Bibliography

2010 Census. "The American Indian and Alaska Native Population," accessed October 3, 2017. http://www.census.gov/prod/cen2010/briefs/c2010br.10.pdf.

Adams, Mick, Peter Mataira, Shayne Walker, Michael Hart, Neil Drew, and Jess John Fleay. "Cultural Identity and Practices Associated with the Health and Well-being of Indigenous Males." *Journal of Indigenous Studies and First Nations and First People's Cultures* 1, no. 1, (2017): 42-61.

Adichie, Chimamanda Ngozi. *The Danger of a Single Story.* Independence, KY: National Geographic Learning, 2016.

Agua Caliente Band of Cahuilla Indians. "News and Events," accessed November 12, 2017. http://www.aguacaliente.org/content/News%20&%20Events/?showStoryID=116.

Alfred, Taiaiake. "Practical (sic) Decolonialization," accessed November 11, 2017. https://www.youtube.com/watch?v=pq87xqSMrDw.

Alfred, Taiaiake. *Wasáse: Indigenous Pathways of Action and Freedom.* Peterborough, Ontario: Broadview Press, 2005.

Aspen Institute. "Fast Facts on Native American Youth," accessed October 1, 2018. http://assets.aspeninstitute.org.

Banaji, Mahzarin R. and Anthony G. Greenwald. *Blind Spot: Hidden Biases of Good People.* New York: Delacorte Press, 2013.

Bancroft, Hubert H. *History of the Pacific States of North American: North Mexican States. 1531-1800.* San Francisco, California: History Company, 1883.

Bauer, William J. *California through Native Eyes: Reclaiming History.*

Seattle, WA: University of Washington Press, 2016.

Blalock-Moore, Nicole. "Piper v. Big Pine School District of Inyo County: Indigenous Schooling and Resistance in Early Twentieth Century." *Southern California Quarterly* 94, (Fall 2012): 361.

Buckley, Thomas. *Standing Ground: Yurok Indian Spirituality, 1850–1990.* Berkeley, California: University of California Press, 2002.

Bush, Jamie L. "Exploring and settling Humboldt Bay." Master's Thesis, Humboldt State University, 2005.

Bushnell, John H. "From American Indian to Indian American: The Changing Identity of the Hupa." *American Anthropologist* 70, no. 6 (1968): 1110-1111.

California Department of Education. "2016 History-Social Science Framework," accessed November 12, 2017. https://www.cde.ca.gov/ci/hs/cf/sbedrafthssfw.asp.

California Department of Public Health. "Humboldt County Maternal Child and Adolescent Health Community Profile, 2017-2018," accessed December 20, 2017. https://www.cdph.ca.gov/Programs/CFH/DMCAH/LocalMCAH/CDPH%20Document%20Library/Community-Profile-Humboldt.pdf.

California Department of Public Health. "Report: More Opioid Prescriptions in Humboldt County than Residents," accessed December 19, 2017. http://www.times-standard.com/general-news/20171026/report-more-opioid-prescriptions-in-humboldt-county-than-residents.

Castañeda, Antonia I. "Engendering the History of Alta California, 1769-1848: Gender, Sexuality, and the Family." *California History* 76, no. 2/3 (1997): 230-259.

Center for Disease Control and Prevention. "Prescription Opioid Overdose Data," accessed December 19, 2017. https://www.cdc.gov/drugoverdose/data/overdose.html.

Chandler, Michael and Christopher Lalonde "Cultural Continuity as a Hedge against Suicide in Canada's First Nations." *Transcultural Psychiatry* 35, no. 2 (1998): 191-219.

Conathan, Lisa. "Recovering Sociolinguistic Context from Early Sources: The Case of Northwestern California." *Anthropological Linguistics* (2006): 211.

Costo, Rupert and Jeannette Henry-Costo, *Natives of the Golden State: The California Indians.* San Francisco, California: Indian Historian Press, 1995.

Costo, Rupert and Jeannette Henry-Costo. *The Missions of California: A Legacy of Genocide*. San Francisco, California: Indian Historian Press, 1987.

Darnell, Regna. "Reflections on Cree Interactional Etiquette: Educational Implications," *Working Papers in Sociolinguistics 57*, (1979): 1-22.

DeLoria, Vine. *Spirit and Reason*. Golden, Colorado: Fulcrum Publishing, 1999.

DeLoria, Vine and Daniel Wildcat. *Power and Place: Indian Education in America*. Golden, Colorado: Fulcrum Publishing, 2001.

Duran, Eduardo and Bonnie Duran, *Native American Postcolonial Psychology*. Albany: SUNY Press, 1995.

Field, Les W. *Abalone Tales: Collaborative Explorations of Sovereignty and Identity in Native California*. Durham, North Carolina: Duke University Press, 2009.

Forbes, Jack. *Native Americans of California and Nevada*. Happy Camp, California: Naturegraph Publishers, 1993.

Freire, Paulo. *Pedagogy of the Oppressed*. New York: Bloomsbury Publishing, 1968.

Fricker, Miranda. *Epistemic Injustice: Power and Ethics of Knowing*. New York: Oxford University Press, 2007.

Goddard, Pliny Earle. *Hupa Texts*. Berkeley, California: The University Press, 1904.

Golla, Victor. *California Indian Languages*. Berkeley, California: University of California Press, 2011.

Gone, Joseph P. "Reconsidering American Indian Historical Trauma: Lessons from an Early Gros Ventre War Narrative." *Transcultural Psychiatry* 51, no. 3 (2014): 387-406.

Gone, Joseph P. "Redressing First Nations Historical Trauma: Theorizing Mechanisms for Indigenous Culture as Mental Health Treatment," *Transcultural Psychiatry* 50, no. 5, (2013): 683-706.

Gone, Joseph P. and Joseph E. Trimble. "American Indian and Alaska Native Mental Health: Diverse Perspectives on Enduring Disparities." *Annual Review of Clinical Psychology* 8, (2012): 131-160.

Hacking, Ian. "Making up People, in Reconstructing Individualism: Autonomy, Individuality, and the Self in Western Thought," edited by Thomas C. Heller, Morton Sosna, and David Wellbery, 222-236. Palo Alto, California: Stanford University, 1986.

Hartmann, William E. and Joseph P. Gone, "Psychological-Mindedness and American Indian Historical Trauma: Interviews with Service Providers from a Great Plains Reservation," *American Journal of Community Psychology*, 57, no. 1-2 (2016): 230.

Heizer, Robert. F. *Eighteen Unratified Treaties of 1851–1852 between California Indians and the United States Government.* Berkeley, California: University of California Berkeley, 1972.

Heizer, Robert F. and Alan J. Almquist. *The other Californians: Prejudice and Discrimination under Spain, Mexico, and the United States to 1920.* Berkeley, California: University of California Press, 1977.

Herman-Stahl, Mindy, Donna L. Spencer, and Jessica E. Duncan, "The Implications of Cultural Orientation for Substance Use Among American Indians." *American Indian and Alaska Native Mental Health Research* 11, no. 1 (2003): 46.

Higham, Scott and Lenny Bernstein, "The Drug Industry's Triumph over the DEA," *The Washington Post*, October 15, 2017, accessed October 31, 2017. https://www.washingtonpost.com/graphics/2017/investigations/dea-drug-industry-congress/?utm_term=.5d0dcce7060f https://www.washingtonpost.com/graphics/2017/investigations/dea-drug-industry-congress/?utm_term=.aedce61daa46.

Hinton, Leanne. *Flutes of Fire: Essays on California Indian Languages.* Berkeley, California: Heyday Books, 1994.

Horse Capture, George, Duane Champagne, Chandler Jackson, and Ben Nighthorse Campbell. *American Indian Nations: Yesterday, Today, and Tomorrow.* New York: Alta Mira Press, 2007.

Indian Health Services. "2009-2011 Health Disparities Fact Sheet," accessed October 1, 2018. http://ihs.gov/newsroom/factsheets/disparities.

Indian Health Services. "IHS 2016 Profile," accessed December 20, 2017. https://www.ihs.gov/newsroom/factsheets/ihsprofile/.

Indian Health Services. "The 2016 Indian Health Service and Tribal Health Care Facilities' Needs Assessment Report to Congress," accessed December 20, 2017. https://www.ihs.gov/newsroom/includes/themes/newihstheme/display_objects/documents/RepCong_2016/IHSRTC_on_FacilitiesNeedsAssessmentReport.pdf.

Johnson, Chiitaanibah. "Native American Student at Sac State Shares her Story," *The State Hornet*, accessed November 11, 2017. https://statehornet.com/2015/10/native-american-student-at-sac-state-shares-her-story/.

Johnston-Dodds, Kimberly. "Early California Laws and Policies

Related to California Indians," *California Research Bureau*, accessed November 7, 2017, http://www.water.ca.gov/pubs/planning/california_water_plan_2005_update__bulletin_160-05_/vol4-tribal-earlycalifornialaws.pdf.

Kang, Jerry. "Immaculate Perception." *Ted Talkx*, accessed August 10, 2017. https://www.youtube.com/watch?v=9VGbwNI6Ssk.

Kang, Jerry and Kristin Lane. "Screening through Colorblindedness: Implicit Bias and the Law." *UCLA Law Review* 58, (2010): 474.

Karp, Michael. *"Lifting the Redwood Curtain: Work, Violence, and Environment, 1850-1948,"* (PhD diss., Saint Louis University, 2015).

Kasser, Tim. "Materialistic Values and Goals," *Annual Review of Psychology* 67, (2016): 489-514.

Kasser, Tim, Katherine L. Rosenblum, Arnold J. Sameroff, Edward L. Deci, Christopher P. Niemiec, Richard M. Ryan, and Osp Árnadóttir. "Changes in Materialism, Changes in Psychological Well-being: Evidence from Three Longitudinal Studies and an Intervention Experiment," *Motivation and Emotion* 38, no. 1 (2014): 1-22.

Kawagley, Angayaqaq Oscar. *Yupiaq Worldview: A Pathway to Ecology and Spirit.* Long Grove, Illinois: Waveland Press, 2003.

KCET Television Network. "We're all Gonna Die Right Here': Talking About the Klamath Salmon Wars," *KCET*, accessed October 16, 2016. https://www.kcet.org/shows/tending-the-wild/were-all-gonna-die-right-here-talking-about-the-klamath-salmon-wars.

Kennedy, Caroline and Ellen Alderman. *In Our Defense: The Bill of Rights in Action.* New York: Perennial, 1991.

Kirmayer, Laurence J. "Psychotherapy and the Cultural Concept of the Person," *Transcultural Psychiatry* 44, no. 2 (2007): 232-257.

Kirmayer, Laurence J. "Rethinking Cultural Competence," *Transcultural Psychiatry* 49, (2012): 149-164.

Kirmayer, Laurence J., Lucy J. Boothroyd, Adrian Tanner, Naomi Adelson, and Elizabeth Robinson, "Psychological Distress among the Cree of James Bay," *Transcultural Psychiatry* 37, no. 1 (2000): 35-56.

Kroeber, Alfred L. *Handbook of the Indians of California.* Washington, D.C.: Bureau of American Ethnology, Bulletin 78, 1925.

Kroeber, Alfred L. *University of California Publications in American Archaeology and Ethnology.* Berkeley, California: University of California Press, 1965.

Kroeber, Alfred L. *Yurok Myths.* Berkeley, California: University of California Press, 1978.

Kroeber, Alfred L. and Edward W. Gifford. *World Renewal: A Cult System of Native Northwest California*. New York: Kraus Reprint Company, 1949.

LaFromboise, Teresa D., Dan R. Hoyt, Lisa Oliver, and Les B. Whitbeck, "Family, Community, and School Influences on Resilience among American Indian Adolescents in the Upper Midwest." *Journal of Community Psychology* 34, no. 2 (2006): 193-209.

Lambert, Diana. "No More Sugar Cubes and Popsicle Sticks?' *Sacramento Bee*, accessed November 12, 2017. http://www.sacbee.com/news/local/education/article170884897.html.

Landry, Alysa. "10-Year-Old Gets Mission Song Stricken from California School District Curriculum," *Indian Country Today*, accessed November 10, 2017. https://indiancountrymedianetwork.com/history/events/10-year-old-gets-mission-song-stricken-from-california-school-district-curriculum/.

Lang, Julian, *Ararapikva*. Berkeley, California: Heyday Books, 1994.

Lara, Kishan. *"Concepts of Giftedness on the Hoopa Valley Indian Reservation."* (EdD diss., Arizona State University, 2009).

Lara-Cooper, Kishan. "K'winya'nya:nma-awhiniw: Creating a Space for Indigenous Knowledge in the Classroom." *Journal of American Indian Education* 53, no. 1, (2014): 3-20.

Lindsay, Brendan C. *Murder State: California's Native American Genocide, 1846-1873*. Lincoln: University of Nebraska Press, 2012.

Littlefield, Alice. "Indian Education and The World of Work in Michigan, 1893-1933," in *Native Americans and Wage Labor: Ethnohistorical Perspectives*, edited by Alice Littlefield and Martha C. Knack. Norman, OK: University of Oklahoma Press, 1996.

Lomawaima, Tsianina. "The Unnatural History of American Indian Education," In *Next Steps: Research and Practice to Advance Indian Education*, edited Karen Swisher and John Tippeconnic, 1-32. Charleston, West Virginia: Clearinghouse on Rural Education and Small Schools, 1999.

Lyons, Sheryl, Jody Green and Cris Plocher. "Humboldt County System Improvement Plan Annual Progress Report: California Child and Family Services Review," *Humboldt Department of Health and Human Services*, accessed August 30, 2016. http://www.childsworld.ca.gov/res/SIPs/2016/HumboldtSIP.pdf.

Madley, Benjamin. *An American Genocide: The United States and the California Indian Catastrophe, 1846-1873*. New Haven: Yale

University Press, 2016.

Madley, Benjamin. "It's Time to Acknowledge the Genocide of California's Indians," *The Los Angeles Times*, May 22, 2016, accessed December 9, 2017. http://www.latimes.com/opinion/op-ed/la-oe-madley-california-genocide-20160522-snap-story.html.

Madley, Benjamin. "Unholy Traffic in Human Blood and Souls": Systems of California Indian Servitude under US Rule." *Pacific Historical Review* 83, no. 4 (2014): 626-667.

Malchiodi, Cathy. *Creative Interventions with Traumatized Children*. New York: Guiford Press, 2015.

Mathes, Valerie. "Nineteenth Century Women and Reform: The Women's National Indian Association." *American Indian Quarterly* 14, no. 1 (1990): 1-18.

Maxwell, Krista. "Historicizing Historical Trauma Theory: Troubling the Trans-generational Transmission Paradigm," *Transcultural Psychiatry* 51, no. 3 (2014): 407-435.

Medina, Vincent. "A Word with Chiitaanibah Johnson." *News from Native California* 29, no. 2 (2015):7.

Medina, Vincent. "Plastic Siege: A New Twist on the Fourth Grade Mission Project." *News from Native California* 27, no. 1 (Fall 2013): 4-5.

McTygue, Nancy. "Enough with Mission Projects Already," *The Source,* (Summer 2012).

Meyer, Manulani. *Ho'oulu our Time of Becoming: Hawaiian Epistemology and Early Writing.* Honolulu, Hawaii: Native Books, 2003.

Million, Dian. *Therapeutic Nations: Healing in the Age of Indigenous Human Rights.* Tucson, Arizona: University of Arizona Press, 2013.

Mills, John E. *The Four Ages of Tsurai: A Documentary History of the Indian Village on Trinidad Bay.* Berkley, California: University of California Press, 1952.

Miranda, Deborah. *Bad Indians: A Tribal Memoir.* Berkeley, California: Heyday, 2013.

Mozingo, Joe. "How a Remote California Tribe set out to Save its River and Stop a Suicide Epidemic," *The Los Angeles Times*, May 19, 2017, accessed October, 13, 2017. http://www.latimes.com/local/california/la-me-salmon-demise-yurok-suicides-20170519-htmlstory.html.

Murphey, Edith V.A. and Lucy Young. "Out of the Past: A True Indian Story told by Lucy Young, of Round Valley Indian Reservation." *California Historical Society* 20, no. 4 (1941): 349-364.

National Congress of American Indians. "2018 Demographics," accessed September 21, 2017. http://ncai.org.

Nelson, Byron. *Our Home Forever: The Hupa Indians of Northern California*. Salt Lake City, Utah: The Howe Bros., 1978.

Norton, Jack. *Centering in Two Worlds: Essays on Native Northwestern California, Culture and Spirituality*. Hemet, California: Center for the Affirmation of Responsible Education, 2007.

Norton, Jack. *Genocide in Northwestern California: When Our Worlds Cried*. San Francisco, California: Indian Historian Press, 1979.

Nowcast KCRA. "Racist homework? West Sacramento School Assigns Controversial Worksheet," *KCRA3*, accessed February 25, 2018. https://www.kcra.com/article/racist-homework-west-sacramen-to-school-assigns-controversial-worksheet/17004436.

O'brien, Sharon. *American Indian Tribal Governments*. Norman, OK: University of Oklahoma Press, 1993.

Perry, Bruce, *What We Have Always Known: A Program Presenting Key Parenting Skills of the Native American Culture*. Chicago: The Child Trauma Academy, 2003.

Platt, Tony. *Grave Matters: Excavating California's Buried Past*. Berkeley, California: Heyday, 2011.

Proudfit, Joely and Theresa Gregor. "The State of American Indian & Alaskan Native Education in California 2016," *San Marcos State University*, accessed November 25, 2017. https://www.csusm.edu/cicsc/projects/projects_docs_images/2016SAIANEC_FINAL.pdf.

Putnam, Robert D. *Bowling Alone: The Collapse and Revival of American Community*. New York: Simon & Schuster, 2000.

Ramirez, Renya. *Native Hubs: Culture, Community, and Belonging in Silicon Valley and Beyond*. Durham, NC: Duke University Press, 2007.

Rawls, James. *Indians of California: The Changing Image*. Norman, OK: University of Oklahoma Press, 1984.

Reed, Kaitlin, "We Are Salmon People: Constructing Yurok Sovereignty in the Klamath Basin" (2014). *Senior Capstone Projects*. 304. http://digitalwindow.vassar.edu/senior_capstone/304.

Rego, Nilda. "Days Gone By: 1860 Massacre of Native American Tribe Prompts Strong Opposition from Brett Harte," *The Mercury News*, March 26, 2014, accessed December 3, 2017. https://www.mercurynews.com/2014/03/26/days-gone-by-1860-massacre-of-native-american-tribe-prompts-strong-opposition-from-bret-harte/.

Reyner, John and Jeanne Eder. *American Indian Education: A History*.

Norman: University of Oklahoma Press, 2004.

Risling Baldy, Cutcha. "Water is Life: The Flower Dance Ceremony." *News from Native California* 30, no. 3 (2017).

Risling Baldy, Cutcha. *We Are Dancing For You: Native Feminisms and the Revitalization of Women's Coming-of-Age Ceremonies*. Seattle, WA: University of Washington Press, 2018.

Sacramento State University. "California Indian History Curriculum Coalition," accessed November 12, 2017. http://www.csus.edu/coe/cic/.

Sacramento State University. "California Indian History Curriculum Coalition Summit at Sacramento State," accessed November 12, 2017. https://www.youtube.com/watch?v=5hW_S6bFKmA.

Sapir, Edward. *Language: An Introduction to the Study of Speech*. New York: Harcout, Brace & Company, 1921.

Schwartz, Shalom H. "Universals in the Content and Structure of Values: Theoretical Advances and Empirical Tests in 20 Countries," *Advances in Experimental Social Psychology* 25, (1992): 1-65.

Secrest, William B. *When the Great Spirit Died: The Destruction of the California Indians, 1850-1860*, Fresno, California: Quill Driver Books, 2003.

Smith, Linda Tuhiwai. *Decolonizing Methodologies: Research and Indigenous Peoples*. London: ZED Books, 1999.

Soza War Soldier, Rose D. "*To Take Positive and Effective Action: Rupert Costo and the California Based American Indian Historical Society*." (PhD Diss., Arizona State University, 2013).

Substance Abuse and Mental Health. "Adverse Childhood Experiences," accessed November 1, 2018. Services Administration. https://www.samhsa.gov/capt/practicing-effective-prevention/prevention-behavioral-health/adverse-childhood-experiences.

Szasz, Margaret Connell. "Foreward." In *Women's National Indian Association: A History,* edited by Valerie Sherer Mathes, ix. Albuquerque, NM: University of New Mexico Press, 2015.

Thompson, Lucy. *To the American Indian: Reminiscences of a Yurok Woman*. Berkeley, California: Heyday, 1916.

Times Standard. "Grand Jury: Humboldt County Kids 'Ill-served' by System Meant to Protect Them," *The Times Standard,* accessed May 30, 2017. http://www.times-standard.com/article/NJ/20170530/NEWS/170539998.

Todd, Zoe. "From a Fishy Place: Examining Canadian State Law

Applied in the Daniels Decision from the Perspective of Métis Legal Orders." *TOPIA: Canadian Journal of Cultural Studies* 36, (2016), 231.

Tolley, Sara L. *Quest for Tribal Acknowledgment: California's Honey Lake Maidus.* Norman, OK: University of Oklahoma Press, 2006.

Trafzer, Clifford E. and Joel R. Hyer. *Exterminate Them! Written Accounts of the Murder, Rape, and Enslavement of Native Americans during the California Gold Rush.* East Lansing: Michigan State University Press, 1999.

Trafzer, Clifford E. and Michelle Lorimer. "Silencing California Indian Genocide in Social Studies Texts." *American Behavioral Scientist* 58, no. 1 (2014): 75.

Union Hill School District. "Union Hill School District Facebook Page," accessed November 30, 2017. https://www.facebook.com/pages/Union-Hill-School-District/122309757825893.

United Nations. "United Nations Office on Genocide Prevention and the Responsibility to Protect," accessed December 1, 2017. http://www.un.org/en/genocideprevention/genocide.html.

United States Congress, Senate Special Subcommittee on Indian Education of the Committee on Labor and Public Welfare, *Hearings on Indian Education: The Study of the Education of Indian Children Part 1*, 90 Cong., 1 and 2 sess. (1968).

University of California Berkeley. "Ararahih'urípih: A Dictionary and Text Corpus of the Karuk Language," accessed December 20, 2018. http://linguistics.berkeley.edu/~karuk/index.php.

Vizenor, Gerald. *Survivance: Narratives of Native Presence.* Lincoln, NE: University of Nebraska, 2008.

Walters, Karina, Selina Mohammed, Teresa Evans-Campbell, Ramona Beltran, David Chaex, and Bonnie Duran. *Bodies Don't Just Tell Stories, They Tell Histories: Embodiment of Historical Trauma Among American Indians and Alaska Natives.* US Library of Medicine National Health Institute, 2011.

Whitbeck, Les B., Dan R. Hoyt, Jerry D. Stubben, and Teresa LaFromboise. "Traditional Culture and Academic Success among American Indian Children in the Upper Midwest," *Journal of American Indian Education* 40, no. 2 (2001): 48-60.

Wiseman, Maury. "Sac State Professor Explains his use of Genocide," *The State Hornet*, accessed November 11, 2017. https://statehornet.com/2015/10/sac-state-professor-explains-his-use-of-word-genocide/.

Wolf, Jessica. "Revealing the History of Genocide against California Native Americans" UCLA Newsroom, accessed August 15, 2017. http://newsroom.ucla.edu/stories/revealing-the-history-of-genocide-against-californias-native-americans.

Yellow Bird, Michael. *Decolonizing the Mind: Healing through Neurodecolonization and Mindfulness.* Produced by Cheryl Easter and Neil Ruckman, 2013 accessed September 27, 2018. Vimeo.com/86995336.

Yellow Bird, Michael and Venida Chenault. "The Role of Social Work in Advancing the Practice of Indigenous Education: Obstacles and Promises in Empowerment Oriented Social Work Practice" In *Next Steps: Research and Practice to Advance Indian Education,* edited by Karen Swisher and John Tippeconnic, 201-238. Charleston, West Virginia: Clearinghouse on Rural Education and Small Schools, 1999.

Yellowhorse Braveheart, Maria and Lemyra M. DeBruyn "The American Indian Holocaust: Healing Historical Unresolved Grief," *American Indian and Alaska Native Mental Health*, 8, no. 2 (1998): 56.

Yurok Today. "Cha-pekw Descendants Raise it up. Ceremonial Leaders Restore the Stone Lagoon Jump Dance, A Sacred Ceremony to Heal the World," *Yurok Today: The Voice of the People*, October, 2012, accessed November 3, 2017. http://www.yuroktribe.org/documents/2012_october.pdf.

Yurok Tribe. "American Community Survey, 5-year Estimates, 2010-2014," *Yurok Tribe,* accessed January 2, 2018. http://www.yuroktribe.org/documents/DRAFT_CEDS_WEB.pdf.

Yurok Tribe. *Constitution of the Yurok Tribe.* Klamath, California: Yurok Tribe, 1993.

Yurok Tribe. "Yurok Tribe Background Information," *Yurok Tribe,* accessed December 10, 2017. http://www.yuroktribe.org/culture/history/history.htm.